ESSENTIAL SKILLS EVERY KID SHOULD KNOW

The Ultimate 3-in-1 Life Skills, Money Skills & Adventure Skills Handbook
for Tween Boys & Girls

FERNE BOWE

Copyright © 2024 Ferne Bowe

Published by: Bemberton Ltd

All rights reserved. No part of this book or any portion thereof may be reproduced in any form by any electronic or mechanical means without permission in writing from the publisher, except for the use of brief quotes in a book review.

The publisher accepts no legal responsibility for any action taken by the reader, including but not limited to financial losses or damages, both directly or indirectly incurred as a result of the content in this book.

ISBN: 978-1-915833-68-6

Disclaimer: The information in this book is general and designed to be for information only. While every effort has been made to ensure it is wholly accurate and complete, it is for general information only. It is not intended, nor should it be taken as professional advice. The author gives no warranties or undertakings whatsoever concerning the content. For matters of a medical nature, the reader should consult a doctor or other health care professional for specific health-related advice. The reader accepts that the author is not responsible for any action, including but not limited to losses both directly or indirectly incurred by the reader as a result of the content in this book.

View all our books at **bemberton.com.**

TABLE OF CONTENTS

BOOK 1. LIFE SKILLS FOR TWEENS

7	**Introduction**
9	Personal Development
21	Friends & Relationships
31	Emotions
41	School and Learning
49	Health and Wellness
59	Money Matters
75	Cooking Skills
83	Happiness Skills
89	Caring & Sharing
97	Communication Skills
107	Practical Skills
113	Personal Safety
121	Emergencies & First Aid
127	Adventure Skills

BOOK 2. MONEY SKILLS FOR KIDS

141   **Introduction**

141   Understanding Money

151   How to Earn Money

167   How to Save Money

179   How to Spend Money Wisely

193   How to Give and Share

199   How to Keep Your Money Safe and Secure

207   An Introduction to Investing

219   Planning for the Future

227   **Conclusion**

229   **Glossary of Key Financial Terms**

BOOK 3. ADVENTURE SKILLS FOR KIDS

235   **Introduction—Searching for Adventure**

239   Preparing for Adventure

251   Building Your Shelter

259   Building Campfires

275   Navigation and Exploration

287   Wilderness Survival

297   Interacting with Nature

305   Creative Adventure Projects for Your Journal

315   The Great Indoors—Bringing Adventure Home

325   Advanced Outdoor Skills

335   Crafting Tools in the Wilderness

345   Creating Your Own Adventures

353   **Conclusion**

357   **Appendix**

LIFE SKILLS FOR TWEENS

How to Cook, Make Friends, Be Self Confident and Health

Everything a Pre Teen Should Know to Be a Brilliant Teenager

FERNE BOWE

BEMBERTON BOOKS

SOMETHING FOR YOU

Thanks for buying this book. To show our appreciation, here's a **FREE** printable copy of the "Life Skills for Tweens Workbook"

WITH OVER 80 FUN ACTIVITIES JUST FOR TWEENS!

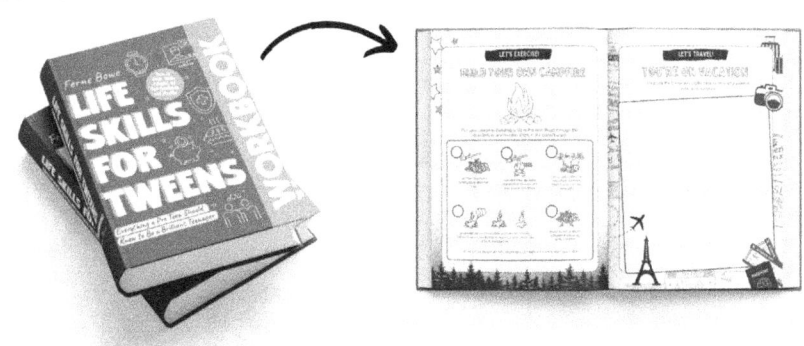

Scan the code to download your FREE printable copy

INTRODUCTION

Congratulations! You're about to become a teenager!

It's an exciting time, but it can also be scary. As you get older, there are many new things you have to learn and deal with. But don't worry, it's perfectly normal to feel anxious about what lies ahead.

As you move through life, you will encounter challenges and obstacles. You can overcome some of these easily, but others may seem impossible. This is where having strong life skills comes in handy. If you can problem-solve and communicate effectively, you will be better equipped to handle whatever life throws your way.

But first up, what are life skills?

> Life skills are abilities that allow you to cope with the demands of everyday life. They can be anything from problem-solving and communication to self-care and money management. Many of these skills take time and practice, but they are essential to living a happy and successful life.

Learning life skills is essential. Many of the jobs you will apply for in the future will require you to have specific life skills. For example, to be a teacher, you must communicate effectively and manage a classroom. If you're going to be an accountant, you will need to be able to manage money and keep track of financial records. So, whether you realize it or not, life skills are essential for almost everything you do.

There are many benefits to having strong life skills. Some of the most important ones are:

- You will be able to handle difficult situations with ease.
- You will be able to achieve your goals and dreams.
- You will be more confident in yourself.
- You will have better relationships with others.
- You will be able to live a happy and fulfilling life.

So, as you can see, having strong life skills is essential for a happy and successful life. To achieve your goals and dreams, you need to start working on your life skills today!

That's where this book comes in. This book is designed to help you develop the life skills you need to make the jump to a teenager. We will cover topics to help you:

- Make friends and build relationships
- Make responsible decisions
- Stay fit and live healthily
- Communicate effectively
- Set goals and achieve them
- Live a life of an adventurer

And so much more.

Each chapter will include tips, illustrations, and real-life examples to help you understand and apply the life skills we are discussing. So, let's get started!

CHAPTER 1

PERSONAL DEVELOPMENT

As you approach becoming a teenager, you will face new challenges and opportunities. These are exciting times! Even though you don't know it yet, everything you do is helping you shape who you will become. Your decisions and actions will have a massive impact on your future.

The world is your oyster, anything is possible, and you have the power to create your destiny.

But before you can conquer the world, there are some essential life skills you need to learn first. These will help you navigate through your teenage years and beyond.

Some of the things you'll need to know include:

- How to manage your time effectively
- How to set goals
- How to stay on track
- How to be confident
- How to motivate yourself

Each of these topics is important in its own right. Still, together, they will form the foundation for a happy, successful teenage experience.

So let's take a closer look at each one.

HOW TO BE A TIME MANAGEMENT SUPERSTAR

Time management is one of the most essential life skills you can learn.

> **What is time management?**
> Simply put, time management is the process of planning and organizing your time to make the most of it.

It sounds easy enough, but it's pretty tricky to do.

There are only 24 hours in a day, and there's only so much you can fit into that time. Effective time management is all about prioritizing your time and using it wisely.

As a teenager, you'll be juggling schoolwork, extracurricular activities, socializing, and perhaps even a part-time job. You must learn to manage your time effectively, or you'll quickly become overwhelmed.

Here are some tips to help you get started:

❶ Make a list of everything you need to do. The best way to do this is to get a piece of paper and write down everything on your mind. Once it's all down on paper, you'll feel much better and see everything more clearly.

❷ Prioritize your tasks. Once you've got everything down on paper, it's time to start working out which tasks are the most important and must be done first. This is called prioritizing.

Ask yourself the most critical task that needs to be completed first. This is usually the task with the most significant consequences if it's not done or the most urgent one. For example, from the list above, doing your homework, or walking the dog, would be more important than playing football with your friends.

Put a number 1 next to the most important task. Then ask yourself, what is the second most important task? Put a number 2 next to that one. Continue doing this until you've numbered all of your tasks.

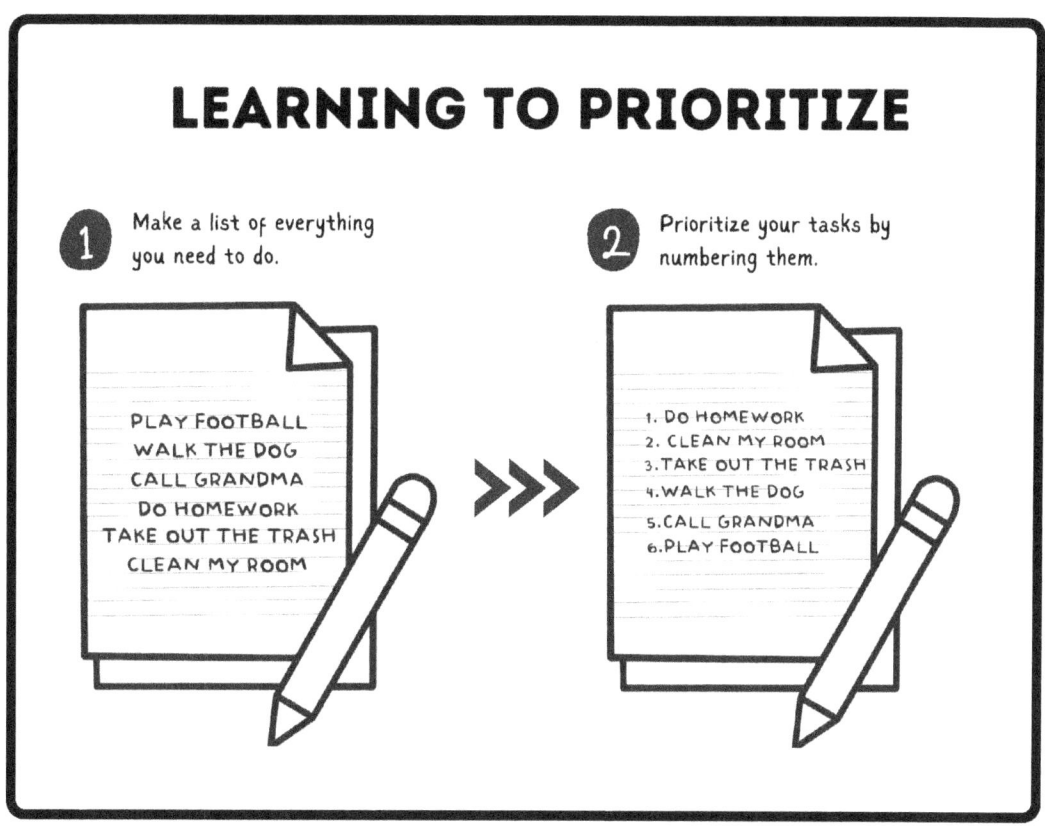

3. **Create a plan.** Once you know what needs to be done and in what order, you can start creating a plan. This can be as simple as writing down what you need to do and when you need to do it.

4. **Get to work.** Now that you've planned everything out, it's time to start working on your tasks. The best way to do this is to start with the most important task and work your way down the list. This will help you ensure that the most important things get done first.

5. **Take breaks.** It's essential to take breaks while you're working on tasks. This will help you to avoid burnout and will keep your mind fresh.

6. **Stick to your plan.** Once you've created your program, do your best to stick to it. This means setting aside specific times for specific tasks and then making sure you actually do those tasks during that time.

HOW TO SET GOALS

Setting goals is another skill you'll need to learn as a teenager.

Goals are simply things that you want to achieve. They can be big or small, long-term or short-term.

The important thing is that you have a clear idea of what you want to achieve and are willing to put in the hard work to make it happen.

Not only will this help you to focus on what's important to you, but it will also give you a sense of purpose and direction.

Here are some tips to help you set goals:

1. **Think about what you want to achieve.** The first step is to sit down and think about what you want to achieve. This could be anything from getting good grades in school to becoming a professional athlete.

2. **Be specific.** Once you've thought about what you want to achieve, try to be as clear as possible. This will help you better focus on your goal and increase your chances of achieving it.

   For example, rather than "getting good grades," you could set the goal of "getting an A in science."

3. **Be realistic.** Make sure that your goal is achievable. There's no point in setting a goal that's impossible to achieve. This doesn't mean that you should only set goals that are easy to achieve, but rather that you should set goals that are challenging but still within reach.

4. **Set a deadline.** If you can, try to set a deadline for your goal. This will help you stay on track and ensure you don't get sidetracked. Without a deadline, it's easy to put off working towards your goal until "someday."

5. **Write it down.** Once you've decided on your goal, write it down. This will help you better remember what you're trying to achieve and keep you accountable. You can also share your goal with someone else to help keep you accountable and on track.

Some people use the SMART goal method to narrow down what they want to achieve. **SMART stands for S-specific, M-measurable, A-attainable, R-relevant, and T-timely.**

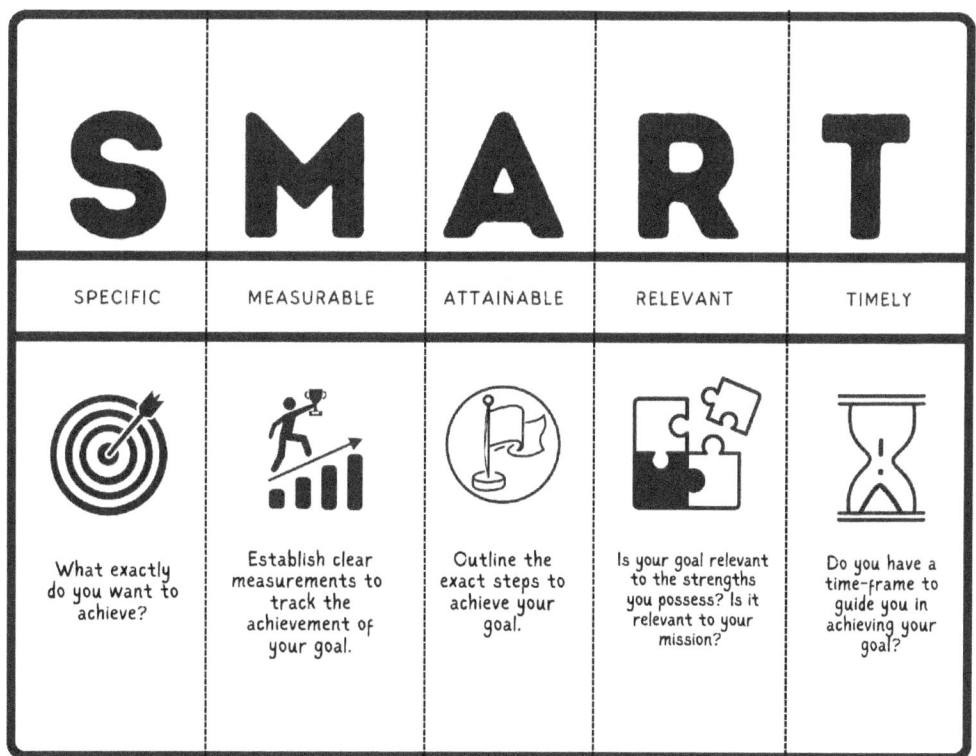

For example, let's say you want to get fit: "I will work out three times a week" is a great start, but it's not very specific.

A more specific goal would be "I will work out for thirty minutes, three times a week, at the gym."

This goal is much easier to achieve because it is more specific. So if we go through the SMART list with the same example.

S-specific: "I will work out for thirty minutes at the gym three times a week."

M-measurable: You can measure this goal by whether or not you actually go to the gym three times a week and work out for thirty minutes each time.

A-attainable: The goal is attainable because it is realistic to go to the gym three times a week.

R-relevant: This goal is relevant because going to the gym is a great way to get fit.

T-timely: This goal is timely because of the amount of time you will spend working out each week, and you can start working out this week.

Now that you know what the SMART goal method is, you can use it to set your own goals.

Have a think about a goal you want to achieve: it could be something related to school, your hobbies, or your future career.

Once you have decided on your goal, use the SMART goal method to make it more specific. Write down your goal and keep it somewhere you can see it often to help you stay on track.

Now that we've covered how to set goals, let's look at how to achieve them.

HOW TO ACHIEVE GOALS

❶ Break them down into smaller pieces

The best way to achieve your goals is to break them down into smaller, more manageable pieces.

This will make them seem less daunting and help you better focus on what you need to do.

> *For example, if your goal is to get an A in math, your first step might be attending all your math classes.*
>
> *Your second step might be doing all the homework and practice problems. And your third step might be to get help from a tutor or teacher if you're struggling.*

By breaking down your goal into smaller steps, you'll increase your chances of achieving it.

❷ Create a plan of action

Now that you've decided on your goal and have broken it down into smaller steps, it's time to create an action plan. **This is simply a list of what you need to do to achieve your goal.**

For each step, you'll want to include a specific action that you need to take.

> *For example, if your goal is to get an A in math, your plan of action might be:*
> *– attend all math classes*
> *– do all homework and practice problems*
> *– get help from a tutor or teacher if needed*

This is just a basic example, but it gives you an idea of how to create a plan of action.

Remember, the more specific your plan of action is, the better.

❸ Take action and stay motivated

Once you've created your action plan, it's time to start taking action. This is where the real work begins.

You'll need to stay focused and motivated to achieve your goal.

One way to do this is to set regular reminders and reward yourself for taking action towards your goal.

- *For example, you could give yourself a small treat after completing each action plan step.*
- *This could be watching an extra episode of your favorite TV show or going for a walk in the park.*

The important thing is to find something that motivates you and helps you stay on track.

❹ Celebrate your achievements

Well done, you've done it! You've hit your goal. This is an exciting moment!

Take time to celebrate your accomplishment.

Once you've celebrated, it's time to set a new goal. This will help you to continue growing and developing as a person.

Remember, goal setting is an important life skill that can help you achieve anything you want. So don't be afraid to set goals and go after them! You can do it.

HOW TO KEEP MOTIVATED AND STAY ON TRACK

Staying on track can be difficult, especially when dealing with teenage life pressures.

There will be times when you feel like giving up or feel like you're not good enough. That's why it's crucial to have a support network of friends and family who can encourage you to keep going.

Here are some other tips to help you stay motivated:

1. **Set yourself regular reminders.** Write your goals down and put them somewhere you'll see them daily. This could be on your fridge, door, or phone.

2. **Find a role model.** Look for someone who has already achieved what you want to achieve and use them as motivation to keep going. *For example, suppose your goal is to play football professionally. In that case, you might look up inspirational quotes or watch videos of other football players.*

3. **Talk to others about your goals.** Sharing your goals with others can help motivate you to stay on track. You might even find a friend who wants to achieve the same goals as you, and you can work together.

4. **Take time to rest and recharge when you need it.** Staying motivated and on track can be exhausting, so make sure you take time to relax and rejuvenate. This could mean working out, getting enough sleep each night, or simply spending some time alone doing something you enjoy.

> ### GO FOR IT!
> No matter what life throws your way, remember that anything is possible with the right skills and mindset! With hard work and determination, you can achieve your goals and become a success. Go for it!

HOW TO BE CONFIDENT

The pre-teenage years can be a tough time. You're dealing with hormonal changes, peer pressure, and the stress of school. It's no wonder that so many teenagers lack confidence.

But being confident is an important life skill you need to learn. It's essential for achieving your goals, standing up for yourself, and enjoying a happy teenage experience.

> **I'VE FAILED OVER AND OVER AGAIN IN MY LIFE. THAT'S WHY I SUCCEED.**
>
> MICHAEL JORDAN,
> BASKETBALL PLAYER

Building confidence takes time and effort, but it's so worth it. Believe in yourself and stay positive. YOU CAN DO IT!

Here are some tips to help you build self-confidence:

1. **Believe in yourself.** You are amazing! The first step to being confident is to believe in yourself. This means accepting yourself for who you are and not comparing yourself to others. You are uniquely you!

2. **Set achievable goals.** Confidence comes from hitting your dreams, so set achievable and challenging goals. *For example, if you want to improve at tennis, practice a few times each week until you see improvement.*

3. **Find confident role models.** Look for people with qualities you admire, such as strength or compassion. You can learn much from observing how they behave and interact with others.

4. **Take risks and step out of your comfort zone.** Confidence comes from pushing outside of your comfort zone and trying new things. So go ahead and take that art class, join the football team or start a club! What's the worst thing that could happen?

5. **Don't be afraid to fail.** Failing is part of life and how we learn and grow. So don't be scared to make mistakes—they're essential to becoming confident.

ACTIVITY

Goal Ladder Visualization

This simple goal-setting activity helps break down big goals into smaller steps.

1. **Write down your DREAM on the top rung of the ladder.** It can be anything, but try to be specific. For example, if you want to improve at football, write, "I want to make the school team."

2. **On the first rung, write down your first goal and what action you need to do to hit that goal.** This will be your first ACTION STEP! For example, "I will attend training sessions 3 times a week" or "I will eat a healthy breakfast every day."

3. Move on to the second rung and set a new goal and what action you will take to achieve it. This is your second ACTION STEP! For example, "I will do some extra training at home" or "I will make sure I get 8 hours of sleep every night."

4. **Keep going until you reach the top of the ladder** (your DREAM). You should now have a list of ACTION STEPS that you need to take to achieve your DREAM!

5. Tick them off as you go

GOAL LADDER

Write your DREAM at the top, and then write each action
& step you'll take to achieve your goal.

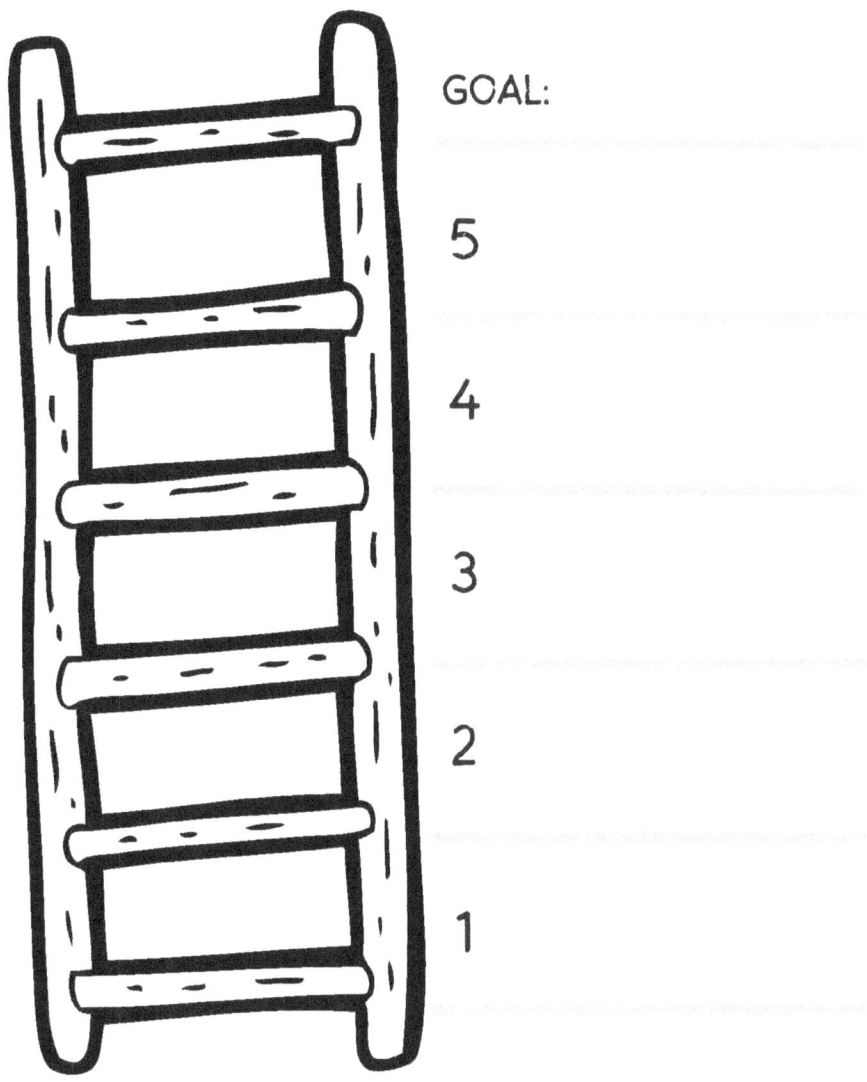

GOAL:

5

4

3

2

1

CHAPTER 2

FRIENDS & RELATIONSHIPS

> FRIENDS ARE AN ESSENTIAL PART OF OUR LIVES. We rely on them for support and guidance as we grow and learn. The friends you make today will likely be with you for life.

This chapter will discuss what makes a good friend, how to make friends, and how to develop healthy relationships.

MAKING FRIENDS

What qualities do you look for in a friend?

Think about the friends you have now. What do you like about them?

Do you have any friends or relatives that you don't see very often, but it's like you never left each other's side when you are together?

These are the types of friends you want to have. They are the ones who make you feel good about yourself and make you laugh. They are supportive and understanding. They are the friends who will be there for you through thick and thin.

When looking for friends, think about the essential qualities to you. Do you want someone who is active and likes to go out and do things? Or do you want someone who is quieter and likes to stay home? We tend to find people who have similar interests. This can help you connect on a deeper level.

HOW TO MAKE FRIENDS

It can be tricky making friends when you're young. If you've joined a new school or moved to a new neighborhood, finding people with similar interests can be tricky. As the new kid, you may feel shy, or like you don't fit in. Just remember they were all new once, and you'll make friends in no time with a bit of effort.

Here are some tips on how to make friends:

1. **Join clubs or teams:** This is a great way to meet people with similar interests outside school.

2. **Be yourself!** You are amazing! You are uniquely you! Don't try to be someone you're not. People will like you for who you are.

3. **Put yourself out there.** Talk to people. Smile. The more approachable you seem, the more likely people will talk to you.

4. **Be a good listener.** Let the other person talk and be interested in what they say. Ask people about their day, their hobbies, or their interests. People love to talk about themselves. By showing an interest in others, they will be more likely to take an interest in you.

5. **Offer help when you can.** People will appreciate it, and it's a great way to make friends. If someone seems lost, offer to show them around the school or help them find their locker. If someone is having trouble with their homework, offer to help.

Remember, making friends takes time and effort. Don't get discouraged if you don't find your best friend overnight.

HOW TO BE A GOOD FRIEND

When you're a good friend, you make the people around you feel good about themselves. You are supportive and understanding. You are there when things are tough, and you celebrate the good times together. You are someone that others can rely on.

Here are some tips on how to be a good friend:

1. **Be there for your friends when they need you.** Be there for them, whether they're having a bad day or having a tough time. Listen to them and offer help if you can.

② **Be honest with your friends.** Don't try to hide things from them or lie to them. They will appreciate your honesty, and it will help build a stronger friendship.

③ **Be respectful of your friends.** Listen to what they have to say and don't judge them.

④ **Be positive.** Offer encouragement when your friends need it. Nobody likes a negative Nancy.

⑤ **Be a good listener.** Listen to them when your friends are talking and be interested in what they say. Let them finish their thoughts.

Always treat your friends with respect. Remember, they are essential people in your life, and you should cherish your friendship.

DEVELOPING HEALTHY RELATIONSHIPS

Although you may not seem ready yet. When you become a teenager, you may start dating or have a serious relationship.

However, not all relationships are healthy. **Healthy relationships, like friendships, are built on trust, respect, and communication.** If you're in a relationship that makes you feel bad about yourself, or if you are constantly fighting, that's not a healthy relationship.

Let's explore what makes a healthy relationship.

Trust

Trust is the foundation on which everything else is built. If you don't trust someone, having a healthy relationship with them will be tough.

What is trust? **Trust is being able to rely on someone.** Knowing that they will be there for you when you need them. Trust is being able to tell someone a secret and know that your secrets are safe with them.

In addition, you should always be honest with the other person. If you're not comfortable with something, tell them. Honesty is the best policy.

RELATIONSHIPS

Building strong, nurturing, and healthy relationships requires trust, respect & communication.

TRUST

Trust is being able to rely on someone. Knowing that they will be there for you when you need them.

RESPECT

Respect is listening to the other person and taking them seriously. It's not interrupting them or talking over them.

COMMUNICATION

Communication is being able to talk to each other about anything and everything.

ENJOY & HAVE FUN

Respect

Respect is essential in any relationship. You should respect the other person for who they are, and they should respect you in return. This includes respecting your opinions, your beliefs, and your boundaries. If there's no respect, there's no relationship.

What is respect? **Respect is listening to the other person and taking them seriously.** It's not interrupting them or talking over them. If you respect someone, you can agree to disagree. You recognize the other person has a right to their own opinion, even if you disagree with it.

Communication

Communication is vital in any relationship. **You need to be able to talk to each other about anything and everything.** It will not be a healthy relationship if you're not comfortable communicating with someone.

If you have a problem with something or someone, talk to the other person about it. Don't bottle things up. It's much better to communicate and work through your problems.

These three things are essential in any relationship, but they're vital when you're growing up.

Finally, remember to have fun! Relationships are all about enjoying each other's company. Laugh, joke, and have fun together. This is what will keep your relationship healthy and strong.

BULLYING

Bullying is a problem that many kids face. It can be tough being bullied, and it can be hard to know what to do. It can make you feel scared, alone, and helpless.

Bullying is when someone repeatedly and purposely says or does mean things to hurt another person. It's not a one-time thing; it's something that happens over and over again.

Bullying comes in many different forms. It can be physical (hitting, kicking), verbal (calling names, making threats), or social (leaving someone out, spreading rumors). It can also happen online, through text messages or social media.

No matter what type of bullying someone uses, it's NEVER okay.

But there are ways that you can deal with bullying and get help.

> Dealing with bullying can be challenging, but you don't have to face it alone. There are people who can help, and there are ways that you can deal with the bully. Remember to stay strong and not let them get the best of you. **BULLIES NEVER WIN IN THE END.**

HOW TO DEAL WITH BULLIES

TELL SOMEONE
Telling someone will help you feel less alone, and it will also help to stop the bullying.

STAY AWAY FROM THE BULLY
If you can, avoid being alone with them and try not to be in places where no one is around.

SUPPORT EACH OTHER
Talk to your friends. If you have a friend who is also being bullied, support each other.

STAND UP FOR YOURSELF
If the bully is saying mean things to you, try to ignore them or walk away.

How to deal with bullies

- **Tell someone.** Talk to a parent, teacher, or friend. Telling someone will help you feel less alone, and it will also help to stop the bullying. You may worry that you're being a tattletale by telling someone, but that's not true. Telling someone about bullying is vital so that it can be stopped.

- **Stay away from the bully.** If you can, avoid being alone with them and try not to be in places where no one is around. This can be hard if the bully is someone you see at school every day, but it's essential to do what you can to stay safe.

- **Support each other.** If you have a friend who is also being bullied, support each other. You can talk to each other about how you're feeling and help each other stay strong.

- **Stand up for yourself.** This can be hard, but it's essential to do what you can to stop the bullying. If the bully is saying mean things to you, try to ignore them or walk away. Tell them to stop and try to get away from them if they hit you.

CYBERBULLYING

Cyberbullying is a different type of bullying over the internet or through electronic devices. **Cyberbullying can include sending mean text messages, posting hurtful comments, or sharing photos on social media sites.**

Kids who are cyberbullied can feel scared, alone, and helpless. If you're being cyberbullied, it's important to remember that you're not alone. There are people who care about you and want to help.

There are a few things you can do to try to stop cyberbullying:

- **Tell a trusted adult about what's going on.** They can help you figure out the best way to deal with the situation. If a classmate or school friend is doing the bullying, talk to your teacher about it.

- **Block the person who is bullying you.** This will make it harder for them to contact you and may stop the bullying.

- **Keep your social media accounts private.** Don't share personal information or photos that could be used to hurt you.

- **Don't respond to the bully.** This can just encourage them and make the situation worse. Walking away and ignoring the bully, however hard, is always the best course of action.

- **Save any evidence of the bullying (texts, emails, photos, etc.).** This can help prove what's happening if you need to report it.

- **Contact the social media site.** Most sites have policies against cyberbullying and will take steps to remove malicious content if it's reported.

With the rise of social media, cyberbullying has become a growing problem. Bullying is never okay. If you're being cyberbullied, don't suffer in silence. Remember, you're not alone. Tell a trusted adult immediately. They can help you figure out the best way to deal with the situation.

GOSSIP

Gossip is another form of bullying.

It involves spreading rumors, secrets, or hurtful things about another person. It can be spread by word of mouth or through social media, text messages, or email.

Gossip can be just as hurtful as saying something to someone's face. It can damage relationships. When you're the subject of gossip, it can be hard to know who to trust and feel like everyone is talking about you behind your back. You may feel alone and like nobody understands what you're going through.

But there are ways that you can deal with gossip.

How to deal with gossip

- **Talk to a trusted adult about what's going on.** This can be a parent, teacher, or counselor. They can help you figure out what to do next.
- **Ignore the gossip.** This can be hard to do, but it's important to remember that what people say is not necessarily true. People gossip because they want to make themselves feel better, not because they care about you.
- **Stand up for yourself.** Talk to the person who is spreading the rumor. Ask them to stop. If people say mean things about you, don't be afraid to speak up and tell them that it's not okay.
- **Stay away from gossips.** If someone is constantly starting rumors or spreading gossip, it's best to stay away from them. There's no reason to put yourself in a situation where you will feel uncomfortable or upset.

Being on the receiving end of gossip can be rough, but remember, it's not about you. People gossip because they want to make themselves feel more important and popular.

> The best thing you can do is to stay away from people who gossip and resist the urge to gossip yourself. **IF YOU WOULDN'T SAY IT TO SOMEONE'S FACE, DON'T SAY IT BEHIND THEIR BACK.**

ACTIVITY

Friendship & Healthy Relationship Rules

Write down some friendship rules that you think are important. Here are some examples to get you started:

- Be honest with your friends.
- Be there for your friends when they need you.
- Listen to your friends and be interested in what they say.
- Offer help and encouragement when your friends need it.

 # FRIENDSHIP

WHAT ARE SOME FRIENDSHIP RULES THAT YOU HAVE?
WRITE DOWN SOME THINGS THAT ARE IMPORTANT TO YOU:

1 _____

2 _____

3 _____

4 _____

5 _____

6 _____

7 _____

8 _____

9 _____

10 _____

CHAPTER 3

EMOTIONS

As you grow older, you will be experiencing lots of new things, some good and some bad. You might find yourself feeling happy one minute and sad the next. It's important to take care of yourself during this time, both physically and emotionally. In this chapter, we will discuss some ways to do just that.

> **What are emotions?**
>
> Emotions are feelings that we experience in response to different situations. They can be positive, such as happiness or love, or negative, like sadness or anger. Emotions can be powerful and affect our behavior, thoughts, and physical health.

Knowing how to deal with these emotions in healthy ways is essential.

When it comes to positive emotions, enjoy them! Positive emotions can make us feel good both physically and mentally. They can also help us perform better at school or work. So don't be afraid to let yourself feel happy, loved, or excited.

ANGER

Anger is a normal emotion but can become a problem if not managed correctly. When you are angry, your heart rate and blood pressure increase, your muscles tense up, and you might even feel like you could hurt someone.

It is natural to feel angry, but it is helpful to find healthy ways to deal with anger before it gets out of control.

HOW TO DEAL WITH ANGER

1. THINK ABOUT WHY YOU'RE ANGRY.
2. TAKE A DEEP BREATH AND COUNT TO 10
3. TAKE YOURSELF AWAY FROM THE SITUATION
4. TALK TO SOMEONE
5. EXERCISE AND 'SWEAT IT OUT'
6. DO SOMETHING CREATIVE

How to deal with anger

Some ways to deal with anger are:

- **Think about why you're angry.** Sometimes figuring out what is making you angry can help you deal with the feeling. Maybe there is something that you can do to change the situation, or perhaps you need to talk to someone about how you're feeling.

- **Take a deep breath and slowly count to 10.** This will help calm you down and give you time to think about what you want to do. Sometimes, slowing down and focusing on your breath can be enough to calm you down. Try taking in a deep breath through your nose and exhaling slowly through your mouth. Count to 10, and repeat. Let your shoulders relax as you do this.

- **Leave the situation that is making you angry.** If you are in a situation making you mad, such as an argument with your parents or a fight with your friends, it might be best to walk away. This will help you avoid saying or doing something you might regret later.

- **Talk to someone you trust about how you're feeling.** This can help you get rid of the anger by talking about it. It can also help you feel better because you are not keeping your feelings bottled up. Your Mom and Dad are a great place to start, but you can also talk to a friend, teacher, or counselor.

- **Do something physical to release the anger.** This could be anything from punching a pillow to going for a run. Physical activity can help release the anger and frustration you might feel and can be a good way of taking you out of the situation.

- **Think about how the situation might have been handled differently.** This can help you learn from the experience and not feel as angry about it. You may find it helpful to write down what you are mad about. This can help you get your thoughts out. Seeing them on paper can also help you make sense of them.

- **Do something creative.** Drawing, painting, cooking, or building something can help you healthily express your anger. It can also help you calm down and focus on something else.

> Remember, anger is a perfectly normal emotion; everyone gets angry from time to time. It might take some time, but eventually, the anger will go, and you will feel better.

The key is to find healthy ways to deal with it.

SADNESS

When we experience sadness, getting out of bed, eating, or even smiling can be challenging. We might feel like we are all alone in the world and that nobody understands what we are going through. We might want to hide away.

But sadness is a normal emotion, and it is okay to feel this way.

There are a lot of ways to deal with sadness. Some people might want to talk about their feelings, while others might prefer to keep to themselves.

HOW TO DEAL WITH SADNESS

1. TALK TO SOMEONE YOU TRUST ABOUT HOW YOU'RE FEELING.
2. WRITE ABOUT YOUR SADNESS.
3. LISTEN TO MUSIC THAT MAKES YOU FEEL HAPPY.
4. GET MOVING.

How to deal with sadness

Some ways to deal with sadness are:

- **Talk to someone you trust about how you're feeling.** This can help you get rid of the sadness by talking about it. It can also help you feel better because you are sharing your feelings.

- **Write about your sadness.** This can be a journal entry or even a letter to yourself. Writing about your feelings can help you understand them better and make them more manageable.

- **Listen to music that makes you feel happy.** Music is a great way to boost your mood and help you forget about your sadness for a little while.

- **Get moving.** Exercise releases endorphins, which are chemicals that improve your mood. So go for a walk, run, or dance around your house to eliminate the sadness.

Remember, it is okay to feel sad sometimes. These tips can help you deal with those feelings and start to feel better.

FEAR

Fear is a natural emotion that is designed to protect us from danger. Everyone experiences it at some point in their life.

There are many reasons why we might feel fearful. We might be afraid of the dark, heights, or animals. We might be scared of something that we know is dangerous or fearful of something new or unfamiliar. It's perfectly natural to feel fear.

> Fear can help us protect ourselves from danger. It can also motivate us to do something we might not have done before, like overcoming our fears of speaking in public. **OVERCOMING FEAR CAN GIVE US A SENSE OF ACCOMPLISHMENT AND MAKE US FEEL MORE CONFIDENT. IT CAN HELP US GROW.**

However, fear can become a problem when it starts interfering with our everyday lives. For example, suppose you are afraid of flying. In that case, this might prevent you from going on holiday or visiting family and friends who live far away. If we are constantly avoiding things that make us afraid, this can hurt our lives.

Sometimes we can feel fear when there is no danger, or the threat is less significant than the fear. This can be really scary, and it can stop us from doing things we want to do.

HOW TO DEAL WITH FEAR

1. TALK TO SOMEONE ABOUT YOUR FEARS
2. WRITE DOWN YOUR FEARS
3. EXPOSE YOURSELF TO THE THINGS THAT SCARE YOU BIT BY BIT
4. TRY TO RELAX

How to overcome fear

There are many ways to deal with fear. Some people might want to face their fears head-on, while others prefer a more gradual approach.

Some ways to deal with fear are:

- **Talk to someone about your fears.** This can help you understand them better and start to work on overcoming them.

- **Write down your fears.** This can help you see them differently and start to work through them.

- **Expose yourself to the things that scare you bit by bit.** This can be very effective in overcoming fear. However, doing this gradually and with someone you trust is essential.

- **Relax.** Relaxation techniques can help you deal with the physical symptoms of fear, such as increased heart rate and sweating.

Remember, you are not alone. Everyone experiences fear. It is a natural emotion that can be helpful to us. But if fear starts to interfere with our lives, there are things we can do to deal with it.

STRESS AND ANXIETY

Anxiety and stress are two of the most common emotions that people experience. They can both be very unpleasant.

Anxiety is caused by worry and fear. It can be caused by events that have already happened or things that might happen in the future. Sometimes we worry about things that are very unlikely to happen.

Stress is the physical response to anxiety. It can cause problems like headaches, upset stomachs, and difficulty sleeping.

Many things can cause stress. At school, you might feel stressed about homework or exams. Or with your friends, you might feel stressed about who will be at a party. It's perfectly normal to feel stressed sometimes.

How to deal with stress and anxiety

While there are many different ways to deal with stress and anxiety, some basic tips can help you get started.

First, **try to understand what is causing your stress and anxiety**. This can be difficult, but once you identify the cause, you can begin to work on addressing it. If you are unsure what is causing your stress or anxiety, many resources can help you figure it out.

Second, it is vital to **manage your stress and anxiety**. This means taking care of yourself both physically and emotionally. Make sure you get enough sleep, eat a healthy diet, and exercise regularly. Taking some time for yourself each day can also help reduce your stress and anxiety.

Finally, try to **avoid things that trigger your stress and anxiety**. This might mean avoiding certain people or situations. If you can't avoid the trigger, try to change how you think about it. For example, if you're anxious about an upcoming test, tell yourself that you are prepared and can do it.

Remember, everyone experiences stress and anxiety in different ways. What works for one person might not work for another. If you don't find the answers you are looking for, **consult a mental health professional**. They can help you find the best way to deal with stress and anxiety.

BASIC TIPS TO HELP DEAL WITH STRESS AND ANXIETY

1. **TRY TO UNDERSTAND WHAT IS CAUSING YOUR STRESS AND ANXIETY.** This can be difficult, but once you identify the cause, you can begin to work on addressing it. If you are unsure what is causing your stress or anxiety, many resources can help you figure it out.

2. **TRY TO MANAGE YOUR STRESS AND ANXIETY** This means taking care of yourself both physically and emotionally. Make sure you get enough sleep, eat a healthy diet, and exercise regularly. Taking some time for yourself each day can also help reduce your stress and anxiety.

3. **AVOID THINGS THAT TRIGGERS YOUR STRESS AND ANXIETY** This might mean avoiding certain people or situations. If you can't avoid the trigger, try to change how you think about it. For example, if you're anxious about an upcoming test, tell yourself that you are prepared and can do it.

ACTIVITY

Stress & Anxiety Action Plan

This is a simple activity, but it can be very helpful in understanding what may be causing your stress and anxiety and working out ways to deal with it.

1. In the first column, write down things that cause you stress or anxiety. Try to put them in order, with the things that cause you most stress at the top; for example, you may include:
   - Taking tests
   - Being around people I don't know well

2. In the following column, for each of the things you wrote down, brainstorm at least two ways to deal with the stress or anxiety it causes. For example:
   - Taking tests:
     - Study ahead of time
     - Take breaks during the test
   - Being around people I don't know well:
     - Talk to someone you do know before going into the situation
     - Bring a friend with you

3. Write down when you will complete it in the last column.

STRESS ACTION PLAN

What's stressing me out?	What I can do about it?	When can I do it?

CHAPTER 4

SCHOOL AND LEARNING

Going to school is an important part of growing up. It's a place where you learn about the world around you, make friends and develop life skills. But for some kids, starting school or moving to a new school can be a bit scary. If you're feeling nervous about starting school, don't worry!

> Remember that **EVERYONE FEELS A BIT NERVOUS ABOUT STARTING AT A NEW SCHOOL.** It's perfectly normal to feel like this. Just take a deep breath and remember that you can do it!

Remember too; there are many great things about going to school, like learning new things and meeting new friends. Of course, one of the most important things about school is that it teaches you how to learn and work hard. These skills will serve you well throughout your life. No matter what you do, always give it your best effort and never give up!

Try to listen to your teachers and do your best at school. This is the best way to learn and get good grades.

But it's also important to be yourself. Don't try to be someone you're not because you'll only end up feeling unhappy.

The most important thing is to have fun and enjoy your time at school. It's a place where you learn new things and make lasting friendships. So go out there and have some fun!

Of course, you'll also have to take regular exams and tests at school. This can be daunting, but remember that everyone gets nervous about these things. Just do your best, and you'll be fine.

GETTING GOOD GRADES AT SCHOOL

Getting good grades at school will help set you up for life. But it can be hard to know where to start. If you're struggling to get good grades, don't worry! We've got some great tips to help you out.

1. **The first step is to make sure you understand the material.** Ask your teacher or a friend if you're unsure about something. The more you know, the easier it will be to do well on tests and exams.

2. **Another critical step is to stay organized.** Keep track of due dates and ensure you have all the materials you need for each class. This will help you stay on top of your work and hand things in on time.

3. **Try to study regularly.** Dedicate some time each day or each week to reviewing the material. This will help you remember things better and get good grades.

4. **Finally, don't stress out!** Getting good grades is important, but it's not worth getting stressed out about. Take a deep breath and do your best. You'll be fine!

HOW TO STUDY EFFECTIVELY

You need to study effectively if you want to do well in school. But what does that mean? And how can you do it? Here are some tips:

1. **Start by making a study plan.** Decide which subjects you need to focus on and devise a study schedule. This will help you stay organized and make the most of your time.

2. **Make sure you have enough space to study.** You need to be comfortable when you're learning, so find a quiet place where you can concentrate.

3. **Create a study environment that works for you.** Some people like to listen to music or have complete silence when they study, while others prefer to be around people. Find what works best for you and stick to it.

4. **Take breaks.** Try to take breaks when studying, especially if you've been working for a while. Get up and walk around, or have a snack. This will help you stay focused and motivated.

DEALING WITH HOMEWORK

As you grow older, you're likely to be set homework. At first, this can be challenging. You may feel like you don't have enough time or are always behind. But don't worry, with a little organization, it's manageable. Here are some tips to help you out.

1. **Make a schedule and stick to it.** Decide how much time you need for each subject and stick to that schedule. This will help you stay organized and avoid last-minute cramming.

2. **Get organized.** Keep track of your homework assignments and due dates. Don't bury your head in the sand! Try to stay on top of things and hand assignments in on time.

3. **Ask for help when you need it.** If you're struggling with a particular subject, don't hesitate to ask your teacher or a friend for help. They'll be happy to assist you.

4. **Take breaks.** Remember to take breaks when doing homework, especially if you've been working for a while. Get up and walk around, or have a snack. This will help you stay focused and motivated.

5. **Stay positive.** When you're doing homework, it's easy to get frustrated. But remember that everyone makes mistakes. Don't get discouraged, and keep trying your best.

6. **Practice, practice, practice.** The best way to improve your grades is to practice. If you can, try solving sample questions or practicing past exams. This will help you become more familiar with the material and do better on tests.

HOW TO ACE TESTS

One of the skills you will learn in school is how to take tests. If you've never taken an exam before, it can be daunting. Tests are usually timed, and you can't bring anything with you into the room.

You may feel under pressure like you're in a race against the clock. But like anything, practice makes perfect!

7 TIPS ON HOW TO ACE TESTS

RELAX
The first thing you need to do is relax. You're more likely to do well if you're calm and focused. So take a few deep breaths, clear your head, and get ready to tackle the test.

TIME YOURSELF

When taking a test, you want to ensure you have enough time for each question. So before you start, decide how much time you want to spend on each section. This will help you stay on track and not run out of time.

READ THE QUESTIONS CAREFULLY
Don't rush through the test. Stop, pause and read each question carefully. This will help you understand what is being asked and ensure you answer the question correctly.

ANSWER THE EASY QUESTIONS FIRST

If you're struggling with a question, try answering the more straightforward questions first. This will give you a better idea of how much time you have left for the more complex questions.

CHECK YOUR WORK
Once you've finished, go back and check your work. Make sure you answered all the questions and that your answers are correct.

TAKE A BREAK

Once you've finished the test, take a break. Get up and walk around, or have a snack. This will help you calm down and clear your head.

DON'T WORRY

If you don't do well on a test, don't worry. It's not the end of the world! Some people do well at tests, while others find them difficult. Tests are just one part of the assessment process. There are other ways to show your knowledge and understanding.

HOW TO REMEMBER INFORMATION

Remembering information is an essential life skill. When you're in school, you will be required to retain a lot of facts. You'll also meet many new people, and it's good to remember their names. If you can place a person's name, you're more likely to make a good impression on them. And if you remember important facts, you're more likely to do well in your studies.

HOW TO EASILY REMEMBER NAMES

- Associate the name with a picture.
- Repeat the name out loud in your first conversation.
- Use the name often.
- Write the name down.
- Rhyme the name.
- Don't be afraid to ask them to repeat it.
- Practice, practice, practice.

You may think you're not good at remembering things, but everyone can improve their memory if they practice regularly. **The brain is a muscle. The more you use it, the stronger it will get.**

Here are some tips to help you remember names, which could also be used to remember facts.

❶ Associate the name with a picture. The human brain is excellent at remembering images. So when you meet someone new, try associating their name with a picture in your head. This will help you remember it better. You could create a funny or silly image as you may remember it better that way.

❷ Repeat the name out loud in your first conversation. Repeating the word aloud will help you internalize and remember it better. For example, if you're introduced to someone called Angie, instead of saying "nice to meet you," say "Hi Angie, it's nice to meet you."

LIFE SKILLS FOR TWEENS **45**

③ Use the name often. When you use someone's name regularly, you're more likely to remember it. So try using the person's name in every conversation you have with them. Not only will this help you remember it better, but it will also make the person feel important and special.

④ Write the name down. When you meet someone, take a few seconds to write their name down. You could put the person's name in your phone contacts or write it on a piece of paper. You could take it further by connecting them with an important fact you've learned about them. For example, if you meet someone called Sarah, you could write "Sarah loves singing" next to her name.

⑤ Rhyme the name. This is a great way to remember someone's name if you're having trouble doing so. Try to think of a rhyme with their name when you meet someone. For example, if someone's name is Anna, you could rhyme it with "banana."

⑥ Don't be afraid to ask them to repeat it. It's okay to make mistakes when trying to remember someone's name. If you forget their name, don't be afraid to ask them to repeat it. And if you still can't remember it, don't worry about it. Just move on and try to remember the person's name the next time you see them.

⑦ Practice, practice, practice. The best way to remember something is to practice. If you can, try repeating the name a few times. This will help embed it in your memory.

The same is valid for remembering facts. If you want to remember something, you need to practice regularly. Some people find it helpful to write the information down, while others prefer to recite it aloud. If you can find a way to make the information exciting or fun, you're more likely to remember it.

Practicing these tips regularly is essential so that they become second nature to you. The more you practice, the better your memory will be. Good luck!

ACTIVITY

Homework Planner

Use the simple homework planner to plan your next assignments.

	Subject	To-do	Due date
☐			
☐			
☐			
☐			
☐			
☐			
☐			

CHAPTER 5

HEALTH AND WELLNESS

Health and wellness are essential aspects of life that we should all strive to maintain. They aren't just about being physically healthy, but also mentally and emotionally healthy.

When it comes to health and wellness, there are a few key things everyone should know and practice.

This chapter will discuss some of the most essential health and wellness topics. We will discuss the importance of eating healthy, staying active, and getting enough sleep.

EXERCISE

One of the most important aspects of good health is staying physically active.

> **EXERCISE IS CRUCIAL FOR OVERALL HEALTH AND WELL-BEING,** and it's especially important during your pre-teen years.

Exercise helps build muscle, improve strength and endurance, and burn calories. It also releases endorphins, which are chemicals in the brain that have mood-boosting effects. In other words, exercise can help improve your mood and reduce stress.

How to exercise more

There are many different ways to stay active and get exercise. You can join a sports team, go for walks or runs, or even play in your backyard. The important thing is to find something that you enjoy and to do it regularly.

If you don't like running, there's no point in forcing yourself to do it. But, it's also good to challenge yourself and push yourself outside of your comfort zone from time to time. This will help you to become stronger and more resilient.

Try to do at least 30 minutes of exercise each day. This doesn't have to be all at once—you can break it up into 10-minute intervals if that's easier for you.

You could:

- Ride your bike or scooter
- Walk to school
- Jump on a trampoline
- Swim
- Play tag with your friends
- Do some pushups or sit-ups
- Run around the block
- Do a simple workout

Try to incorporate your exercise into your daily routine so that it becomes a habit. For example, if you usually watch TV after school for an hour, try doing a 20-minute workout and then watching TV for the remaining 40 minutes.

Alternatively, you could incorporate exercise into your school day, so instead of driving to school, walk or ride your bike.

. . . .

HEALTHY EATING

Another aspect of good health is eating a balanced and healthy diet. **Eating healthy foods helps our bodies to function correctly and to stay strong**. It also helps us maintain a healthy weight, which is important for our physical and mental health.

A balanced diet includes foods from all the major food groups: fruits, vegetables, grains, dairy, and protein. It's important to eat a variety of different foods from each group so that we get all the nutrients our bodies need.

How to eat healthily

We have covered the need for a balanced diet above, but how do you actually put this into practice?

There are a few simple tips that can help you to make healthier choices:

1. **Eat a healthy breakfast every day:** Breakfast is the day's most important meal. It helps jumpstart your metabolism and give you energy for the day ahead.

2. **Make half your plate fruits and vegetables:** Fruits and vegetables are packed with nutrients essential for good health. Try to include a variety of different colors and types to get a variety of nutrients. You should aim for at least 5 servings of fruit and vegetables every day.

3. **Avoid processed foods:** Processed foods (such as chips, cookies, cakes, and ice cream) are often high in sugar, salt, and unhealthy fats and low in nutrients. Try to eat less of these foods and instead focus on eating whole, unprocessed foods (such as fruits, vegetables, whole grains, and lean protein).

4. **Limit sugary drinks:** Sugary drinks are often high in sugar and provide very little nutritional value. Instead of sugary drinks, try to drink water, milk, or 100% fruit juice.

5. **Enjoy everything in moderation:** It's okay to enjoy your favorite foods from time to time. Just remember to eat them in moderation (small amounts) and balance them with healthier choices.

6. **Be active:** As we mentioned, exercise is vital for good health. Try to be active for at least 30 minutes each day.

7. **Drink plenty of water:** Water is essential for our bodies to function properly. It helps to transport nutrients and to keep our cells hydrated. Try to drink 8 glasses of water each day.

There are many aspects of good health, but eating a balanced diet and regular exercise will help your body function properly and stay strong. Try to incorporate healthy eating and exercise into your daily routine so that they become habits. These habits will help you to stay healthy throughout your life.

HOW TO ENSURE YOU GET ENOUGH SLEEP

Getting enough sleep is another part of good health. **During sleep, our bodies rest, recharge and rebuild tissues, muscles, and bone.**

A good night's sleep usually means around 8 hours of uninterrupted sleep for adults and 10 hours or more for children. If you don't get enough sleep, you may feel tired during the day, have trouble concentrating, and you may be more likely to get sick and feel stressed out. **Sleep is quite literally your superpower!**

There are a few things you can do to help improve the quality of your sleep:

1. **Establish a regular sleep schedule** and stick to it as much as possible. This means going to bed at the same time each night and getting up at the same time each morning, even on weekends.

2. **Create a bedtime routine to help you relax before sleep.** This could involve things like reading or taking a bath.

3. **Avoid screens (TV, phones, laptops) in the hour leading up to bedtime** as the blue light from screens can make it harder to fall asleep. It's a good idea to switch off all electronic devices in your bedroom or remove them from the room altogether.

4. **Create a calm and inviting environment in your bedroom.** This means making sure it's dark, quiet, and cool. Your bedroom should be a place where you feel relaxed and comfortable.

5. **Get regular exercise during the day.** Exercise helps to promote good sleep. It helps tire out your body and releases endorphins, which can help you to relax and fall asleep more easily.

Tips to recharge your superpower!

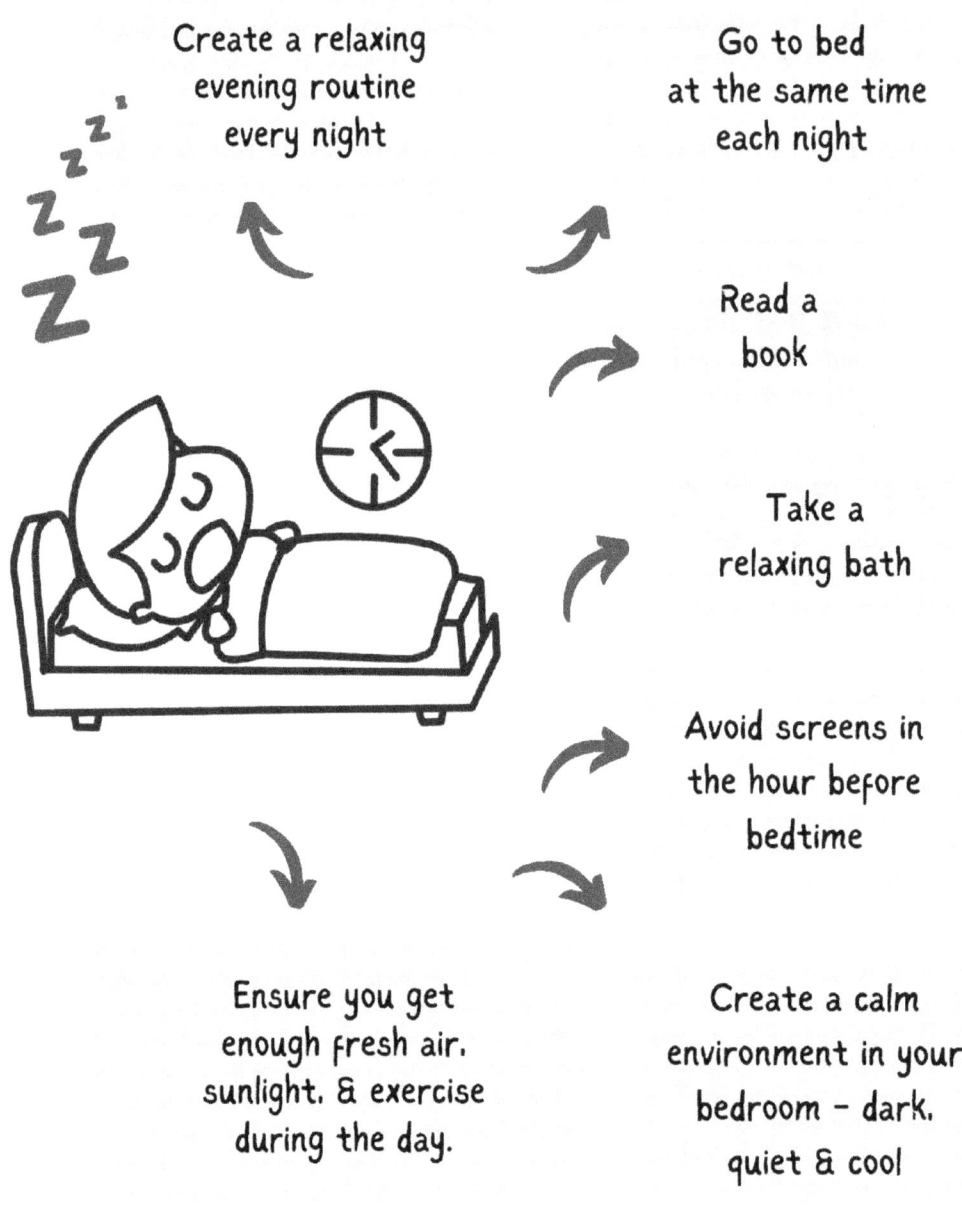

- Create a relaxing evening routine every night
- Go to bed at the same time each night
- Read a book
- Take a relaxing bath
- Avoid screens in the hour before bedtime
- Create a calm environment in your bedroom – dark, quiet & cool
- Ensure you get enough fresh air, sunlight, & exercise during the day.

THE IMPORTANCE OF GOOD HYGIENE

Another aspect of good health is keeping our bodies clean. This means washing your hands regularly, brushing your teeth twice a day, and showering or bathing.

Throughout the day, our hands come into contact with many different surfaces, and they can pick up bacteria and other germs. If we don't wash our hands, we can spread these germs to other people or onto surfaces. This can lead to illnesses such as colds, flu, and stomach bugs.

When you should wash your hands:

- before, during, and after preparing food
- before eating food
- after using the restroom
- after coughing, sneezing, or blowing your nose
- after handling animals or animal waste
- after handling garbage

How to wash your hands

To wash your hands properly, use warm water and soap and scrub all over your hands for at least 20 seconds. Be sure to get in between your fingers and under your nails. Rinse well and dry with a clean towel.

How to brush your teeth

Brushing your teeth twice a day helps keep them healthy. Brushing removes plaque—a sticky film of bacteria—from your teeth. If plaque isn't removed, it can harden and turn into tartar, leading to gum disease.

To brush your teeth properly, **use a pea-sized amount of toothpaste on your toothbrush**. Aim the toothbrush at a 45-degree angle towards the gum line and use gentle circular motions. Be sure to brush on the inside surfaces of your teeth and use a light back and forth action on the chewing surfaces of your molars. Spit the toothpaste out after brushing.

Lastly, showering or bathing will help keep your skin clean and healthy. Use a mild soap or body wash and avoid scrubbing your skin too hard. Rinse the soap off, and then dry yourself with a clean towel.

Body smells and puberty

As you grow older, you might notice your start to smell different. This is perfectly normal! As your body goes through puberty, you might sweat more, and your skin will produce more oil. This can lead to body odor.

Puberty usually occurs between 10 and 14 for girls and between 12 and 16 for boys.

There are a few things you can do to help reduce body odor:

- Firstly, **shower or bathe every day.** This will help to remove sweat and bacteria from your skin.

- Secondly, **wear clean clothes.** You should wash your clothes regularly, especially items like socks and underwear.

- Thirdly, **use an antiperspirant or deodorant.** These products can help to mask body odor.

- Fourthly, **eat a healthy diet.** Eating foods that contain lots of fiber can help reduce body odor as they help flush toxins out of your body.

- Lastly, **drink plenty of water.** Staying hydrated will help to keep your skin healthy and free from bacteria.

ACTIVITY

Exercise Log

Regular exercise is essential for good health. It can help to improve your mood, reduce stress, and boost your energy levels.

Over the next week, keep track of your daily exercise. This could be going for a walk, a bike ride, or a swim. It could also be playing football, basketball, or soccer.

You can also include other activities that make you move, such as dancing, skipping, and running.

At the end of the week, add up all the minutes you exercised for each day. Then calculate the total number of minutes you exercised over the week.

How much exercise did you do this week?

Did you do more or less exercise than you thought you would?

How do you feel after completing this activity?

EXERCISE LOG

FILL OUT EACH DAY WITH YOUR DAILY EXERCISE. AT THE END OF THE WEEK, ADD UP ALL THE MINUTES YOU EXERCISED.

MONDAY
Activity: ☐

Minutes _____

TUESDAY
Activity: ☐

Minutes _____

WEDNESDAY
Activity: ☐

Minutes _____

THURSDAY
Activity: ☐

Minutes _____

FRIDAY
Activity: ☐

Minutes _____

SATURDAY / SUNDAY
Activity: ☐

Minutes _____

○ ○ ○ ○ ○ ○
m t w t f s s

Total Minutes _____

CHAPTER 6

MONEY MATTERS

One of the most important things you will learn in this book is how to handle money. It is helpful to start learning about money as early as possible to make the most of it and be responsible with your finances when you are older.

There are a few things you need to know about money.

- **Firstly, you need to know how to earn it.** Money doesn't grow on trees—it comes from working hard. When you're young, this usually comes from doing chores around the house or getting an allowance from your parents. As you get older, you may start to earn money from part-time jobs.

- **Secondly, you need to know how to save it.** Let's say you have your eye on a new bike that costs $200. You can either save up for it over time or borrow the money from your parents (or someone else) and pay them back over time.

- **Thirdly, you need to know how to spend it.** Just because you have money doesn't mean you should go out and spend it all! You need to be mindful of what you are spending your money on and whether or not it is something you need. You might feel you need a new PlayStation 4 straight away, but is that a need? Or are you just wanting it because all your friends have one?

Learning about money is an important life skill, and it is something that will benefit you for the rest of your life. The more you know about money, the better off you will be financially.

Before we get started, let's look at some money-related words.

- CASH: This is paper money or the coins you have in your wallet or piggy bank.

- INCOME: This is the money that you earn. For example, if you receive a $50 per month allowance from your parents, that is your income.

- EXPENSES: This is the opposite of income—it is the money we spend on things. For example, if you spend $10 on a new toy, that is an expense.

- BUDGET: This is a plan that helps us track our income and expenses to save money.

- SAVING IS WHEN YOU PUT SOME OF YOUR MONEY ASIDE FOR LATER.

- INVESTING: This is when you use your money to make more!

- DEBT: This is when you owe somebody money.

Now that we have examined money-related words, let's dig deeper and learn more about these topics.

HOW TO BUDGET YOUR MONEY

Budgeting is an important life skill to learn. **It is planning for your future spending.** This means looking at your income and working out how much you need to save each month and what you can afford to spend.

For example, let's say you are saving for a new pair of jeans that cost $100. You will need to work out how much money you have coming in each month and how much you can afford to put away each month until you have enough for the jeans.

When you start earning money, you may find that you spend it each month as you get it. But even if you put a small amount of money away, it's a good idea to start saving some each month to have money for later. You never know when you might need it!

> If you can start a habit of saving when you're younger, it will become easier to save when you're older and earn more money.

HOW TO SAVE MONEY

One popular method for learning to save is the jar system. This is where you have different jars for different savings goals.

For example, you might have a "new jeans" jar and a "new pet" jar.

You divide it every time you get money and put it into your different jars. This can be a fun way to save, and it also helps you see how much you are saving for each goal.

As you grow older, you may want to adopt another popular method: the 50/30/20 rule. In this case, you divide your money into three categories—**50% for essential expenses, 30% for things you really want, and 20% for savings.**

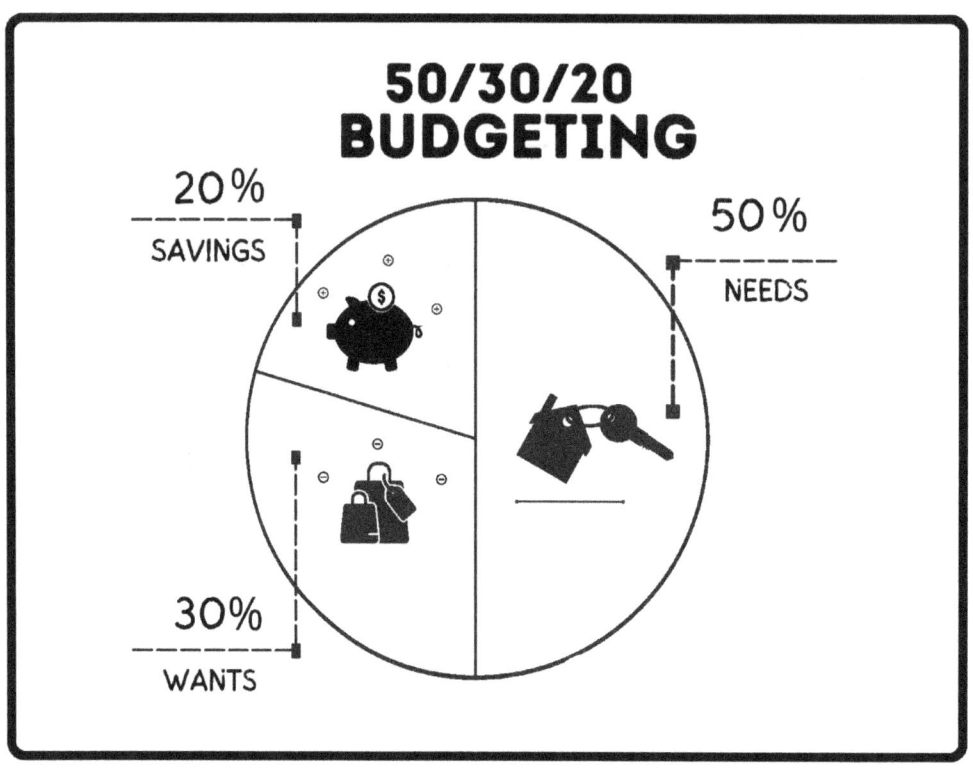

For example, if you received $100 birthday money, you would divide it up like this:

- *$50 for essentials—this could be clothes or food*
- *$30 for wants—this could be a new toy or game*
- *$20 for savings—this could be put into your piggy bank or a savings account*

The 50/30/20 rule is a good starting point, but you may need to adjust it depending on your income and expenses.

There are many ways to budget, and finding a system that works for you is vital. The most important thing is to be mindful of your spending and try to put some money away each month.

HOW TO SPEND MONEY WISELY

Now that you have a good idea about budgeting and how to save money, let's talk about spending money wisely.

When you choose to spend your money, think about whether you are buying something you need or if it is something you just want.

- **Needs are things that we cannot live without, such as food and shelter.**
- **Wants are things we would like to have but are not essential.**

   For example, you might need a new pair of shoes because your old ones are too small. But you might want a new toy because you've seen it advertised.

It is crucial to distinguish between needs and wants to spend your money wisely.

> **THINK ABOUT WHETHER YOU NEED SOMETHING BEFORE YOU BUY IT.** If you can wait a little while, you might be able to save up and buy it later.

LIFE SKILLS FOR TWEENS

Consider how much something is worth. Just because something is expensive does not mean it is a good value.

> *For example, a new pair of shoes might cost $100. But if you only wear them for a few months and then they are too small, it was not a wise purchase.*
>
> *On the other hand, a toy that costs $20 but will provide hours of fun is better value. It is helpful to consider both the price and the quality when making a purchase.*

Finally, **try to be aware of sales and discounts.** You might be able to get the same toy for $10 if you wait for a sale. Or you might be able to find a coupon for $20 off your purchase.

Keep your eyes open for these deals to save money on the things you want to buy.

Here are a few tips to help you spend money wisely:

1. **Buy items on sale:** This is a great way to get something you want while spending less money.

2. **Plan ahead:** If you know you are going to want something in the future, you can start saving for it now.

3. **Buy used items:** Used items are often just as good as new items but cost less. There are often bargains to be found at garage sales and thrift stores. You can also find great deals on second-hand items online with your parent's help.

4. **Compare prices:** It pays to shop around and compare prices before making a purchase.

5. **Be patient:** If you can wait to buy something, you might be able to get it at a lower price or find a better deal.

By following these tips, you can learn to spend your money wisely. And remember, the best way to save money is to avoid spending it in the first place!

HOW TO SPEND MONEY ONLINE

These days, we can buy almost anything we want online. But just because we can buy something doesn't mean we should!

When you are spending money online, you need to be careful. Just like in a store, you need to consider whether you are buying something you need or if it is something you just want.

Spending online is easy and can be done with just a few clicks. But if you're not careful, you can spend a lot of money without even realizing it.

Here are a few tips to help you spend money wisely online:

1. **Always ask your parents:** Before making a purchase, ask your parents or an adult if it is okay.

2. **Compare prices:** Many different websites sell the same things. So it pays to shop around and compare prices before making a purchase.

3. **Only buy from reputable websites:** This is the most important rule when buying anything online. Do you know the site? Have you heard of it before? You should consider these things before giving your credit card information to any website. If you're unsure, ask your parents or another adult for help.

4. **Read the reviews:** Before you buy something, read the reviews. This will help you avoid buying something that is not worth the money.

5. **Look for coupon codes:** You can often find discounts and coupons online. Be sure to check for these before you make a purchase.

Following these tips can teach you to spend your money wisely online. With some care, you can find great deals and save money on the things you want to buy.

UNDERSTANDING CREDIT CARDS, DEBIT CARDS & BUY NOW PAY LATER

When you buy things online or at the shops, you will often see the option to pay with a credit or debit card. But what are these? And how do they work?

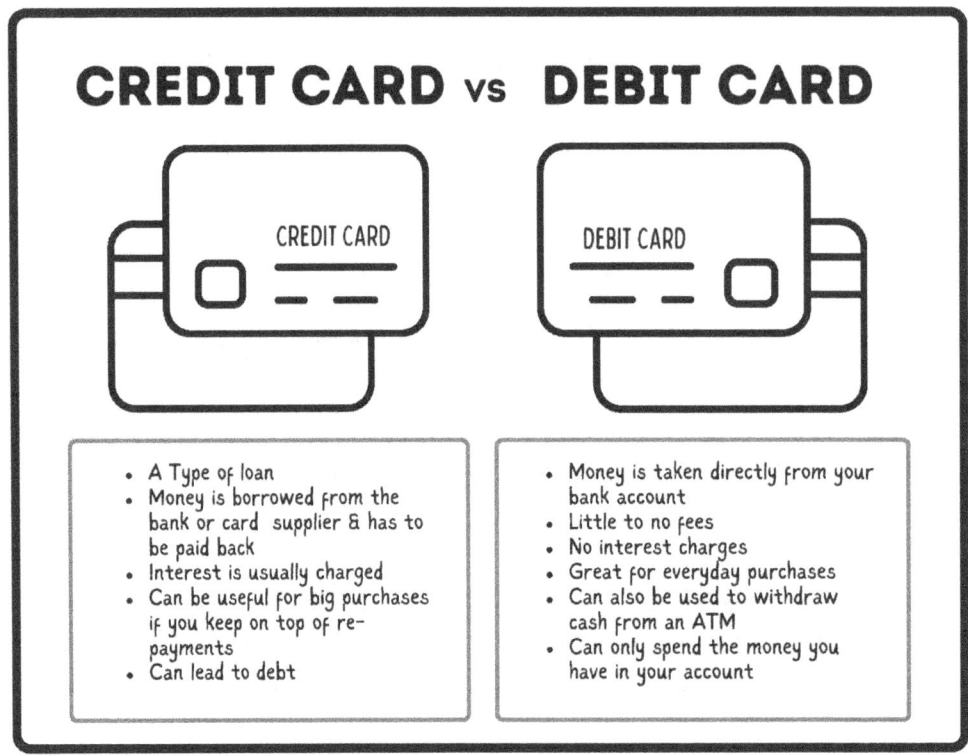

Credit cards

> CREDIT CARDS are a type of loan. You borrow money from the bank when you use a credit card. You will need to pay this money back with interest.

If you don't pay back the money you owe, the bank or card supplier will charge you a fee. This is called interest.

For example, imagine you spend $100 on your credit card. The bank will charge you interest; let's say it's 10%. This means you will owe the bank $110.

If you don't pay this back, the bank will charge you another 10% interest on the $110. So now you owe the bank $121.

As you can see, the interest can quickly add up, and you can end up owing a lot of money to the bank. This is why you must be careful if you use a credit card.

Debit cards

> DEBIT CARDS are different from credit cards. When you use a debit card, the money is taken directly from your bank account.

This means you can only spend the money you have in your account. You cannot borrow money like you can with a credit card.

> *For example, let's say you have $100 in your bank account. You use your debit card to buy something that costs $50. This means there is now $50 left in your account.*

If you try to spend more than you have in your account, the transaction will be declined.

Both credit and debit cards can be used to make purchases online or in the shops. While they may look like the same bits of plastic, they are very different, and you should be careful with both of them. You don't want to end up spending more money than you have!

Here are a few things to keep in mind when using credit or debit cards:

- **Ask your parents before you use their card.**
- **Always know how much money you have in your account.** This will help you avoid spending more money than you have.
- When you are older, if you get a credit card, ensure you **understand the terms and conditions and keep on top of your monthly payments.**
- **Keep your credit or debit card in a safe place.** This will help prevent someone from stealing and using it without your permission.

Many apps now allow parents to control their child's spending. This can be a great way to help teach young adults about money and how to spend it wisely.

Buy now pay later

Even though you may not have seen it, you've probably heard of "buy now, pay later." This is where you can buy something today and pay for it over time. More and more online websites offer their customers this payment option.

> *For example, let's say you want to buy a new jacket that costs $200. The website offers you the option to pay for it over 3 months. This means you would pay $66.67 per month for 3 months.*
>
> *At the end of the 3 months, you would have paid off the jacket in full.*

This may sound like a great idea, but there are some things you should know before you do this.

First, **this is debt**. This means you are borrowing money from the company to pay for the jacket.

Second, **you will be charged interest if you don't make your payments on** time. This means you will end up paying more than the original price.

> *For example, let's say you have three months to pay for your jacket. If you pay it all in those 3 months, there is no interest to pay. This is called 'Interest-Free.' But if you don't pay it all in those 3 months and still owe $50, the company will charge you interest on that $50.*
>
> *The interest rate can be anywhere from 10% to 25%. This means your $50 debt could turn into a $60 or even a $75 debt!*

So, while "buy now, pay later" might sound like a great idea, you must be careful before using this option. Be sure you can afford the monthly payments and will pay them off within the interest-free period.

If you are unsure about something, ask your parents or an adult you trust for help. They will be able to give you some good advice.

You can learn to spend your money wisely with a bit of care. Whether using a credit card, debit card, or cash, remember to think about what you are buying and why. By doing this, you can avoid making impulsive purchases that you may later regret.

HOW TO MAKE MONEY

Now we know how to spend money wisely, let's talk about how to make money.

Making money is not always easy. When you're younger, you might rely on an allowance from your parents. But as you get older, you'll need to find ways to make your own money.

There are many ways to earn money, some of which you can do even if you're still a kid.

Money-making ideas

- **Do odd jobs:** You can earn money by doing odd jobs for your neighbors or family friends. This could include mowing lawns, washing cars, raking leaves, or shoveling snow.
- **Have a lemonade stand:** This is a great way to earn money in the summer. You only need a pitcher, some lemonade mix, and a table or stand to set up your business.
- **Do chores:** You can also earn money by doing chores around the house. This could include taking out the trash, cleaning up your room, or doing the grocery shopping.
- **Have a yard sale:** This is a great way to earn money and get rid of things you don't need anymore. You can set up a table in your front yard and sell items like clothes, toys, or books.
- **Make and sell crafts:** If you're creative, you can make things like jewelry, cards, or paintings and sell them to people. You can set up a table or sell your items online at a local market.
- **Be a pet sitter:** If you love animals, you can earn money by caring for people's pets while they are out of town. This could include feeding, walking, and playing with the pet.
- **Baby-sit:** If you're responsible and good with kids, you can earn money by babysitting for families in your neighborhood.
- **Sell your stuff:** If you've got toys or games you no longer play with, try selling them online with the help of an adult. eBay, Facebook Marketplace, Gumtree, and Craigslist are just some platforms to buy and sell second-hand goods.

These are just a few ideas to get you started. There are many other ways to make money. The important thing is to be creative and think of something you're interested in.

How to turn a money-making idea into a reality

If you have an idea about how to make money, the next step is to turn that idea into a reality.

First, you must **research and determine if there is a market for your product** or service. This means finding out if people are willing to pay for what you're offering.

Next, you need to **create a plan**. This will help you figure out what to do to get your business up and running.

Once you have a plan, you need to **start taking action**.

> *For example, say you want to wash cars in your neighborhood.*
>
> *To turn this idea into a reality, you need to do the following:*
>
> *— Do some research and figure out how much people are willing to pay for car washes.*
>
> *— Create a plan including what supplies you need and where you will wash the cars.*
>
> *— Start advertising your business by hanging up flyers or posting them online.*
>
> *— Start washing cars!*

These are just a few things you need to do to make your idea a reality. Remember **making money takes time and effort, but it is worth it**! When you have your own money, you can spend it however you like. Just be sure to follow the tips above to spend it wisely!

HOW TO GET A JOB

Now that you know how to make money from your hobbies let's talk about how to get a job. You may not be old enough to get a job now, but it's never too early to start thinking about it!

There are many different types of jobs out there.

The best way to figure out what job is right for you is to think about what you're interested in. Do you like working with people? Do you like animals? Do you like being outdoors? These things can help you narrow down the type of job you're looking for.

Another way to figure out what job is right for you is to think about what things you're good at. Are you good at math? Are you good at writing? Are you good at cleaning? These things can help you find a job that's a perfect fit for you.

Once you know what job you're looking for, the next step is to apply for jobs. The best way to do this is to look online or in the newspaper for job postings. You can also ask your parents or other adults if they know of any openings in their workplace.

The last step is to go for an interview. This is where you'll meet with the hiring person and tell them why you're the best person for the job.

Remember, it's never too early to start thinking about your future career! By following the tips above, you'll be on your way to finding a job you love.

OPENING YOUR FIRST BANK ACCOUNT

When you start earning money, you will need somewhere to keep it safe. This is where a bank account comes in handy!

There are different types of bank accounts, but the most common for young adults is a kids' account. This type of account is designed specifically for children and young people.

When you open a kids' account, you will usually get a card that allows you to withdraw money from cash machines (ATMs). You may also be able to set up a standing order or direct debit, which is when money is automatically transferred from your account to another account regularly.

> *For example, you could set up a standing order to pay your pocket money into your savings account each week.*

Most banks will also offer an app that you can use to check your balance and make payments.

HOW TO USE AN ATM MACHINE

An ATM machine (or cash point) is a helpful way to get cash when needed. You can take money from your account by inserting your bank card into the machine.

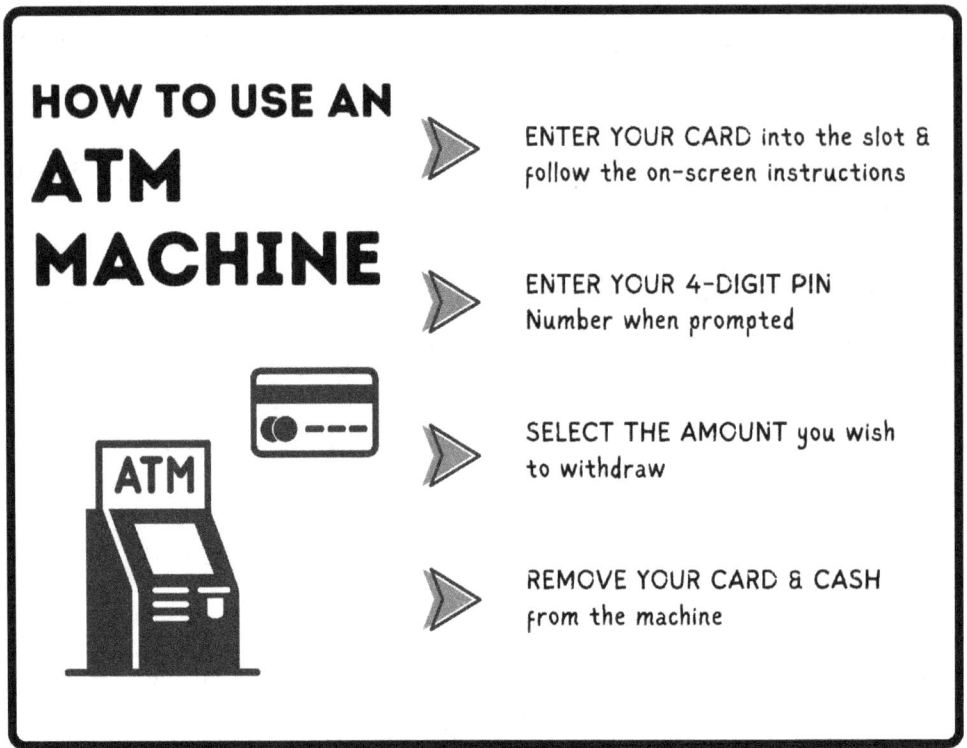

Most machines will allow you to take out different amounts of cash, so you can choose how much you need. Remember that once you have taken the money out, it is gone from your account. So be sure you only take out what you need.

Some machines will also allow you to check your balance. This can be a handy way to track how much money you have in your account.

There are a few simple things you should know before using one.

First, **some ATM machines will charge you a fee for using them**. Look at the screen beforehand to see how much money they might charge you.

Second, **you need to know your PIN number**. This is the 4-digit number that you use to access your bank account.

If you don't know your PIN number, you need to contact your bank to get it. Once you have your PIN number, keep it in a safe place. You don't want anyone else to find out what it is and use your account without your permission.

Third, **you need to have your bank card with you**. This is the card that has your name and account number on it.

Most ATM machines will only accept cards with a Visa or MasterCard logo.

Finally, **take your bank card and cash** when you are finished using the machine. Do not leave them behind.

ACTIVITY

Savings Tracker

Saving money can be difficult, but if you're organized and start early on in life, it's a habit that will benefit you throughout your life. One way to help you save money is by using a savings tracker.

Try to think of something you really want that you can save towards. This could be a new pair of jeans, a top or a new games console. Now let's use the worksheet to try to save towards that goal.

1. Write what you're saving for, the amount of money you need, and the due date for when you want to hit your goal.
2. Each time you save some money towards your goal, enter the amount next to the piggy. This could be daily, weekly, or monthly.
3. Try to make saving towards your goal a regular habit. You'll hit your goal in no time.

SAVINGS TRACKER

Saving For : _____

Amount : _____   Due By : _____

Total :

Notes : _____
_____

CHAPTER 7

COOKING SKILLS

Cooking is an essential life skill. It allows you to make tasty food and teaches you about math, science, and nutrition. Cooking is a great way to get creative, and it's a fun activity to do with friends or family.

With just a few basic ingredients and some basic techniques, you can learn to make a variety of dishes in no time without spending a lot of money. Plus, cooking at home is healthier than eating out. You know what's in your food and can control what you eat.

If you're not sure where to start, don't worry. There are plenty of recipes online that are easy to follow. You can also watch cooking tutorials on YouTube. With a bit of practice, you'll be able to cook delicious, healthy meals that everyone will love.

Let's get started with some basics.

- COOKING SAFELY. Cooking can be great fun, but you should always take precautions to stay safe. Only cook when you're under adult supervision, never leave cooking unattended, and always use the correct utensils.

- BASIC HYGIENE. Always wash your hands before cooking, and clean your work surfaces and utensils. This will help prevent bacteria from spreading and ensure your food is safe to eat.

- HANDLING RAW MEAT. Always wash your hands and utensils thoroughly after handling raw meat. Use a separate cutting board for meat; never put cooked food on the same plate as raw meat.

- CLEANING UP. After you've finished cooking, you need to clear up.

- FILL THE SINK WITH HOT, SOAPY WATER. Add your pots and pans and let them soak for a few minutes. Use a scrub brush to clean them off, then rinse them under hot water. Finally, dry them with a dish towel.

- MEASURING. When cooking, you need to measure your ingredients accurately. This will help ensure that your food comes out as you want it to. There are various measuring devices, such as cups, spoons, and tablespoons.

HOW TO MEASURE INGREDIENTS

For wet ingredients, such as milk or water, you'll need to use a liquid measuring cup. Pour the ingredient into the cup until it reaches the line marking the desired amount.

You'll need to weigh or use a spoon to measure dry ingredients, such as flour or sugar.

BASIC COOKING TERMS

Before you start cooking, it will help you to understand some basic cooking terms. Here are a few of the most common ones:

- **Boil:** To cook food in boiling water on a stovetop in a pan.
- **Saute:** To fry food in a small amount of hot oil or butter on the stovetop.
- **Simmer:** To cook food over low heat, so the liquid is just below boiling point.
- **Roast:** To cook food in an oven at a high temperature.
- **Steam:** To cook food by boiling it in steam.
- **Grill:** To cook food on a grill over hot coals or gas heat.

CUTTING TECHNIQUES

One of the most important things about cooking is cutting food into the correct sizes. This will ensure that your food cooks evenly and is ready to eat when you want it to be. Here are a few basic cutting techniques that you should know:

- **Cutting in half:** To cut a piece of food in half, place the knife at one end and slice down the middle.

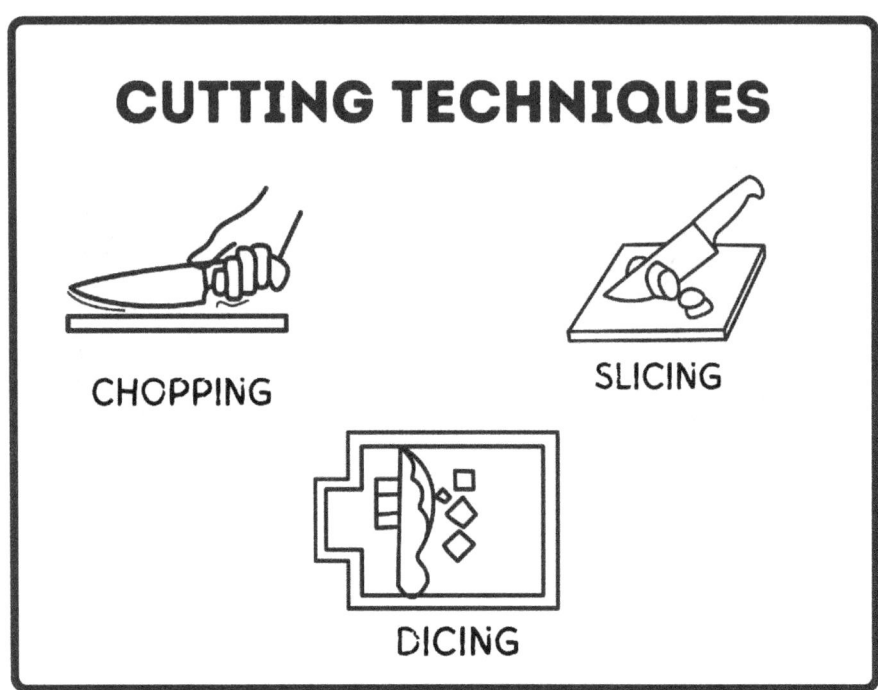

- **Dicing:** To dice a piece of food, place the knife at one end and cut it into small cubes.

- **Chopping:** To chop a piece of food, place the knife at one end and cut it into small pieces.

- **Slicing:** To slice a piece of food, place the knife on top of the food and slice down. Make sure to use a gentle motion so you don't cut yourself.

HOW TO READ A RECIPE

A recipe is a set of instructions that tells you how to cook a particular dish. It will list the ingredients you need and the steps you need to take to make the dish.

When you're reading a recipe, make sure to pay attention to the following things:

- **Ingredients:** These are the items you need to make your dish. Make sure you have all of the ingredients before you start cooking. If you don't have something, you'll need to substitute it or leave it out.
- **Time:** How long will the dish take to prepare and cook? You'll need to plan ahead to prepare your dish when you want to eat it.
- **Temperature:** What temperature should the oven be set to? What type of stove should the dish be cooked on?
- **Serving size:** How many people will this recipe serve?

Now that you've mastered the basics. With an adult, have a go at creating this delicious meal… spaghetti & meatballs with a tasty salad!

HOW TO COOK SPAGHETTI & MEATBALLS

This recipe for Spaghetti and Meatballs is a classic dish everyone will love.

SERVES 4   20+40 MIN

INGREDIENTS:
- 1 pound of ground beef
- 1/2 cup minced onion
- 1/4 cup grated Parmesan cheese
- 1 egg
- 1/4 teaspoon black pepper
- 1/4 teaspoon salt
- 1/2 cup bread crumbs
- 1 can (14.5 ounces) of crushed tomatoes
- 1/4 cup tomato sauce
- 1 teaspoon dried basil
- 1/4 teaspoon dried oregano
- 1/4 teaspoon garlic powder
- 1 pound spaghetti
- Parmesan cheese, for serving

INSTRUCTIONS:

1. In a large bowl, combine ground beef, minced onion, Parmesan cheese, egg, black pepper, and salt. Mix well.
2. Add bread crumbs and mix well.
3. Shape mixture into 1-inch balls. You should have enough for about 16 balls in total.
4. Heat some oil in a large pan on medium heat. Add your meatballs and cook them for about 10 minutes, turning them regularly, until they are brown all over. Turn off the heat and place the meatballs on a plate.
5. In a large saucepan, heat the crushed tomatoes, tomato sauce, basil, oregano, garlic powder, and pepper over medium heat until hot. Once the sauce is bubbling nicely, add your browned meatballs, turn the heat down and simmer for 10 minutes, until the sauce has thickened and the meatballs are cooked through.
6. Cook the spaghetti according to package directions in boiling water.
7. Serve the meatballs and spaghetti with Parmesan cheese or a cheese of your choice.

Enjoy your delicious Spaghetti and Meatballs!

Remember, you can adjust the recipe to suit your tastes. If you like more sauce, add more tomato sauce. Add more bread crumbs if you want your meatballs to be a little crunchier. The possibilities are endless!

Now that you know how to cook your first dish, let's try making a salad!

WALNUT AND BLUE CHEESE SALAD

This salad is excellent as a side salad but can also be the main meal.

Please note that the salad contains nuts; if you or any of your family members suffer from nut allergies, simply omit the nuts.

SERVES 4   10 MIN

SALAD INGREDIENTS:
- 2 cups lettuce (any variety), chopped
- 1 cup cherry tomatoes, halved
- 1/2 cup crumbled blue cheese
- 1/2 cup chopped walnuts
- 1/4 cup vinaigrette or make your own dressing

DRESSING INGREDIENTS:
- 2 tablespoons of olive oil
- 1 teaspoon of lime juice
- 1/2 teaspoon of mustard
- Salt and pepper to taste

INSTRUCTIONS:
1. If you're making your own dressing, combine the dressing ingredients in a jar and shake well
2. Combine chopped lettuce, cherry tomatoes, blue cheese, and walnuts in a large bowl.
3. Drizzle the dressing over the salad and mix well.
4. Serve salad chilled or at room temperature.

Enjoy your delicious salad!

Remember, you can always add or remove ingredients to fit your own tastes. Add some cooked bacon or ham if you want a more savory salad. If you want a sweeter salad, add some dried cranberries or raisins. The possibilities are endless!

ACTIVITY

Cook a Delicious Meal

Now you know the basics of cooking, with the help of an adult, it's time to try cooking a tasty meal yourself.

1. Scan the QR code below with your camera
2. Download your FREE Cookbook for Tweens (featuring 20 easy-to-follow recipes)
3. Choose from one of the delicious breakfast, lunch, dinner, or snack recipes
4. Follow the recipe and get creative in the kitchen
5. Enjoy!

How did you get on?

What did you find tricky?

Did you enjoy it?

CHAPTER 8

HAPPINESS SKILLS

Do you wake up each day with a smile on your face? Or look forward to something during the day, and go to bed at night with a sense of achievement?

These are all habits of happy people.

> **But what exactly is happiness?**
>
> Happiness is a state of mind. It's not about having everything in life; it's about doing things you enjoy and being grateful for what you have.

Happiness is important because it leads to a more fulfilled life. When you're happy, you're more likely to have positive relationships and better health, and what's more, it's contagious. You're more likely to be happy when you're around happy people.

In this chapter, we'll explore happiness and what you can do to stay positive, even when things are tough. You'll learn about the power of positive thinking and how to find your happy place.

So let's get started on your journey to happiness!

HOW TO FIND THINGS YOU'RE GOOD AT

It can be challenging to find things you're good at. You may feel like you're not good at anything or that everyone is better than you. But everyone has talents and skills; it's just a matter of finding what yours are.

> Hobbies are a great way to find things you're good at. If you enjoy doing something, chances are you're good at it or will become good at it. Try out different hobbies and activities until you find something you enjoy. Once you find something you're passionate about, it will be easier to find things you're good at.

Remember, it doesn't matter what other people think, be proud of the things that make you happy. It's better to be into something that makes you happy and passionate about than to be good at something that doesn't interest you.

Just believe in yourself and don't give up. Pursue your passions and do whatever it takes to find things you're good at. You'll be surprised at what you can accomplish when you set your mind to it.

Many people fear trying new things because they're afraid of failing. But it's important to remember that everyone fails at some point. **The key is to keep trying.**

You may not be good at something the first time you try it, but that doesn't mean you should stop. In fact, people often give up too quickly because they don't see results immediately. But if you stick with it, you'll eventually get better and start seeing results. **Practice makes perfect.**

Remember that everyone has to start somewhere. Pursue your passions and do whatever it takes to find something you're good at.

Another way to find things you're good at is by taking classes or joining clubs. This can help you explore new interests and meet people with similar interests. It's a great way to see what you like and don't like.

No one is good at everything. Everyone has different talents and skills. It's just a matter of finding what yours are.

HOW TO BE MORE POSITIVE

Life can be tricky sometimes. Things might not go your way, and it can be easy to get down. But it's important to remember that **you always have the power to choose how you react to things.** You can either let the bad things bring you down or choose to stay positive.

If you take a step back and look at the bigger picture, you'll see that there's always something to be grateful for.

It's important to stay positive because your attitude can affect everything in your life. If you're constantly negative, you'll start to see the world in a negative light. But if you're positive, you'll begin to see the good in everything. Being positive can be contagious. If you're around positive people, it can rub off on you. And before you know it, you'll be seeing the world in a different light.

LIFE SKILLS FOR TWEENS

One way to stay positive is by writing down three things you're grateful for every day. This can be anything from the sun shining to getting a good grade on a test. It doesn't matter how big or small; just write down three things that made you happy that day.

Another way to stay positive is to do something nice for someone else. This can be anything from holding the door open for someone to volunteering at a local shelter. When you make other people happy, it will, in turn, make you happy.

It's also important to **surround yourself with positive people**. This can be friends, family, or even co-workers. If you're constantly around negative people, it will be harder for you to stay positive. But if you're around upbeat people, it will be easier for you to see the good in things.

FIND YOUR HAPPY PLACE

Everyone needs a happy place where they can go to relax and feel at peace. For some people, it's the beach; for others, it's the mountains. It doesn't matter where it is, as long as it makes you happy.

If you don't have a happy place, there's always time to find one. Start by thinking about what makes you happy. Do you like being outdoors or indoors? Do you like being around people or being alone? Once you figure out what makes you happy, you can start looking for a place that fits those criteria.

If you're unsure where to start, try looking online for ideas. There are lots of websites and blogs that have lists of happy places. Or you can ask your friends and family if they have any suggestions.

It may not happen overnight, but don't give up if you don't find it immediately. Just keep looking, and you'll eventually find the perfect place for you. It could be at home, in your garden, on your bike, or on top of a mountain. It doesn't matter where it is, as long as it makes you happy.

Once you find it, you'll know it. And you can go there anytime you need to relax and feel at peace.

HOW TO MAKE YOUR OWN FUN

When you're a kid, it's easy to find things to do. But when you're a tween, it can be more challenging to find something that is fun and interesting.

One way to make your own fun is by trying new things. If there's something you've always wanted to do, go for it! There's no time like the present to try new things.

Another way to make your own fun is by creating your own games. If you're bored, get creative and make up your own rules. You can even invite your friends to join in on the fun.

> Finally, remember that it's okay to be bored sometimes. It's not always necessary to be doing something. Sometimes it's nice to just relax and do nothing. So if you're ever feeling bored, don't worry. Just take a deep breath and relax.

ACTIVITY

Gratitude Journal

One way to stay positive is to start a gratitude journal. Every day, write down three things you're grateful for.

It could be as simple as, "I'm grateful for my bed because it's so comfortable." Or, "I'm grateful for my dog." Over time, you'll start to notice that you're grateful for more and more things. And when you're feeling down, you can look back at your journal and remember all the good things in your life.

WEEKLY GRATITUDE JOURNAL

○ ○ ○ ○ ○ ○ ○
m t w t f s s

Month: _____

- Monday
- Tuesday
- Wednesday
- Thursday
- Friday
- Saturday
- Sunday

CHAPTER 9

CARING & SHARING

When you grow older, you will start to take on responsibilities.

> Responsibilities are things we have to do even when we don't want to or when it's inconvenient. They might include going to school or work, caring for our families and pets, or doing chores around the house.

In this chapter, we will explore how to take care of animals, look after our family, and what we can do to care for our planet.

HOW TO LOOK AFTER A PET

One of the most significant responsibilities that you might have is taking care of a pet. Pets are often like family members; they rely on us for food, water, shelter, and love.

> **When you take care of a pet, you are responsible for its well-being.** This means ensuring it has everything it needs to be healthy and happy.

For example, if you have a dog, you will need to walk it every day, give it food and water, and take it to the vet for regular check-ups.

Cats are a bit easier to take care of than dogs, but they still need care and attention. They must be fed and have fresh water daily, and their litter box must be cleaned regularly.

Although your pet may not be able to speak, they can still communicate their needs. Over time by watching your pet, you can learn how to interpret their body language so that you begin to understand what they are trying to tell you.

> *For example, a wagging tail usually means that a dog is happy. In contrast, a growling noise can mean they feel threatened or angry.*

Pets can teach us much about showing care and concern for others. They rely on us for their basic needs, and in return, they give us companionship and love.

HOW TO CARE FOR PLANTS

Caring for a plant is a great way to learn about responsibility. Plants rely on us for their basic needs, and we must ensure that we give them the care they need. This can be a rewarding experience, as it is satisfying to see a plant grow and thrive under your care.

How to grow your own vegetables

Growing your own food is a great way to be more environmentally friendly and save money. It's also satisfying to watch your plants grow and enjoy your labor's fruits (or vegetables). If you're interested in trying it, here are some tips on getting started.

❶ Choosing your vegetables

First, you'll need to choose what kind of plant you want to grow. Do you want a fruit or a vegetable? Some vegetables are easier to grow than others, so if you're a beginner, you might want to start with something like tomatoes or lettuce. Once you've decided what you want to grow, it's time to get some seeds. You can either buy them from a garden center or online.

❷ Planting your seeds

Once you have your seeds, it's time to plant them. You'll need some pots or planters and some potting soil. Make sure you read the instructions on the seed packet so you know how deep to plant the seeds. Once they're in the ground, water them well and put them in a sunny spot. Keep an eye on them, and water them every day or so. In a few weeks, you should start to see your plants growing!

③ Looking after your vegetable plants

Once your plants are big enough, you can transfer them to a garden bed or bigger pots. Again, make sure you read the instructions on the seed packet so you know how much space they need. Once they're in their new home, continue to water them regularly.

If you take care of your plants, you should be able to enjoy fresh fruits and vegetables all summer long!

How to look after a houseplant

If you don't have the space to grow your own vegetables, or you're not ready to take on the responsibility of a pet, then a house plant might be a good option.

> Although they might not be as exciting as a puppy or a kitten, house plants can make great pets. They're low maintenance, look pretty, and can help purify the air in your home. If you're thinking of getting a house plant, here are some tips on how to take care of it.

① Choosing your house plant

First, you'll need to choose the right plant for your home. Some plants need a lot of sunlight, while others can thrive in low-light conditions. Look at your home and decide which room would be best for your plant. Once you've found the perfect spot, it's time to buy your plant.

② Looking after your house planet

When you get your plant home, it's important to check the care instructions and give it a good watering. Check the soil and ensure it's moist before putting your plant in its new pot. Once it's in its pot, give it more water and put it in its new home.

Now that your plant is settled, it's time to take care of it. Water it when the soil is dry, or according to the instructions, and give it some feed every month. You should also dust the leaves occasionally to help them stay healthy. If you take good care of your plant, it should thrive for years!

CARING FOR THE ENVIRONMENT

As a teenager, you will have more opportunities to make a difference in the world around you. One way you can do this is by taking care of the environment.

The earth is our home, and it is vital to take care of it. Unfortunately, humans have had a negative impact on the environment in many ways. We pollute the air with harmful gases, we pollute the water with chemicals, and we destroy habitats by cutting down trees. These activities have caused many problems, such as climate change, air pollution, and water shortages.

But there are things that you can do to help. You might be thinking... what difference can I make? I'm just one person...

But every little bit helps. **If everyone plays their part, it can make a big difference.**

Here are some things that you can do to help care for the planet:

- **Reuse**

Reduce the rubbish you create by reusing things instead of throwing them away. For example, you could use an old coffee mug as a plant pot or turn an old t-shirt into a cleaning cloth.

- **Recycle**

When you recycle, you are turning waste materials into new products. This reduces the amount of rubbish that goes to landfills and helps conserve resources.

> *For example, old newspapers can be recycled into new paper, while plastic bottles can be made into fleece jackets. Try to encourage your family and friends to recycle too.*

- **Rot**

Composting is a great way to reduce the waste that goes to landfills. It involves using decaying organic matter, such as food scraps and garden waste, to create a nutrient-rich soil enhancer for your plants.

Not only does this reduce the amount of rubbish that goes into the ground, but it also provides a valuable resource for your garden. Anyone can compost; in fact, it's easy to do. All you need is a compost bin, which you can usually buy from your local garden center.

- **Refuse**

One of the best ways to reduce the amount of rubbish you create is to simply refuse things you don't need. For example, say no to plastic straws in your drinks, freebies that you know you'll never use, or plastic carrier bags.

> EVERY TIME YOU REFUSE SOMETHING, YOU ARE HELPING TO REDUCE THE AMOUNT OF WASTE THAT GOES TO LANDFILLS.

- **Save water**

Turning the tap off when you're not using it can save a lot of water. *For example, turn the tap off when brushing your teeth while scrubbing away.*

- **Save energy**

You can help to save energy by turning off lights and electrical appliances when you're not using them. It only takes a second, but it can make a big difference. *For example, turn off your bedroom light when you leave the room, and unplug your phone charger when you're not using it.*

- **Walk or cycle**

Whenever possible, **try to walk or cycle instead of taking the car.** Not only is this good for the environment, but it's also good for your health.

- **Buy local**

Support your local farmers and businesses by buying locally produced food and goods. This helps reduce the energy used to transport goods from one place to another.

- **Grow your own**

You can save money and eat healthily by growing your own fruit and vegetables. It's also good for the environment because it uses no fossil fuels (energy from things like oil and coal).

We all need to do our bit to take care of planet Earth. It's the only home we have, and we need to ensure that it's a safe and healthy place for future generations. Remember, every little bit makes a difference. Small changes can have a significant impact when everyone does their bit.

SHARING THE WORLD WITH OTHERS

We share the world with billions of other people and must learn to live together peacefully.

Here are some things that you can do to make the world a better place for everyone:

- **Respect other people**

It's important to respect other people, even if they are different from you. This means listening to what they say and treating them with kindness and understanding.

- **Respect other cultures**

There are many different cultures worldwide, and it's important to respect them all. This means being open-minded and tolerant of others, even if they don't share your beliefs or values.

- **Stand up to discrimination**

Discrimination is when people are mistreated because of their race, religion, or other factors. It's wrong, and it needs to be stopped.

If you see someone discriminated against, don't be a bystander—speak up and do something about it.

- **Be an ally**

An ally speaks up for others, even if they are not directly affected by the issue.

> *For example, suppose you see someone being bullied because of their race, religion, or sexuality. In that case, you can be an ally by speaking up and standing up for them.*

- **Respect nature**

We share the world with billions of other living things and must respect them. This means taking care of the environment and not harming or polluting the planet.

FAMILIES

Our families are usually the people who care for us and support us the most, and we must do the same for them.

Here are some things that you can do to show your family that you love and appreciate them:

- **Spend time with them**

One of the best ways to show your family that you care is to simply spend time with them. This can be anything from having a meal together to going for a walk or even just sitting and talking.

- **Help out around the house**

Another great way to show your family that you care is to help out around the house. This could be doing the dishes, vacuuming the floor, or taking the dog for a walk.

- **Be kind and respectful**

It's not always easy, but try to be kind and respectful to your brothers, sisters, and parents, even when you disagree with them. This means listening to what they say and treating them respectfully.

- **Say, "I love you."**

Sometimes the best way to show your family that you care is to simply say, "I love you." These three words can mean so much and will let your family know you appreciate them.

ACTIVITY

Start a School Recycling Program

Recycling is a great way to help the environment, and it's something everyone can do. If you're interested in starting a recycling program at your school, here are some tips for getting started.

1. **Talk to your teacher or principal about your idea.** They'll need to approve the program before you can start.

2. **Start collecting materials.** You'll need to find a place to put the recycling bin and ensure everyone knows where it is. Paper, plastic, and metal can all be recycled. Encourage your classmates to put their recyclable materials in the bin. You can also put up signs to remind people to recycle.

3. **Take them to a recycling center.** You can usually find one at your local grocery store. Once you've recycled all your materials, you can start the process again!

CHAPTER 10

COMMUNICATION SKILLS

As you grow older and become a teenager, you'll deal with many different people, from friends and family to teachers and employers. You'll probably be faced with a lot of challenging situations too. That's why it's helpful to have good communication skills.

But what is communication exactly?

> Communication is the process of exchanging information between two or more people. It can be verbal (using words), nonverbal (using body language or facial expressions), or written (using text messages, emails, etc.).

Often we think of communication as speaking and listening. But it's also important to listen and understand the other person's point of view, use body language effectively, and resolve conflicts peacefully.

This chapter will cover all of these communication skills and more. So whether you're dealing with a difficult situation or just want to chat with your friends, you'll be prepared!

HOW TO IMPROVE YOUR COMMUNICATION SKILLS

Here are some general tips on how to improve your communication skills:

1. **Listen more than you speak.** One of the best ways to improve your communication skills is to simply listen more. When you're in a conversation, try to hear what the other person is saying and understand their point of view. This is sometimes called active listening.

② Be firm and assertive but not aggressive. It's good to be able to stand up for yourself and express yourself in any relationship. But it's also good practice to do this in a way that doesn't hurt the other person. When assertive, you can communicate your needs clearly and calmly without being aggressive.

③ Don't be afraid to say "no." It's okay to say no sometimes, especially if you're not comfortable with what the other person is asking of you. Just be sure to do it in a way that doesn't upset or offend the other person. For example, you could say, "I'm sorry, but I don't feel comfortable doing that," or "No, thank you."

④ Be aware of your body language. Body language is a form of nonverbal communication. It includes your facial expressions, how you hold yourself, and your eye contact. All of these things can affect the way the other person perceives you. So it's good to be aware of your body language and ensure it sends the right message.

⑤ Put your phone away. It's easy to get distracted by our phones when communicating with someone. But this can make the other person feel like they're not valued. So put your phone away and give the other person your full attention.

Before we move on to specific communication skills, let's look at some key parts of being a great communicator.

THE IMPORTANCE OF EYE CONTACT

Making eye contact is an integral part of communication. It's a way to show the other person that you're interested in what they're saying and helps build trust.

Our eyes are often the first thing people notice about us; when you enter a room or meet someone for the first time, making eye contact is a sign of confidence. It shows that you're not afraid to meet someone's gaze and are comfortable in your own skin.

Eye contact is also essential for displaying emotion. **When we make eye contact with others, we are more likely to feel connected to them.** On the other hand, avoiding eye contact can make us seem untrustworthy.

When greeting someone, look them in the eye and give them a smile. During a conversation, try to maintain eye contact with the other person. And when you're saying goodbye, make sure to end with eye contact and a friendly expression.

> By making eye contact, you'll come across as more confident and trustworthy, and you'll also be able to connect with others on a deeper level.

THE IMPORTANCE OF BODY LANGUAGE

Experts agree that almost 80% of communication is nonverbal, meaning body language plays a significant role in how we communicate with others.

But what exactly is body language?

> Body language is the way we use our bodies to communicate. It includes our facial expressions, how we hold ourselves, and our eye contact.

Body language can be positive or negative. Positive body language is when we use our bodies to show that we're happy, interested, and engaged in the conversation. Negative body language is when we use our bodies to show that we're bored, uncomfortable, or uninterested.

Some examples of positive body language include:

- Smiling
- Nodding your head
- Keeping an open posture
- Making eye contact

On the other hand, some examples of negative body language include:

- Crossing your arms
- Slouching
- Avoiding eye contact
- Yawning

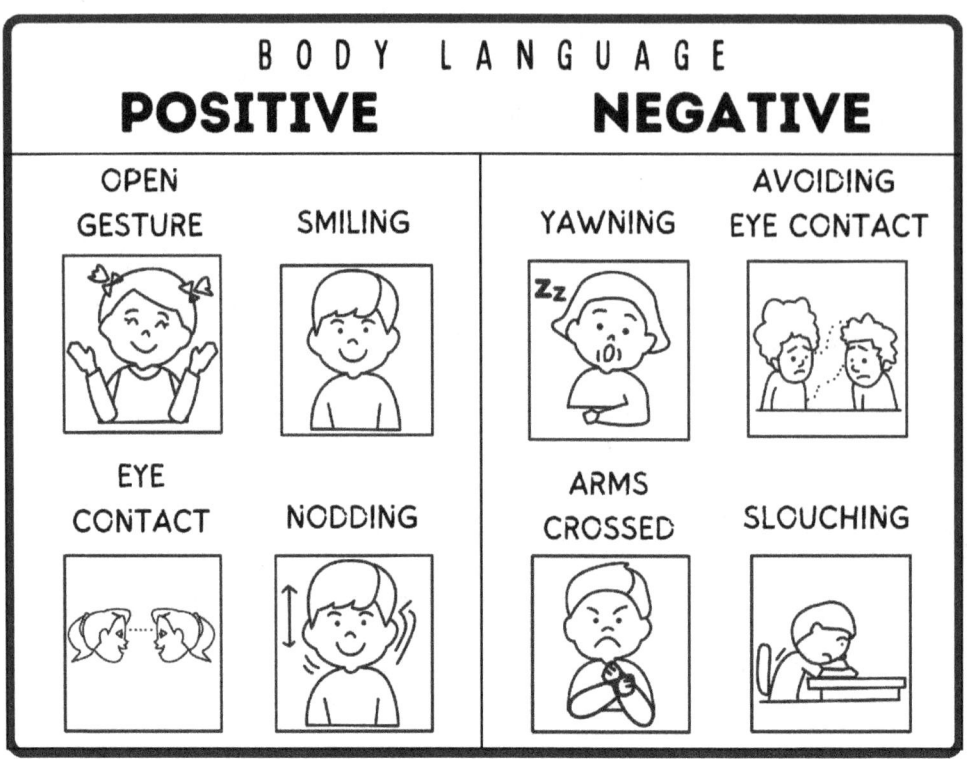

It's essential to be aware of your own body language and the body language of the person you're talking to. This will help you understand how the conversation is going and whether or not the other person is interested in what you're saying.

> *For example, standing with your arms crossed and your head down, you might appear angry. But if you're standing with your arms open and your head up, you might come across as friendly and approachable.*

Your body language can also affect the way the other person feels. If you look at the other person and smile, they will likely feel happy. But if you're looking away and not making any eye contact, they might feel like you're not interested in what they have to say.

So it's helpful to be aware of your body language and ensure it sends the right message. The next time you're in a conversation, pay attention to your body language and see if it's conveying the message you want to send.

THE IMPORTANCE OF ACTIVE LISTENING

Active listening is a communication technique that requires you to fully engage and listen to what the other person is saying. It's important because it shows that you're interested in the conversation and value what the other person says.

> Active listening requires you to do more than just hear the other person's words. It also requires you to try to understand the meaning behind those words. This means paying attention to the tone of voice, body language, and facial expressions.

It can be easy to get distracted when trying to communicate with someone. But we might miss important information or cues if we're not listening carefully.

The next time you're in a conversation, try to practice active listening. Pay attention to the other person, give them your complete focus, and listen to what they're saying.

By actively listening, you'll be able to communicate more effectively and connect with others on a deeper level.

Now let's explore some specific communication scenarios and how you can use these skills.

HOW TO TALK ON THE PHONE

It's no secret that communication is key in any relationship. But what about when you're communicating with someone over the phone? Phone conversations can be tricky, but they don't have to be! Many of us don't like talking on the phone, but it's an important life skill to learn.

Here are some tips to help you improve your phone conversation skills:

1. **Start by introducing yourself.** This may seem like a no-brainer, but it's important to remember! When you answer the phone, introduce yourself to the other person—"Hi, this is Sarah."

2. **Be aware of your tone of voice and SMILE.** The way you sound on the phone can be just as important as the words you're saying. So make sure you smile. Believe it or not, your tone of voice can be affected by your facial expressions. So if you smile while you're talking on the phone, the other person will be able to hear it in your voice.

③ Use open-ended questions. These questions can't be answered with a simple "yes" or "no." For example, "How was your day?" or "What did you do this weekend?" Open-ended questions will help keep the conversation going and prevent it from becoming a one-word exchange of answers.

④ Avoid interrupting the other person. This is an essential conversation rule that applies to phone conversations as well. Let the other person finish what they're saying before you speak. Not only is it rude to interrupt, but it also makes it harder to follow the conversation.

⑤ Be an active listener. Just like in face-to-face conversations, really listen to what the other person is saying on the phone. This means giving the person your full attention.

⑥ Avoid distractions. It can be tempting to multi-task when you're on the phone. Still, avoid distractions like checking your messages or browsing the internet. This will help you stay focused on the conversation and prevent missing anything important.

⑦ Use positive body language. Even though the other person can't see you, they'll be able to sense your energy through the phone. So if you're slouching or rolling your eyes, they'll be able to tell. Instead, sit up straight and use positive body language to project a positive image.

⑧ End the conversation properly. This means saying goodbye in a friendly way and not just hanging up abruptly.

Communicating effectively on the phone is an important life skill that will help you in all aspects of your life, from work to personal relationships. So remember to use these tips the next time you're on the phone, and you'll make a great impression.

HOW TO BE SOCIAL IN DIFFERENT SITUATIONS

One-on-one

When talking to someone one-on-one, try to make eye contact and focus on the conversation. You can ask questions about the other person or share stories from your own life. It's also an excellent opportunity to get to know someone better.

In a group

In a group setting, be aware of the other people around you. Make sure you're not talking over anyone and that you're listening when others are talking. You can share your thoughts and opinions, but make sure to respect the views of others as well.

At a party

At a party, it's important to socialize with as many people as possible. Talk to people you know and also try to meet new people. Parties are an excellent opportunity to have some fun and let loose.

By following these tips, you'll be sure to socialize effectively in any situation.

Now that we've gone over the basics of socializing let's move on to more advanced topics.

HOW TO BE A GOOD LISTENER

Listening is an important life skill that is often underrated. We communicate with others every day, but we don't always take the time to really listen to what they're saying.

Here are some tips to help you become a better listener:

❶ Pay attention. This means giving the other person your full attention and listening to what they're saying. Try to avoid distractions like your phone or the tv. By giving someone your full attention, you're showing them that you care about what they have to say.

❷ Show that you're listening. You can do this by making eye contact, nodding your head, and using verbal cues like "uh-huh" and "I see."

❸ Ask questions. Asking questions shows that you're interested in the conversation and want to know more. It also shows that you're listening to the other person's words. For example, if someone is telling you about their weekend, you could ask them what they did or how they enjoyed it.

❹ Repeat back what you've heard. This is an excellent way to ensure you've understood the other person correctly. It also shows that you were paying attention to the conversation. For example, "So what you're saying is that you're upset because your friend didn't invite you to her birthday party."

❺ Avoid interrupting. It can be tempting to jump in and share your own experiences or stories. Try to resist the urge and let the other person finish speaking.

❻ Avoid giving advice. Sometimes people just want to be heard and don't necessarily want your advice. Unless they've asked for it, try to avoid giving advice and just listen to what they have to say.

By following these tips, you'll be sure to become a better listener and have more productive and enjoyable conversations with others.

Of course, not all communication is verbal, so let's look at some nonverbal scenarios.

HOW TO WRITE A THANK YOU NOTE

Thank you letters are a lovely way to show your appreciation. Whether it's a gift, an act of kindness, or simply a thank you to a party, taking the time to write a thank-you note is always appreciated.

It doesn't have to be long or overly formal and can be written by hand or typed up, whichever you feel more comfortable with. Most importantly, taking the time to write it shows that you care. It's also a great habit to get into!

Here are some tips to help you write a great thank you letter:

1. **Write it as soon as possible.** The sooner you write the note, the more sincere it will seem. If you wait too long, it becomes a hassle, and the recipient can tell.

2. **Start with a greeting.** This can be as simple as "Dear Mr./Mrs. Smith" or "Dear Uncle John."

3. **Express your gratitude.** Be specific about what you're thanking the person for. For example, "Thank you so much for the generous gift card to my favorite shop. I really appreciate it."

4. **Mention how you'll use the gift or how you enjoyed it.** For example, "I can't wait to use it to buy a new dress for my birthday party."

5. **Reiterate your thanks.** You can say something like "Thank you again" or "I'm truly grateful for your kindness."

6. **End with a closing.** If it's a close friend or family member, you can use "Love" or "With love," For a more formal letter, "Yours truly" or "Respectfully" are good choices.

If you're still stuck, here's a basic template you can adapt next time.

> *Dear (name),*
>
> *Thank you so much for (gift/act of kindness). It was (how it was used/enjoyed). I really appreciate it. Thank you again.*
>
> *Sincerely,*
> *(Your name)*

By following these tips, you'll be sure to write a thank you letter that is both heartfelt and well-formed.

ACTIVITY

Write a Thank You Note

Using the examples above, write a thank you letter to a friend or family member. It could be for a specific present they gave you or a general letter of thanks for something they have done for you.

How did it make you feel sending a thank you letter?

How do you think the recipient felt when they received your letter?

CHAPTER 11

PRACTICAL SKILLS

As you become a teenager and more independent, you will be expected to take on more responsibilities, from doing household chores to fixing your bike. To help you make the transition, here are some practical skills that will come in handy:

HOW TO KEEP YOUR ROOM TIDY

As you get older, you will be expected to keep your own space tidy. An excellent way to start is by making your bed every day and putting away any clothes lying around. Then, set aside time each week to clean your room. Start by decluttering—get rid of anything you don't use or need. Then, dust all surfaces and vacuum or sweep the floor.

Of course, the best way to keep your room tidy is to keep it clean in the first place. Here are a few tips to help you:

1. Hang up your clothes and put them away as soon as you take them off

2. Put away any books, toys, or games that are lying around

3. Make sure all surfaces are clean before you go to bed

4. Wipe up any spills straight away

HOW TO DO YOUR OWN LAUNDRY

Washing clothes is a necessary but sometimes tedious chore. To make it a little easier (and to avoid ruining your clothes), here are some tips on how to do your laundry:

1. **Sort your clothes into piles—white, dark, and delicate.** Delicates include anything that might shrink or bleed in color, like wool, silk, and denim.

2. **Check the labels on your clothes before you wash them.** Different fabrics have different care instructions. For example, some clothes need to be washed in cold water, while others can handle hot water.

3. **Add the right amount of detergent.** Too much and your clothes will be stiff, too little and they won't come out clean.

4. **Don't overload the washing machine.** This will make it harder for your clothes to get clean and could damage the machine.

5. **Select your cycle.** If you're not sure, go with the normal cycle.

6. Once the cycle is done, immediately remove your clothes from the washing machine and **put them in the dryer, or hang them up to dry.** Otherwise, they'll start to smell.

And that's it! With a bit of practice, laundry will be a breeze.

HOW TO CHANGE A BIKE TIRE

As you get older, you'll probably use your bike more often—whether for commuting to school or just for fun. But as any bike owner knows, you will have to change a bike tire sooner or later. It's not as difficult as it might seem, and it's a good skill to know how to do.

Here's what you'll need:

- a new inner tube (make sure it's the right size for your wheel!)
- a bike pump
- a tire lever (or two)
- a patch kit (optional)

First, **you'll need to remove the wheel from the bike.** You can usually do this by loosening the bolts that hold the wheel in place. If you're unsure how to do this, consult your bike's manual.

Once the wheel is off, press the tire valve to remove any air, and then use the tire lever to pry off one side of the tire. Be careful not to puncture the inner tube!

Remove the inner tube entirely and inspect it for any holes or punctures. If you find a hole, you can try to patch it with the patch kit.

Inflate the new inner tube slightly and fit it inside the tire. Make sure it's not twisted.

Use the tire lever to put the tire back on, starting with the side you removed first. Again, be careful not to puncture the inner tube.

Inflate the tire to the correct pressure and reattach the wheel to the bike. You're now ready to hit the road!

HOW TO READ A BUS OR TRAIN TIMETABLE

Public transport can be a great way to get around, but it can also be confusing if you don't know how to read a bus or train timetable. Once you know how to read it, it's actually quite simple.

BUS TIMETABLE

FROM ST. PAUL'S CATHEDRAL TO BUCKINGHAM PALACE — FREE BUS RIDE

BUS STOPS	DAY TIMES						
ST. PAUL'S CATHEDRAL	08:34	10:12	11:45	13:45	14:30	16:30	18:45
TOWER OF LONDON	08:46	10:14	11:57	13:57	14:34	16:42	18:48
THE SHARD	08:48	10:22	11:59	13:59	14:42	16:44	18:50
TATE MODERN	08:56	10:29	12:14	14:07	14:44	16:52	18:58
LONDON EYE	09:03	10:38	12:23	14:14	14:52	16:59	19:05
WESTMINSTER	09:12	10:43	12:28	14:23	14:53	17:04	19:14
DOWNING STREET	09:17	10:49	12:34	14:28	15:08	17:13	19:19
OXFORD CIRCUS	09:30	10:56	12:41	14:34	15:15	17:19	19:25
BUCKINGHAM PALACE	09:38	11:04	12:49	14:41	15:19	17:26	19:32

Timetables are usually organized by the destinations or stops, with the times that the bus or train will arrive at each stop listed in the columns.

To figure out when the bus or train you need will arrive, first find your stop on the timetable. Then look at the column next to it to see when it is scheduled to arrive.

> Remember that sometimes buses or trains can be delayed, so it's a good idea to arrive at the stop a few minutes before the scheduled arrival time.

If you're unsure, ask a staff member or another passenger. People are usually happy to help.

Now that you know how to read a bus or train timetable, you're one step closer to being a public transport pro!

ACTIVITY

Cleaning Planner

Using the room cleaning planner, list what you need to do to clean an area in the house. Note what items you might need, e.g., a vacuum, cleaning liquids, or cloths.

DATE

NOTES

FOCUS AREA

TO DO LIST:

○ _____
○ _____
○ _____
○ _____
○ _____
○ _____
○ _____
○ _____
○ _____
○ _____

CHAPTER 12

PERSONAL SAFETY

As you get older, you will become more independent and will probably start going places by yourself. Being aware of personal safety when you're out and about to stay safe and sound is essential.

Here are some general things you can do to stay safe when you're out and about:

1. **Be aware of your surroundings** and who or what is around you. If you feel unsafe, trust your instincts and move to a different area.

2. **Avoid walking alone at night.** If you must, walk in well-lit areas and stay in busy areas.

3. **Never accept rides from strangers.**

4. **Carry a cell phone with** you to call for help if needed.

5. **Trust your instincts.** If something doesn't feel right, it probably isn't.

6. **Make sure someone knows where you are** and who you're with.

Personal safety is important, but don't let it stop you from living your life. By following these simple tips, you can help keep yourself safe.

HOW TO USE PUBLIC TRANSPORT SAFELY

Public transport is a great way to get around, but it's important to be aware of your surroundings and take steps to stay safe.

Here are some tips for using public transport safely:

1. **Plan your journey,** so you know which route you're going to take and where you'll get off.

2. If you can **travel during daylight hours** when more people are around.

3. **Be aware of your belongings** and keep them close to you at all times.

4. **Trust your instincts**—if something doesn't feel right, get off the bus or train and find another way home.

5. **If someone follows you, go to a busy, well-lit place and call for help.**

Following these simple tips can help ensure your journey is safe and enjoyable.

HOW TO STAY SAFE ONLINE

Just as you need to be aware of your surroundings when you're out and about, you must also be mindful of what you're doing online.

The internet is a wonderful place full of information and opportunities. You can find anything you want online, and it's a great place to connect with friends and family.

However, some risks are also associated with using the internet, and it's essential to be aware of them.

- **Privacy:** Ensure you're not giving away too much personal information online. Don't share your address, phone number, or school name with people you don't know.

- **Scams:** There are a lot of scams online. A scam is when someone tries to get you to give them your money or personal information by pretending to be something they're not. For example, a scam might ask you to click on a link in an email or to download something, and then they'll try to steal your information.

- **Strangers:** Don't talk to strangers online. If someone you don't know starts messaging you, or if you see something that makes you uncomfortable, report it to a trusted adult.
- **It's always there:** once you post something online, it's there forever. Even if you delete it, someone might have copied or screenshot it. Be careful what you post online because many people can see it.

HOW TO STAY SAFE ONLINE

PRIVACY
Don't share your personal information with people you don't know.

SCAMS
Stop & think before you click on a link in an email or message.

STRANGERS
Be careful. If you see or hear something that makes you uncomfortable report it.

IT'S ALWAYS THERE
Be careful what you post online, it can be seen by lots of people and is always there.

HOW TO KEEP YOUR PERSONAL INFORMATION SECURE

It's important never to share your personal information online; this includes:
- Your address
- Your phone number
- Your school name
- Your bank details
- Your passwords

You can take a few other steps to keep your personal information safe and secure.

❶ Use strong passwords: Your password should be difficult to guess, and it should be different for each account.

– Make your passwords strong

> *For example, instead of using your dog's name, combine your dog's name with his favorite snack and turn your password into a fun sentence.*
>
> *E.g., Fidoloves5bones!*

Making your password longer and using a mix of letters, numbers, and symbols makes it more difficult for someone to guess.

– Don't use easy-to-guess words like your name or your birthday.

– Try to use different passwords for different accounts. Some people use the same password for everything, but this is a bad idea because if someone guesses your password, they could access all of your accounts.

❷ Activate two-step verification: This is an extra layer of security that you can use to protect your accounts. When you activate two-step verification, you must enter a code sent to your phone each time you try to sign in. This makes it more difficult for someone to get into your account.

❸ Update your software and apps regularly: Keeping your software and apps up-to-date fixes any security vulnerabilities and makes it more difficult for someone to hack into your device.

❹ Be careful when you're on a shared device: Be careful if you use a shared device, like a school computer. Always log out of your accounts after using them, and don't save your passwords.

❺ Think before you post: Before posting something online, ask yourself if you would be happy for everyone to see it. If the answer is no, then don't post it. Remember, once you post something online, it's there forever.

❻ Be careful about what you share on social media: Social media is a great way to stay connected with friends and family. Still, you need to be careful about what you share. Don't share personal information like your address or phone number; be careful about what you post online. Something that may seem funny or harmless today could come back to haunt you in the future.

7. **Be skeptical:** if something seems too good to be true, it probably is. Don't click on links or download files from strangers; be wary of emails asking for personal information. They may be Phishing scams. Phishing scams are emails or websites that try to get you to give away your personal information. They might look like they're from a trusted source, but they're not.

8. **Keep your online friends online:** It's a good idea only to add people you know and trust to your social media accounts. If you have online friends, be careful about what information you share and don't offer to meet up with them in person.

9. **Report anything that makes you uncomfortable:** If you see something on social media that makes you uncomfortable, or if you receive a message from someone that makes you feel unsafe, report it. The social media platform or email provider will investigate the incident and take appropriate action.

10. **Only download apps from trusted sources:** There are a lot of fake apps out there, and it can be tricky to tell the difference between a real app and a fake one. Only download apps from trusted sources, like the App Store or Google Play.

11. **Be a good digital citizen:** Digital citizenship is the way we behave online. We should be respectful of others and treat people online the way we would want to be treated ourselves. We should also obey the law online, just like in the real world.

HOW TO SPOT FAKE NEWS

Not everything you see online is true. Much of what you see may be fake news — news that is made up or inaccurate. There are several reasons why people spread fake news, but often it's done to try and influence people's opinions or to get them to buy something.

Here are some tips for how to spot fake news:

1. **Check the source or website:** Fake news often pops up on social media, so check the source before sharing it. Fake news websites often have weird or unfamiliar URLs and may not have much information about themselves. Usually, a quick Google search will reveal if the story is true or not.

② Check the date: Fake news stories often get circulated repeatedly, even if they're not true. Check the date to see if the story is recent.

③ Check the photos: Fake news stories often use fake or stock photos. If the images in the story look strange or like they've been Photoshopped, it's probably fake news.

④ Check the comments: If a story is fake, you'll often see people commenting on it to say it's not true. Pay close attention to the comments to see if other people question the story's authenticity.

⑤ Ask an adult: If you're not sure if a story is true or not, ask an adult you trust for their opinion. They may have some insights that you don't.

ACTIVITY

Password Activity

Creating strong passwords helps keep you safe online and prevents scammers from accessing your personal information. Let's look at a quick activity to try to create stronger passwords:

1. Take a look at the following list of passwords and tick the ones that would be easy for someone to guess:

   ☐ password   ☐ abc123

   ☐ 1234   ☐ letmein

   ☐ qwerty   ☐ Trustno1!

   Some passwords on the list above would be easy to guess because they are common words, have simple patterns of letters, or have few characters.

2. Now let's try to create some strong passwords using longer, memorable sentences.

   A. Write down your favorite animal

   _____

B. Write down their favorite food

_____

C. Write down your age

_____

D. Add an Uppercase and one symbol

_____

E. Now combine all of them into one sentence

_____

> *For example: if your favorite animal is a dog, their favorite food is bones, and you are 10 years old, your new password could be:*
>
> *Dogslovebones10!*

Making your password longer and using a mix of letters, numbers, and symbols makes it more difficult for someone to guess.

CHAPTER 13

EMERGENCIES & FIRST AID

One of the most important things to know when you're growing up is how to deal with emergencies. Emergencies can happen anytime, anywhere, and it's good to be prepared for them.

It could be a natural disaster, like a tornado or a hurricane. It could be a man-made disaster, like a fire. Or it could be something medical, like an injury or an illness.

No matter what kind of emergency it is, there are some basic things you can do to stay safe and help out.

Here are some tips for dealing with emergencies:

1. **If you can, stay calm:** One of the most important things you can do in an emergency is to stay calm. This will help you think clearly and make smart decisions. It will also help other people around you remain calm.

2. **Stop! Check and Assess:** Before you do anything else, stop and take a few seconds to assess the situation. Are there any dangers that you need to be aware of? Are there things that could explode or catch on fire? Is there hazardous material that you need to avoid?

3. **Call for help:** If there's an emergency and you need help, call 911 (or 999 in the UK). They'll help you get to safety and connect you with the right people who can help. The operator will ask what emergency service you need—police, fire, or ambulance. Give them your name, your address, and the type of emergency you're dealing with.

4. **Help others if it's safe to do so:** In an emergency, the people who are calm and helpful often become the most valuable. If you can, help out other people in danger or who need help.

5 Follow the instructions of emergency responders: When emergency responders arrive, they'll tell you what to do. Follow their instructions and don't try to take things into your own hands.

A BASIC GUIDE TO FIRST AID

If someone is injured or ill, it's helpful to know some basic first aid.

> First aid is the initial care you can give an injured or sick person. It's important to remember that first aid is not a substitute for professional medical care. Still, it can be lifesaving in an emergency.

But before you start first aid, you need to assess the situation. Is it safe for you to approach the person? If not, call for help.

Here are a few basic first aid techniques that everyone should know:

How to deal with bleeding

If someone is bleeding, you should try to stop the bleeding as quickly as possible.

Apply pressure to the wound with a clean cloth or bandage. Raise their arm if the bleeding is coming from their hand or fingers.

If the bleeding is severe, do not remove the object causing the bleeding (such as a knife or glass)—this could worsen the injury. In that case, call 911 and ask for an ambulance.

How to deal with choking

If someone is choking, something is stuck in their throat, and they cannot breathe. This is usually caused by food or a small object. Try to stay calm and don't panic.

Ask the person if they can speak or cough—if they can, it means that their airway is only partially blocked.

Have them try to cough up the object. If that doesn't work, stand behind them and give them five quick slaps between their shoulder blades with the heel of your hand.

If they can't speak or cough, their airway is completely blocked, and you will need to give them abdominal thrusts (also known as the Heimlich maneuver).

To do this, stand behind the person and put your arms around their waist. Make a fist with one hand and place it between their belly button and ribs. With your other hand, grasp your fist and pull upwards—repeat this movement until the object is removed. If you can't clear the blockage, call 911 and ask for an ambulance.

How to deal with burns

Burns occur when the skin comes into contact with a hot object or substance, such as fire or boiling water. If someone has a burn, try to cool the area as quickly as possible. This will help to reduce swelling and pain.

Run cool water over the area for at least 10 minutes or until the pain eases.

If the burn is severe, or if the burn is still painful after 20 minutes, call 911 and ask for an ambulance.

How to deal with sprains or broken bones

A sprain is a stretch or tear of a ligament (the tissue that connects bone to bone). While a broken bone is a crack or break in the bone. Both injuries can be extremely painful.

If you think someone has a sprain, try to immobilize the area as much as possible. You don't want to move the injured area any more than necessary.

If you suspect a broken bone, seek medical help immediately.

If you think the person has a sprained ankle, have them prop their foot up on something and avoid putting any weight on it. If they have a sprain in their arm, have them hold it close to their body. Apply ice to the area for 20 minutes to help reduce swelling.

No one ever expects to be in a situation where they must use first aid. But hopefully, by reading this, you now feel a little more prepared if you ever need to use it.

> Remember, the most important thing is to stay calm. First aid is not about being a medical expert—it's about being able to assess a situation and taking action to help someone in need. And sometimes, that can make all the difference.

ACTIVITY

Emergency Role-plays

Emergencies are just that, emergencies. They can be stressful and scary, and you never know when they will happen or how you will react. But you can practice with your friends and family so that you will be prepared in the event of an emergency.

Here are a few role-play scenarios you could act out to help you prepare:

Scenario 1: One of your friends is injured at the park, and you don't know what to do.

Solution: If your friend is injured, firstly assess the injury. If a severe injury, such as a head injury, or your friend is not responding, do not try to move them. Call 911 and wait for help to arrive. If the injury is less severe, like a cut or a sprain, you can help your friend by taking them home, cleaning the wound, and applying pressure to stop the bleeding.

Scenario 2: You're at home alone when your mom falls down the stairs.

Solution: If your mom falls down the stairs, you should first call 911. Then try to help your mom by checking to see if she's responsive and by seeing if she's bleeding. If she's not responding, check for a pulse and start CPR if you know-how. If she responds, do not move her and wait for help to arrive.

Scenario 3: There's a fire in your building.

Solution: If there's a fire in your building, the first thing you should do is evacuate the building. Once you're outside, shout for help and call 911. Don't go back into the building, even if you think you can put out the fire yourself. Let the professionals handle it.

These are just a few scenarios to help you get started. **Remember never to call emergency services for jokes or pranks—only use it in real emergencies.** And always be prepared and try to stay calm in an emergency.

CHAPTER 14

ADVENTURE SKILLS

The thrill of adventure is something that many people crave. Exploring new places, meeting new people, and having new experiences is exciting. But what does it really take to be an adventurer?

There are specific skills and qualities that all adventurers possess.

Firstly, **they are brave**. Adventurers are willing to take risks and step outside of their comfort zone. They are also physically fit and have a good sense of direction.

In addition, **adventurers are resourceful**. They know how to make the most of what they have and are not afraid to get their hands dirty. They are also independent and self-reliant, able to take care of themselves in any situation.

Finally, **adventurers are curious**. They are constantly exploring and learning, always looking for new challenges. If this sounds like you, you have what it takes to be an adventurer!

Let's dig deeper into the practical skills required to be a great adventurer and how you can start learning these skills now!

HOW TO PACK FOR AN OUTDOOR TRIP

Packing for an outdoor adventure can be daunting, especially if you're new to camping or hiking. But with some planning and preparation, it doesn't have to be.

The first step is to **make a list of everything you need**. This includes all the essentials like food, water, shelter, clothing, and other items you think you might need.

Once you have your list, start packing your backpack. The key is to pack light and ensure that everything is secure and within easy reach.

Here are some tips for packing your backpack:

1 Use a lightweight backpack that is comfortable to carry.

2 Pack the heaviest items first and distribute the weight evenly.

3 Use compression sacks to reduce the size of your belongings.

4 Make sure all your gear is secure and won't fall out when you're on the move.

5 Pack essential items like food and water within easy reach.

Now that you know how to pack for an outdoor adventure, it's time to get out there and explore! Remember to be prepared, stay safe, and have fun!

HOW TO BUILD A CAMPFIRE

Building a campfire is an essential skill for any adventurer. Not only will it keep you warm and dry, but it can also be used for cooking.

> Before attempting to build a campfire, always ensure you have adult supervision. While fires can be great fun, they can be extremely dangerous. So be sensible and always listen to the adult in charge.

You need three things for a fire to burn: Heat, Oxygen, and Fuel. This is called the FIRE TRIANGLE.

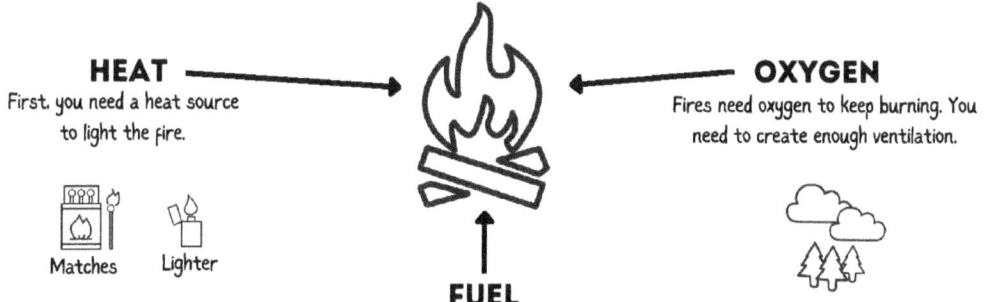

HEAT
First, you need a heat source to light the fire.

Matches   Lighter

OXYGEN
Fires need oxygen to keep burning. You need to create enough ventilation.

FUEL
The fuel is what the fire will actually burn, e.g. paper and wood

Leaves, Paper, Pine Needles, Lint or Cotton — TINDER

Twigs, Sticks, and Branches — KINDLING

FIREWOOD

5 STEPS ON HOW TO SAFELY START AND PUT OUT YOUR CAMPFIRE

1 Choose a safe location. Then make a loose pile of tinder. Don't pack them too tightly. Your fire needs airflow gaps.

2 Use the twigs, sticks and branches to build a kindling teepee around the tinder.

3 Being very careful, light the tinder from all sides using your lighter or some matches.

4 As your fire grows, add on more dry twigs and branches, and eventually, start feeding it with larger pieces of firewood. Leave some space to allow sufficient airflow.

5 To safely put out your fire, you must cut off one of the elements of the Fire Triangle. You can do it by dousing the fire with water or covering it with sand. You can also let the firewood burn out (just be sure there's no fuel surrounding the area to avoid it from catching fire again.)

LIFE SKILLS FOR TWEENS

Building a campfire is not as difficult as it may seem. The first step is to **find a safe location away from anything that could catch fire**. Once you have found a safe spot, gather your wood. You will need three types of wood:

1. Tinder: This is small, dry material that will catch fire easily. Examples of tinder include dry leaves, paper, and twigs.

2. Kindling: This is slightly larger than tinder and will help get the fire going. Examples of kindling include small sticks and twigs.

3. Fuel: This is the largest wood you will need and will keep the fire burning. Examples of fuel include logs and branches.

Once you have gathered your wood, it's time to start building your fire. The first step is to create a tinder nest. This is a small pile of tinder that you will use to start the fire.

Once you have your tinder nest, add some kindling on top. Then, use your matches or lighter to ignite the tinder. Once the kindling is burning, add more wood gradually until you have a roaring campfire! Remember to stay away from the flames and never leave your fire unattended.

With these tips, you'll be a campfire pro in no time!

HOW TO BUILD A DEN

One of the best things about being an adventurer is that you can build your own home away from home. And there's no better place to do this than in a den!

> Building a den is a great way to practice problem-solving and engineering skills. It's also a lot of fun!

There are two main types of dens: natural and man-made.

Building a den is a great way to spend time with friends or family. It's also a great way to learn new skills.

How to build your natural den

Natural dens are made from materials that you find in nature, such as sticks, stones, and leaves. Building a natural shelter is a great way to reconnect with nature and your surroundings. It's also a great way to practice your problem-solving skills.

Here are some tips for building your own natural den:

1. Look for a sheltered spot away from the wind and rain.

2. Find a tree with low-hanging branches.

3. Gather sticks and twigs and place them around the tree trunk.

4. Weave smaller sticks and twigs between the larger ones to create a wall.

5. Add leaves, moss, or ferns to your den for extra insulation.

6. Make a roof for your den by placing sticks and branches across the top.

7. Cover your roof with leaves, moss, or ferns.

Now it's time to enjoy your new home!

How to build a man-made den

Man-made dens are built using man-made materials like tarps and rope.

Here are some tips for building your own man-made den:

1. Find a suitable location sheltered from the wind and rain.

2. Build your frame: Use the sticks or branches to create a frame for your den.

3. Cover the frame: Place the tarp over it and secure it with rope.

4. Make it cozy: Add leaves, moss, or ferns to your den for extra insulation.

With these tips, you'll be a Den-building pro in no time!

Of course, you can build your man-made den anywhere you have some space, but if you're going to make it indoors, here are a few things to keep in mind:

1. Choose a room you can close off from the rest of the house. This will help to keep your den private and cozy.

2. Place blankets, sheets, or towels over furniture to create walls.

3. Add pillows and cushions for extra comfort.

4. Make a roof for your den by draping a blanket or sheet over a rope or clothesline.

5. Use flashlights or lanterns to light up your den at night.

Now that you know how to build a den, it's time to get creative! So grab some blankets and start creating!

HOW TO NAVIGATE USING A MAP AND COMPASS

One of the most important skills for any adventurer is navigating using a map and compass. After all, getting lost in the wilderness is not fun!

The first step is to find your location on the map. This can be done using landmarks, contour lines, or GPS coordinates.

Once you have found your location, it's time to orient the map. This means aligning the map so that it matches the direction you are facing.

Next, use your compass to find the north. Once you have found north, draw a line on the map from your location to where you want to go.

Now it's time to start walking! As you walk, check your compass and map to ensure you are still on course.

HOW TO READ ANIMAL TRACKS

One of the best ways to learn about animals is by studying their tracks. This can tell you what kind of animal it is, what it was doing, and where it was going.

The first step is to find an excellent spot to look for tracks. A sandy beach or muddy riverbank is a great place to start.

Once you have found a good spot, it's time to start looking for tracks. The best way to do this is by using a magnifying glass. This will help you to see the details of the tracks.

Once you have found some tracks, it's time to start identifying them. The best way to do this is by using a field guide. This will help you identify the animal based on the shape, size, and number of toes on the tracks.

Following these simple steps, you can read animal tracks like a pro. Happy tracking!

HOW TO FIND YOUR WAY BACK IN THE DARK

One of the best skills for any adventurer is learning how to find your way back in the dark. After all, you never know when you might find yourself in a situation where it's not safe to use a light.

There are two main ways to find your way back in the dark: using the stars and your sense of hearing.

If you want to use the stars, the first step is to find the North Star. This brightest star in the sky can be found using the Big Dipper as a guide. Once you have found the North Star, draw an imaginary line from it to the horizon. This line will point due north.

If you want to use your sense of hearing, the first step is to find a noise you can hear from a distance away. This could be a train, a plane, or even a river.

Once you have found a noise, walk towards it until you reach your destination.

And that's it! You can now find your way back in the dark. Happy exploring!

ACTIVITY

Vacation Adventures

Tick off each activity in the Vacation Adventures worksheet. Happy Exploring!

Tick off each activity as you achieve it!

YOU'VE GOT THIS!

The pre-teen years are full of changes, not just physically but emotionally and mentally too. Having a solid foundation of life skills will make the big jump to teenagerhood that much easier. This book has taught you some valuable skills that will hopefully help you succeed in life, no matter what challenges come your way.

Many of the skills we've covered are not taught at school but will help you manage day-to-day life. For example, you'll always have to budget your money, whether buying a coffee or making a large purchase. Learning how to handle your finances now will save you so much stress in the future.

Other skills, like time management and goal setting, will help you not just in school but in every area of your life. If you can learn to manage your time efficiently and set realistic goals, you'll be able to achieve anything you put your mind to.

Remember that taking care of your physical and mental health is key to a happy and successful life. Eat healthily, exercise regularly, and make sure to take time for yourself to relax and de-stress. That includes putting your adventure skills to good use and getting outside to enjoy this wonderful world. If you can do all these things, you'll be well on your way to a bright future.

Finally, life is a journey, and there's always room to learn new things. Even if you don't feel like you need it right now, learning new skills will only benefit you in the long run. So keep your mind open, be willing to try new things, and don't be afraid to fail.

Good luck. You've got this!

Thanks for reading! I hope you enjoyed this book and that it was helpful to you. If you have any questions or want to learn more about the topics covered, feel free to reach out to me on social media or via email.

Take care of yourselves, tweens! The world is yours for the taking!

— *Your Friend, Ferne Bowe*

MONEY SKILLS FOR KIDS

A Beginner's Guide to Earning, Saving, and Spending Wisely

Everything Tweens Should Know About Personal Finance

FERNE BOWE

INTRODUCTION

Welcome to *Money Skills for Kids*.

Have you ever stared longingly at the newest video game or the latest gadget, wishing you had a bit more money to buy it? Maybe you saved up your allowance, only to realize you're a few dollars short; or perhaps you've thought about earning more, but you're not sure how to start. If any of this sounds familiar, don't worry—you're not alone.

Understanding money and how it works can sometimes feel like trying to decode a secret language. That's where this book comes in.

In a world where a handful of coins, a few pieces of paper, and some digital numbers on a screen can transform into books, toys, and even family vacations, understanding money is like having a superpower. This book is your personal guide to start developing this power!

This book will take you on a fascinating journey to discover what money really is and how you can earn it, save it, and even spend it (wisely, of course!). But we won't stop there. We'll explore how you can grow your money, learn the art of budgeting, and keep your money safe and secure.

Each chapter is filled with interesting facts, a hands-on activity, and real-life examples to make learning about money engaging and fun. By the time you reach the end of this book, you'll have uncovered the secret to making smart money choices. These skills will serve you well now and when you're grown up.

Here's a sneak peek at some of the information we'll cover:

- The fascinating world of money and how it works
- The art of budgeting and saving like a pro
- The important difference between needs and wants
- A beginner's guide to growing your money through investing
- How to keep your money safe and secure

While the following chapters are written for kids, we encourage parents to join us in this learning journey. Their participation will help ensure the lessons we cover move from the pages of this book into your everyday life. This way, you're not just learning about money in theory, but also becoming a confident money manager in practice.

We hope you and your parents will find *Money Skills for Kids* to be a valuable tool and a rewarding educational adventure.

Are you ready? Let's embark on this exciting journey together!

Please note: This book's information is general and designed to be for information only. While every effort has been made to ensure it is accurate, it is for general educational purposes only and is not intended, nor should it be taken, as professional financial advice. It is essential to consult with a qualified financial advisor before making any financial decisions. The author and publisher are not responsible for any actions taken based on the information presented in this book.

CHAPTER 1:

UNDERSTANDING MONEY

WHAT IS MONEY?

Have you ever wondered what money truly is? Well, it's more than just the coins you can feel in your pocket or the colorful notes stashed in your wallet. At its core, money is a tool that holds a particular value, kind of like a key that can unlock numerous goods and services for you.

Money is your ticket to trade. It allows you to exchange what you have—your money—for the things you want or need. That's why money is often called a "medium of exchange." Think of it like swapping. You give a certain amount of money, and in return, you receive a product or service. It's like the universal language of trade that everyone understands.

> *For example, say you want to buy a shiny new bike for $250. To make that bike yours, you have to hand over $250, and in return, you get the bike. Simple.*

The money we use is issued by the government and comes in different shapes and sizes—coins and banknotes—each symbolizing a different value that everyone acknowledges and accepts.

When people talk about money, they often use the term "currency." This refers to the physical forms of money, such as coins and banknotes, specific to a particular country.

Every country has its own unique currency. For example, in the United States, they use the dollar. If you go to Japan, you'll need yen. In the United Kingdom, they use pounds. If you're visiting India, you'll be spending rupees. And in Mexico, you'll come across pesos. These are all different types of currency, each used within their own countries. Money might look different in every country, but it all serves the same purpose—it's a key to trade.

DID YOU KNOW? Dollar bills are not made of ordinary paper. They are made of a special paper called "currency paper," composed of 75% cotton and 25% linen fibers. This combination makes them more durable and helps them withstand the wear and tear of everyday use. Still, the average life of a one-dollar bill is only 18 months.

HISTORY OF MONEY

Imagine you want a new video game, but instead of going to the store to buy it, you have to find someone willing to trade the video game for something you already own. Maybe they want your skateboard, and you could agree to swap it for the video game. Sounds pretty complicated, doesn't it? Well, that's what people did before money existed. They used trading (or "bartering") to get the things they needed.

Now, let's say it is a long time ago and you have a cow, but what you really want is a horse. In this case, because there was no money, you would have had to find someone who had a horse but who wanted a cow, and who was willing to agree to the exchange. They would have to agree that it was a fair trade, and you'd have to walk your cow to the person's farm to make the trade.

As you can see, bartering was not an easy thing to do. It was not always possible to find someone willing to make a trade, people had to carry their goods long distances, and it was not always easy to agree on the value of the items they were trading to make sure the trade was fair and of equal value.

144   ESSENTIAL SKILLS EVERY KID SHOULD KNOW

That's why physical money was created. Money solved the issues involved in trading because the value was recognized and agreed upon by everyone to ensure that the exchange was equal. Plus, money was easier to carry around than a cow or a horse.

> **DID YOU KNOW?** Money dates back thousands of years. The earliest coins were made of precious metals like silver and gold, but the first use of paper money was in ancient China around the 7th century.

The next time you go out to the store to buy a loaf of bread, just be glad you can use the coins or notes in your pocket instead of carrying a cow!

DIFFERENT FORMS OF MONEY

When you think of money, you probably think of cash. If so, you're right—cash is a form of money! But there are other forms of money, as well.

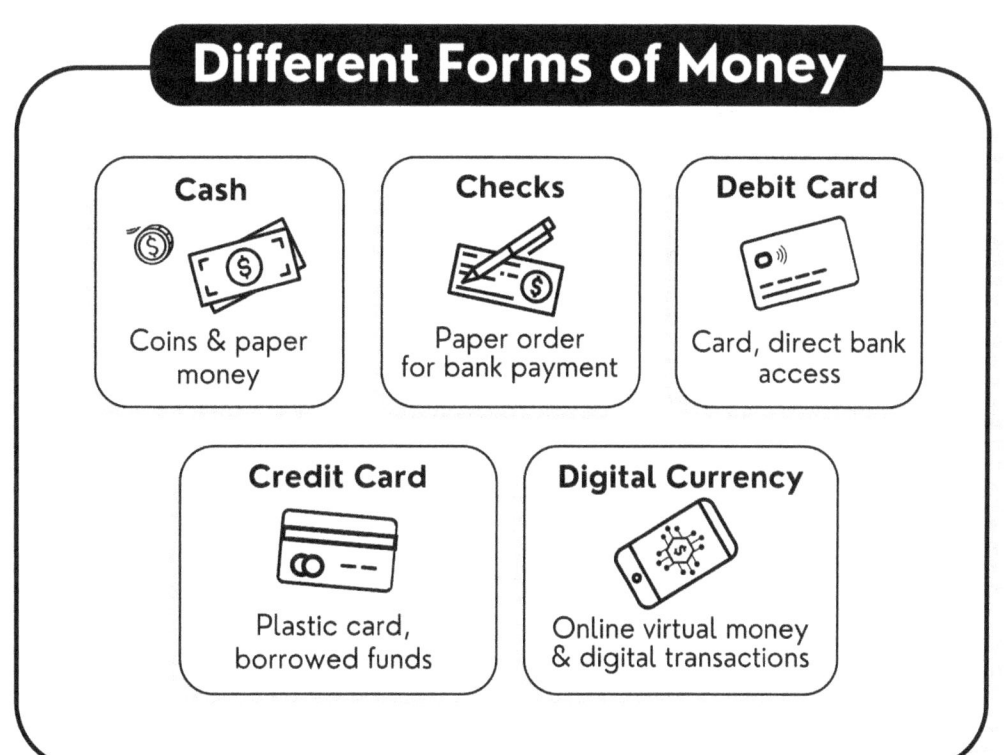

MONEY SKILLS FOR KIDS   **145**

Here are some of the different forms of money:

Cash

Cash is the simplest form of money, consisting of coins and paper money.

Checks

Checks are numbered pieces of paper issued by banks saying it's ok to pay someone by having the money deducted from your bank account. Other forms of money have become more popular, and checks aren't used as much today.

Debit Cards

A debit card is a special card that works like a combination of a check and cash. It's issued by a bank and used to buy things, just like you would with cash. But instead of carrying around cash, you can use a debit card to pay for things.

When you use a debit card, the money for your purchase is taken straight from your bank account. Banks usually don't give debit cards to kids, as you need an adult account. However, there are a number of accounts designed for kids and their parents that offer prepaid debit cards.

Prepaid debit cards for kids are usually managed by parents through an app. This means parents can put money on the card, control how it is used, and have visibility on purchases. Some apps also have features that allow parents to assign pocket money when chores are completed. This is a great way to help kids learn about money management and spending responsibly.

Credit Cards

A credit card is issued by a bank and can be used to make purchases. It works a bit differently than a debit card. When you use a credit card, you buy things now but pay for them later.

Every month, you'll get a bill from the bank for the things you bought on your credit card. It's essential to pay this bill on time. If you don't pay the total amount every month, the bank will charge you extra money, called interest. Interest is a percentage of the balance that you still owe. This means you have to pay more money back to the bank.

The bank decides how much money you can spend with the credit card. The bank is lending you this money to make purchases, and you must pay it back. If you can't pay it back in one month, the bank charges you interest on the remaining balance. As with debit cards, banks typically don't issue credit cards to kids.

Digital Currency

Digital currency is a type of money that is unlike coins, checks, or paper money. It exists only online and has no physical form you can touch. It's like money that lives inside a computer.

Instead of being accounted for and transferred through banks like traditional money, digital currency uses electronic codes stored in computers. So, when you use a digital currency, it's all happening electronically.

> **DID YOU KNOW?** Most of the money we use today exists in the form of electronic money or numbers on a screen, stored electronically in banks or online accounts. If everyone tried to take out all their money as physical cash, the banks would quickly run out of money. So, even traditional money is a form of digital money.

Other forms of digital money, such as cryptocurrencies, only exist on screens and computers. Cryptocurrencies like Bitcoin and Ethereum are examples of digital currencies that have no physical cash associated with them.

HOW MONEY IS USED IN EVERYDAY LIFE

Money is a standard tool of value that we use every day. It's essential because our economy—the system that tracks how people spend and earn money—is founded on the principles of money.

We use money to buy the things we need or want. This includes products (like toys, video games, and food) and services (like getting a haircut, seeing a dentist, or paying a builder).

But we don't always have to spend the money we earn as soon as we get it. It's also a good idea to save money. When you save money, you set it aside for the future. This could be to buy something bigger, like a bicycle, or to pay for any unexpected expenses, like buying a new video console if yours suddenly stops working. Or, it could be used to fund your retirement when you stop working later in life.

When you work, you earn money. Whether you do chores at home, like mowing the lawn or babysitting, or a full-time job when you get older, you earn money in exchange for your hard work. Once you've earned money, you decide how to spend it (or save it) on the things you need, such as food, clothes, a car, and a house. You wouldn't survive if you couldn't buy the stuff you needed.

Money makes the world go round. If people stopped spending, stores would have to close and people would lose their jobs and wouldn't have money to spend. That's why a healthy economy is a bit like a seesaw. It's about having a good balance between saving money (for future needs) and spending money (to buy the things you need now and keep the economy going).

YOUR KNOWLEDGE ABOUT MONEY

Fill in the blanks:

1. What's another word for money? _____
2. Money is also known as a _____
3. Money is issued by each country's _____
4. What's another name for trading? _____
5. What was created to solve the problems that resulted from trading? _____
6. What are you charged if you don't pay off your balance on a credit card? _____

Match the country with its currency:

Mexico ○   ○ $ Dollar

India ○   ○ ₱ Peso

United States ○   ○ ₹ Rupee

United Kingdom ○   ○ ¥ Yen

Japan ○   ○ £ Pound

Circle the Correct Answer:

1. Which currency exists only online?

   Credit Card   Debit Card   Check   Digital Currency

2. Which card is used to buy things now and pay for them later?
   Debit card   Credit card

3. Which card deducts money directly from your bank account?
   Credit card   Debit card

CHAPTER 2:

HOW TO EARN MONEY

To save and spend money, first, you must earn it.

WHY IT'S IMPORTANT TO START EARNING MONEY AT A YOUNG AGE

It's often only when you really want something, like a cool Lego set or craft kit that your parents won't buy for you, that you start thinking about earning money. But wouldn't it be great to have your own money to buy it immediately?

That's why starting earning money as early as possible is a good idea. When you earn your own money, you can save it up for the things you want in the future. You can also save up for even bigger things, like your very first car!

There are many benefits to earning money at a young age.

❶ Building a Strong Work Ethic

Earning money at a young age builds a strong work ethic. A work ethic is the set of values that you set for yourself in the workplace. It's how you behave while performing your work.

For example, a strong work ethic involves:

- Working hard to make something the best it can be
- Checking for mistakes
- Submitting work on time
- Helping others

- Showing up for work on time
- Staying focused
- Working well with others

❷ Learning the Value of Money

When you earn money, you begin to understand its value. Everything has value and is worth something. The effort and time you put into work produces value in the form of money.

> *For example, if you want a scooter that costs $89, you will have to work and earn at least $89 to pay for it.*

In this case, you exchange your hard-earned money ($89) for the item. This helps you understand and appreciate the value of money and the work required to earn it.

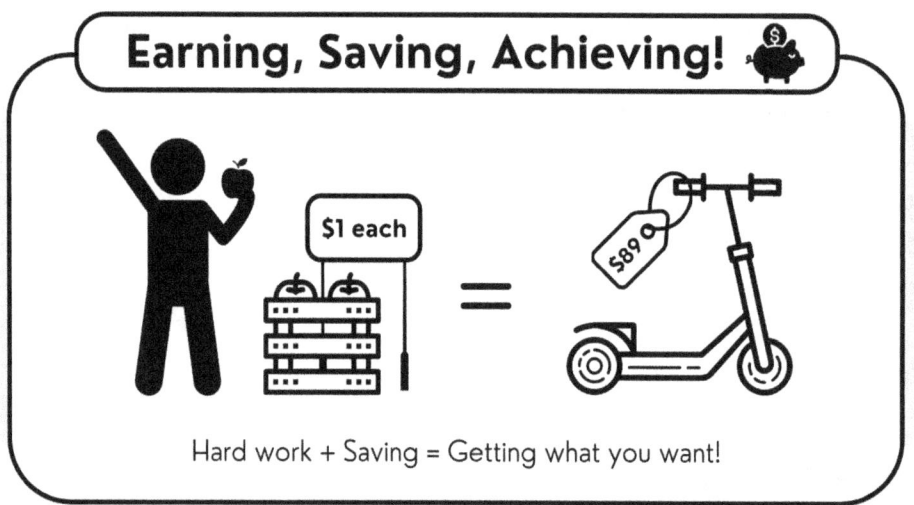

❸ Developing Communication Skills

Earning money teaches you how to communicate with different people outside school or at home. Communication at work may be different from what you are used to. It usually requires a more formal and professional approach.

You'll gain experience working with people of different backgrounds, ages, races, and personalities, and this will teach you how to interact and communicate with all types of people.

❹ Developing Problem-Solving Skills

Earning money teaches you how to solve problems and work well with others.

> *For example, say you have a book to sell for $5. The person buying the book hands you a $20 bill. How much change do you give back?*

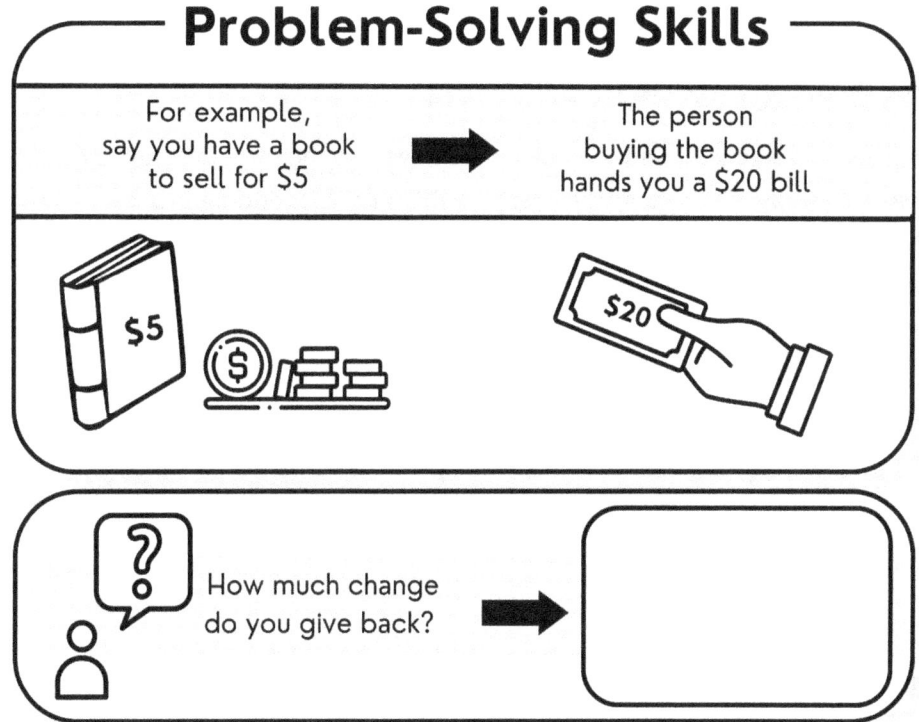

In this instance, you're learning how to handle money and how much change to give back.

❺ Developing Teamwork

It's never too early to learn how to work as a team. Earning money will give you experience working with others, helping each other, relying on each other, and learning from each other to achieve a goal—not for yourself, but for a group of people.

❻ Building Your Resume

Earning money and gaining work experience helps you develop skills that can benefit your future. It may help you get a scholarship for college or land your first job after high school. Having skills and work experience also sets you apart from others and shows your willingness to take on responsibilities.

❼ Understanding the World of Work

Earning money at a young age helps you discover what you do and don't enjoy about work. It begins to shape what you might want or not want from a future job.

Early exposure to various work settings and experiences will make you more comfortable and confident in the working environment when you are older.

❽ Understanding the Cost of Living

Earning money gives you a sense of how much things cost and the effort required to afford the things you need or want. It helps make you more responsible about spending money.

It feels great to earn your own money and purchase the things you want without depending on someone else to buy them. Making money at a young age helps you learn to be responsible with your money. This way, when you are older, you can do the things you want without worrying about how to pay for them.

Developing good habits of earning and managing money when you're young makes your life easier and more fulfilling as you get older.

. . . .

WAYS TO EARN MONEY

Money certainly doesn't grow on trees. If it did, we wouldn't have to work and would all be rich! Earning money comes from hard work, but there are plenty of opportunities to make money, even at a young age.

Here are some ways to earn money when you're a kid:

❶ Allowance or Chores

You can earn money by receiving an allowance for doing chores around the house or getting good grades in school.

> *For example, your parents might agree to give you $10 a week for doing the dishes, taking out the trash, doing the laundry, cleaning a particular area of the house, feeding the dog or cat, or keeping your grades at a B or above.*

❷ Part-Time Jobs

You can also make money by doing part-time jobs.

> *For example, you can babysit, mow lawns, rake leaves, shovel snow, or wash cars for people in your neighborhood.*

You could also get a part-time job in a cafe or restaurant when you're older.

③ Entrepreneurial Ventures

Another way to make money is by starting a small business based on your hobbies and interests. This is called an entrepreneurial venture.

> *For example, you could create crafts or make items to sell, offer pet-sitting or dog-walking services to your neighbors, or bake and sell delicious treats.*

This is a fun way to turn your passions into a profitable venture and earn money doing what you love.

> **DID YOU KNOW?** Some professional video gamers make millions of dollars by competing in e-sports tournaments. They play video games at a high level and earn money from prize pools, sponsorships, and streaming their gameplay online.

PASSIVE INCOME – HOW TO EARN MONEY WHILE YOU SLEEP

Wouldn't it be great to make money even while you're sleeping? Believe it or not, there's something called passive income that allows people to do just that.

156 ESSENTIAL SKILLS EVERY KID SHOULD KNOW

Passive income is money that you earn without actively working for it. It's like a money-making machine that keeps running, even when you're not actively involved.

There are lots of different ways to earn passive income. Some examples include owning a rental property, writing a book that continues to sell, or making an app that keeps getting downloaded. All these sources of income require lots of hard work and effort up front, but once they're set up and take off, they can make money regularly.

Let's look at the example of Ryan.

> *Ryan is a 7-year-old boy who has become a millionaire by reviewing toys on YouTube. Every time someone watches one of his videos, he earns a small percentage of the advertising money YouTube generates from his videos. The more viewers he has, the more money he makes.*
>
> *Let's say he earns $0.003 every time someone views his video, and it gets 1,000 views. In this case, he would make $3.*
>
> *1,000 x $0.003 = $3*
>
> *Now imagine he gets a million views. He would make $3,000.*
>
> *1,000,000 x $0.003 = $3,000*
>
> *What makes this form of passive income so unique is that Ryan has built a loyal following of viewers. Whenever he uploads a new video, people watch it because they enjoy his content. And since his fans come from all over the world, Ryan continues to earn money even when he's fast asleep!*
>
> *But Ryan's success didn't happen overnight. It took time, effort, and creating content that people enjoyed.*

Passive income is a great way to earn money because it enables you to make money even when you're not actively working. However, it's essential to know that it isn't easy. Launching successful passive income business ventures takes dedication, time, and a lot of hard work. But the rewards can be worth it, as it can provide you with financial freedom. This may be something you want to explore as you get older.

HOW TO TURN A MONEY-MAKING IDEA INTO A REALITY

If you're ready to venture out and start your own business, a few steps are involved in the process.

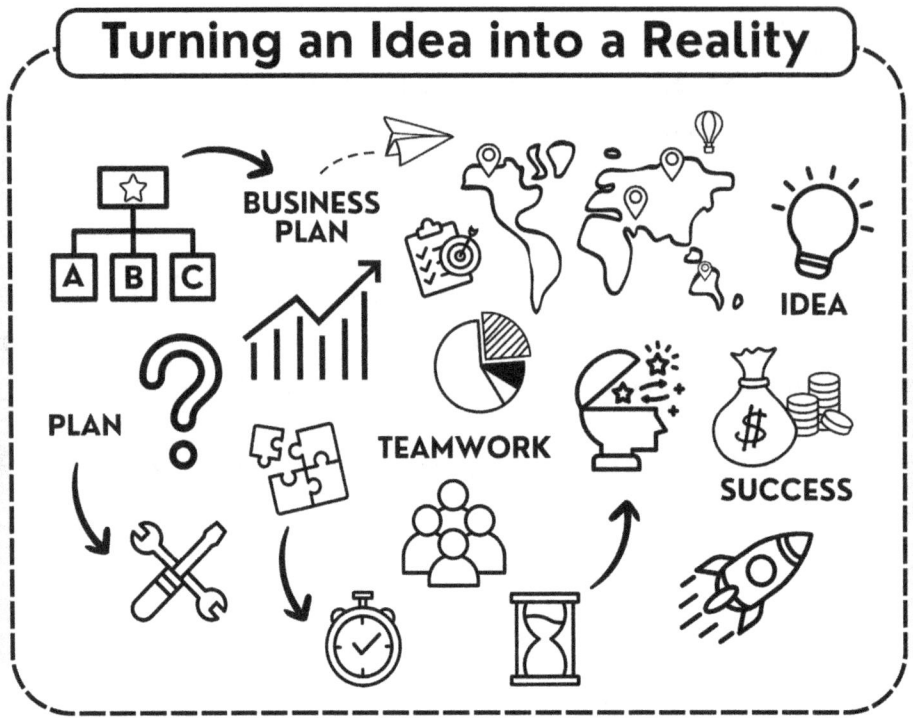

❶ Come up with an idea.

Think about something you enjoy doing and that you can really get excited about. Start with something simple, like baking and selling cookies.

❷ Conduct market research.

Think about who your customers will be. Everyone likes cookies, so they could be neighbors, friends, teachers, or just about anybody!

Also, think about who your competition will be. Is anyone else selling homemade cookies near you, and how is their business doing? This will tell you if there is a market for what you sell (for example, homemade cookies) and how successful your business could be. What kind of cookies do they sell, and how much do they charge?

❸ Find something to make you stand out.

Find something that will set you apart from your competition.

> *For example, you could sell a type of cookie that no one else sells, or you could sell cookies as "sandwiches" and have vanilla or chocolate icing in the middle of two cookies.*

It's important to develop something to differentiate your cookies from those of your competitors.

❹ Create a business plan.

Write your business plan. A business plan is like a roadmap for your business, guiding you and keeping you on track for success.

Your business plan should include the following:

- Who you are
- Your experience
- What product or service you're going to sell
- Your target customers
- The research you've compiled on your competitors and how you'll differentiate yourself from them
- How will you advertise and sell your product
- An estimate of sales, expenses, and profit
- Next steps and milestones
- Future goals

❺ Get the word out.

Once you've created your business plan, it's time to get the word out and start selling. How are you going to market your business? Think of ways to promote your product or services. Will you advertise on social media, create flyers, or focus on word of mouth?

: For example, if you created a cookie business, you could start by telling everyone you know. You could put flyers in schools or local businesses and use social media platforms to spread the word.

DID YOU KNOW? The game "Among Us" became super popular among kids and teens because of word of mouth. It started with a small group of players who loved the game and shared their excitement with their friends. Soon, everyone wanted to play, and it became a massive sensation because people talked about it and recommended it to others!

UNDERSTANDING PROFIT

Once you've come up with your own money-making idea, you must understand the fundamentals of profit before you can turn it into a reality. Most businesses exist to make money, so understanding profit is critical to any new venture.

Profit is the money you make when you sell your products or services, after you take away the expenses, like materials, labor, and other overhead costs.

For instance, imagine you're selling homemade jewelry. The profit is the money that remains after you pay for the materials, such as beads, bracelets, or chains.

So, if each necklace costs you $10 in materials and you sell them for $20, your profit is $10 per necklace. However, it's important to remember that materials aren't your only costs when you make your own products. You must also include overhead costs like labor, advertising, and electricity.

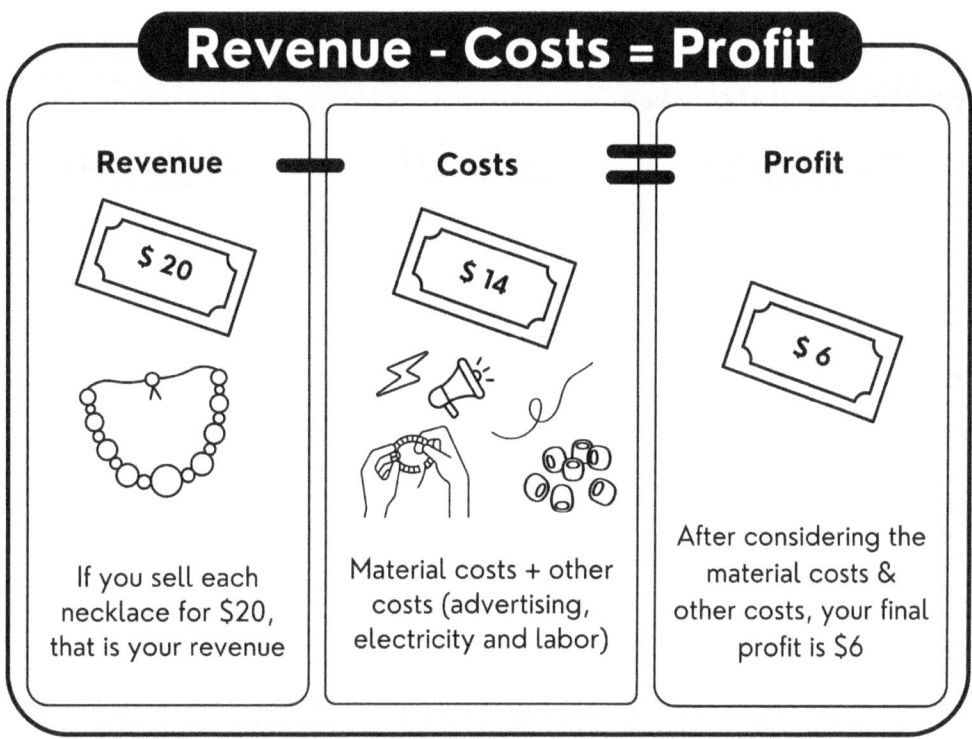

By ensuring your revenue exceeds your costs, you can create a positive profit and make money! A clear understanding of profit will help you manage your costs and take the next steps to turn your money-making idea into a reality.

HOW TO GET A PART-TIME JOB

Another way to earn money is to get a part-time or full-time job. Part-time jobs are often available to teenagers or students looking to gain work experience and earn some extra cash. These jobs include working at a local store, restaurant, or cafe.

Here are the steps it takes to get your first part-time job.

❶ Determine your interests and strengths.

Think of something you're interested in, good at, or enjoy doing.

> *For example, suppose you're interested in food and enjoy meeting new people. In that case, you might consider working in a cafe.*

❷ Search for job openings.

To find out who is hiring, list all the cafes near you. Call each cafe and ask if they are hiring, or stop by and ask them in person.

❸ Prepare a resume.

Once you find out who is hiring, you need to prepare and submit a resume. A resume is a document that outlines your skills, work experience, education, and achievements.

A resume includes the following information:

- Name
- Address
- Phone number
- Email address
- Objective—A short description of yourself and your goals
- Work experience—Any jobs or volunteer work you've had
- Your education—The name and address of your school, your grades, and any coursework that ties in with the job you are applying for
- Additional skills

Here is an example of a resume:

Example Resume

Jane Doe
123 Main Street Anytown, CA 12345
(123) 456-7890 | jane.doe@email.com

About Me

I am a friendly, organized High School Student looking for part-time work in retail. I love learning new skills, and working in a team.

Experience

Assistant, ABC Cafe — July - Dec 2023
- Serving coffee at local cafe
- Valuable experience in customer service

Babysitting — Jan - Dec 2023
- Babysitting for children aged 3-9, in my local area

Education

High School Senior — Class of 2023
Anytown High School, Anytown, CA

Awards

- National Honor Society
- President's List
- AP Scholar with Distinction

Skills

- Experience using cash & credit payments
- Serving customers food & drink
- Excellent communication skills
- Strong organizational & time management skills

Interests

I am captain of the school basketball team, and I also play lacrosse. I have a passion for travel and speak Spanish fluently.

❹ Interview

If the cafe you're applying to likes your resume, they may invite you in for an interview. In an interview, someone from the cafe will sit down and talk with you, face to face. They may ask about your experience and why you want to work there. You should always be polite and answer all questions honestly.

The best way to earn money is to work hard. Hard work always pays off. It shows employers that you are responsible and motivated, and that you take pride in your work.

With the money you earn from working, you can now buy what you need and want.

CREATE YOUR OWN BUSINESS IDEA

ACTIVITY TIME!

Think of a fun business idea that you would like to turn into a reality. It could be a product (like baking cookies) or service (like walking dogs.)

YOUR BIG IDEA

  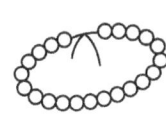 

a. What will you sell or offer? [Your Product or Service]

_____

b. What makes it unique?

_____

c. What is the main goal of your business?

☐ Make money   ☐ Help others   ☐ Have fun

MARKETING

a. Who are your customers (kids, parents, etc.)? [Target customers]

_____

_____

_____

b. How will you let people know about your business? Will you make posters, create a website, or tell your friends? [Promotion ideas]

_____

c. What will your business be called? [Business name]

_____

d. Create a unique logo or symbol for your business. Think about colors, shapes, and images that represent your business. [Logo design]

FINANCES

a. How much money do you need to start your business?

_____

b. How much will it cost to make each product or provide your service?

_____

c. How much will you charge for your product or service?

_____

d. What will be your profit? How much will you make after you take out your costs?

_____

Remember, this activity is all about using your imagination and having fun. Fill in the gaps with your creative ideas for your own business. You can also discuss your ideas with friends and family for feedback and support. Have fun being an entrepreneur!

CHAPTER 3:

HOW TO SAVE MONEY

Once you've earned money, you can save or spend it. Let's start by talking about the importance of saving money. Saving is when you set aside a portion of your money for the future.

THE IMPORTANCE OF SAVING

Saving money is an important habit to develop, especially when you've worked hard to earn it. By setting aside a portion of your earnings each month, you can achieve your future goals and afford things that you may not be able to afford right now.

For example, imagine you want to buy a new pair of shoes that cost $200, but you currently have only $50. To reach your goal, you'll need to save $150. It's essential to plan how much money you can set aside each month to reach your savings target.

If you can save at least $30 per month, it would take you five months to save $150. When you combine this amount with the $50 you already have, you'll have a total of $200, which is enough to buy the shoes.

Starting with $50, by saving $30 a month for five months, you would have a total of $200 to buy your dream shoes.

Saving Money Allows You to Put It Aside for Emergencies

While it's good to set aside money for things you want or need, it's also good to have money set aside for unexpected emergencies.

> *Suppose you have a pet dog, and your parents agreed to let you have it on the condition that you take care of all its expenses. Suddenly, your dog starts limping and requires veterinary care. If you've regularly set aside money each month, you will have the funds to take your dog to the vet immediately.*
>
> *If your dog has a broken leg or any other health issue, it's crucial to get professional help as soon as possible. This is why it is essential to save money. Otherwise, you might have to borrow money from someone else or delay the necessary medical treatment for your dog, which isn't the best option for your furry friend.*
>
> *By saving money, you can be prepared for unexpected situations and ensure your beloved pet receives the care it needs promptly.*

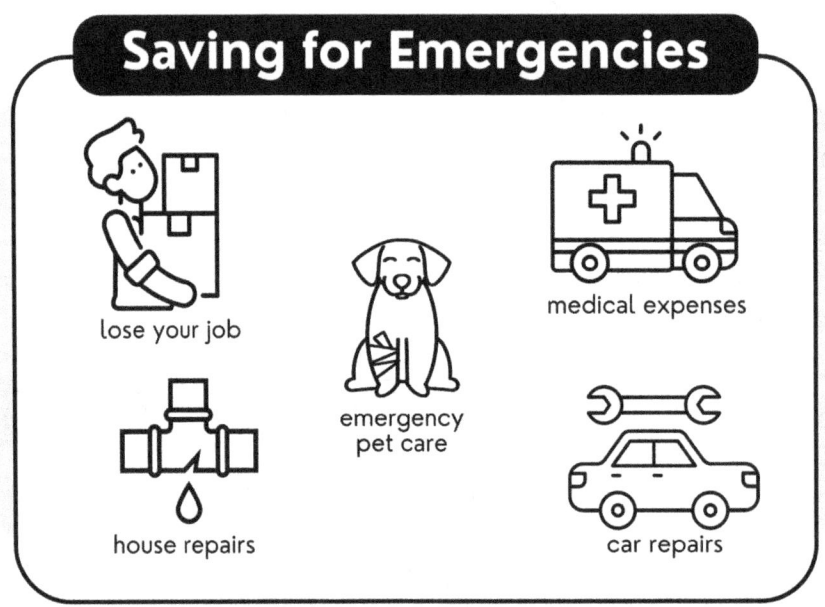

Saving Money in a Bank Earns You Interest

When you deposit money into a savings account at the bank, the bank pays you for keeping it there. This is called interest.

Interest is like a reward for saving your money. It's usually a percentage of the amount you have held at the bank.

- *For example, let's say you have $100 in a savings account, and the bank agrees to pay you an interest rate of 4% yearly. That means they'll give you $4 as interest at the end of the year.*

- *To calculate interest, you can use a simple formula: Multiply the amount you have saved ($100) by the interest rate (0.04, which is the decimal equivalent of 4%).*

- *So $100 X 0.04 = $4.00*

There is also another type of interest called compound interest. Compound interest is interest earned on interest. This means you not only make interest on your initial deposit, but also on the interest you have already earned.

Using the same example, let's see how compound interest works.

- *In the first year, you had $100 in your savings account, and the bank paid you $4.00 in interest (4% of $100). At the end of the first year, your savings account has grown to $104.00 ($100 + $4.00).*

- *Now, in the second year, you earn interest not only on your initial $100, but also on the interest you earned in the first year. Using the same interest rate of 4%, you would earn $4.16 in interest (4% of $104). By the end of the second year, your savings account would have increased to $108.16 ($104 + $4.16).*

- *Do you see how the interest went from $4.00 in the first year to $4.16 in the second year? This is because you earned interest on top of the interest you made the previous year.*

This cycle of earning interest on the initial amount plus the interest continues year after year, making your savings grow faster. It's like a snowball rolling down a hill that grows bigger and bigger each year. The more money you deposit, the more interest you earn; the longer you leave it in the account, the faster it grows.

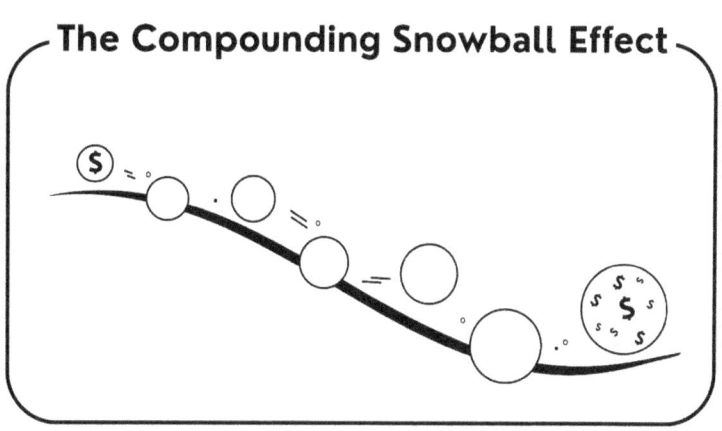

The Compounding Snowball Effect

This is why it's important to start saving early and to regularly add to your savings. It allows your money to work for you and grow over time.

Did you know that if you saved just $1 every day starting at the age of 10 and let it grow with a 5% interest rate, by the time you were 18, you would have around $3,600? And if you continued saving until you were 25, you will have about $8,000! The power of starting early and letting compound interest work its magic can make your money grow over time.

HOW TO SET SAVINGS GOALS

To keep yourself motivated and have a clear target to work towards, it's helpful to set goals when saving money. An excellent way to set effective goals is to remember the word "SMART."

S = Specific (What exactly are you saving for?)
M = Measurable (How much do you need to save?)
A = Achievable (Is your goal realistic and achievable?)
R = Relevant (Why is this goal important to you?)
T = Time-bound (How long will it take you to achieve your goal?)

> *Let's say you have your heart set on getting a new bike. You're really excited about riding around on your own wheels. Setting a savings goal for buying a bike gives you a strong motivation to save more and save faster. You'll do your best to set aside as much money as possible in a shorter amount of time so you can get that bike sooner.*
>
> *Here's how you can save using the SMART saving method:*
>
> *S = Specific: Save money for a new bike.*
> *M = Measurable: Determine how much the bike costs and how much you need to save.*
> *A = Achievable: Set a goal that you can realistically reach.*
> *R = Relevant: Understand why getting the bike is essential to you.*
> *T = Time-bound: Decide when you want to reach your savings goal.*
>
> *For example, if the bike you want costs $200, you can set a goal of saving $20 each week. In 10 weeks, you'll have enough money to buy the bike.*

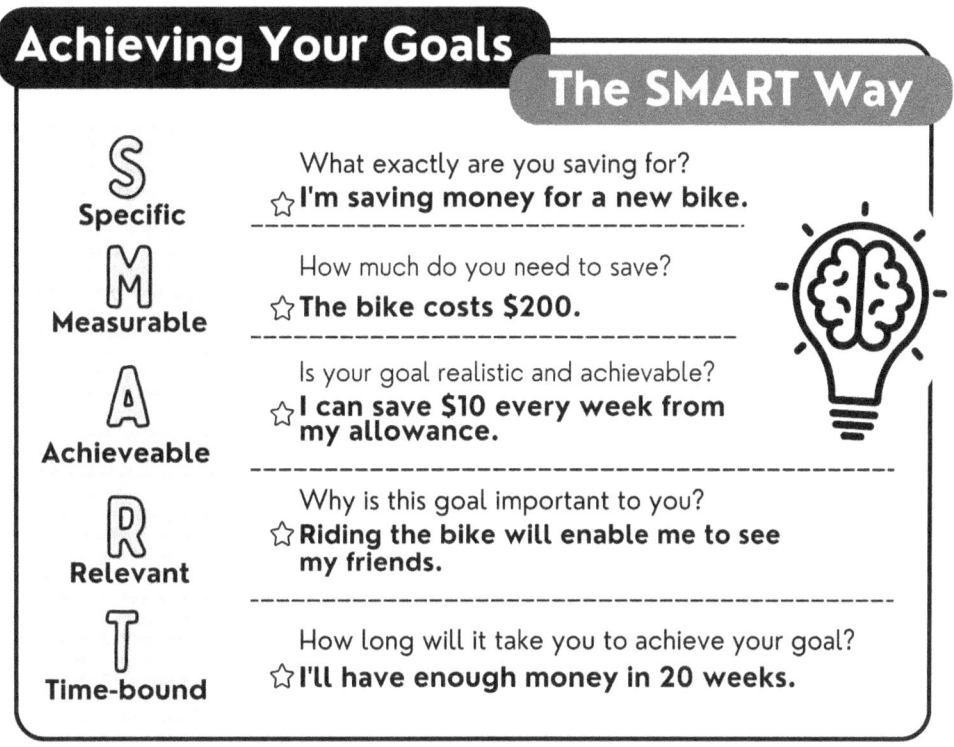

Remember, using the SMART saving method, you can easily set savings goals and buy what you want over time.

When it comes to savings goals, they can be categorized into different timeframes:

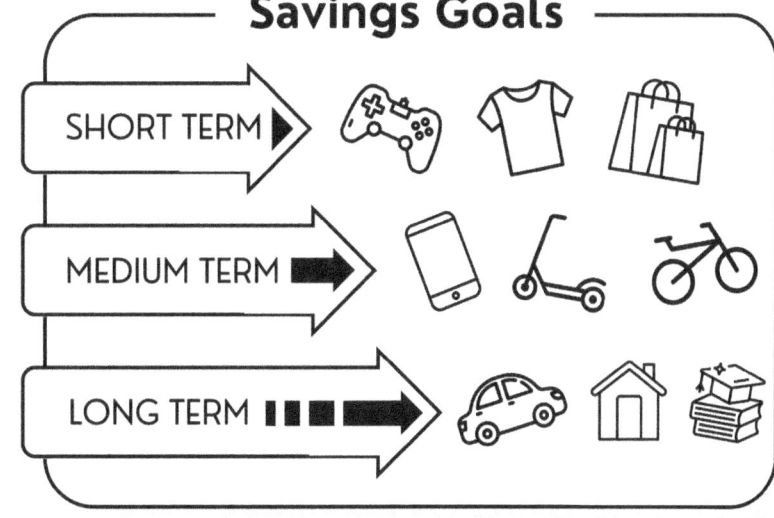

Short-Term Savings Goals

These are goals that can usually be reached within weeks or months. An example is saving up to buy a toy or a new video game.

Medium-Term Savings Goals

These goals usually take about a year to accomplish. An example is saving for a bike or a scooter.

Long-Term Savings Goals

These are goals that require several years of saving to achieve. Examples include saving for college tuition or a car.

By setting SMART savings goals and categorizing them based on their timeframes, you'll have a clear roadmap to follow and a sense of accomplishment as you reach each milestone. Remember, saving money is a journey. Setting goals can make it an exciting and rewarding adventure!

HOW TO SAVE MONEY

Saving money is a great habit to develop, and there are several ways to reach your savings goals. You just need to find the method that works best for you.

Here are a few methods you can try:

- **Piggy bank:** Start by regularly putting a small amount of money aside into a piggy bank. While it won't earn you interest, seeing your piggy bank fill as you keep adding more money is fun.

- **Savings account:** Open a savings account at a bank. This is a great way to keep your money safe and earn interest on your savings.

- **Savings app or online saver:** Explore different savings apps or online platforms to help you save towards your goals. These tools often offer interest and allow you to set savings goals so you can track your progress. Some even automate your savings so you can put a small amount into your account regularly.

Different Methods to Save

Piggy Bank — A simple way to save money

Savings Account — Keeps your money safe while earning interest

Savings App or Online Saver — A simple way to save online

Remember, finding the saving method that suits you best will make it easier and more enjoyable to reach your savings goals. Start saving today and watch your money grow!

HOW TO OPEN A SAVINGS ACCOUNT

When you start earning money, having a safe place to keep it is crucial. A savings account at a bank is a secure place to deposit and store your money while earning interest over time.

Here are some things to consider when choosing the best bank for your savings account:

- **Convenience:** Look for a bank that is easy to access whenever you need to deposit or withdraw money.

- **Customer service:** Make sure the staff at the bank are friendly, helpful, and knowledgeable and that you are comfortable dealing with them.

- **Fees:** Some banks charge fees to manage your account. Check what expenses the bank charges on your savings account, such as maintenance fees for falling below a minimum balance. Shop around for banks with fewer and lower fees so you can keep more of your savings.

- **Interest rates:** Different banks offer different interest rates. Look for the bank with the highest interest rate to help your savings grow faster.

Once you've chosen a bank, it's time to open your account. Some banks require you to do this in person, while others allow you to do it online.

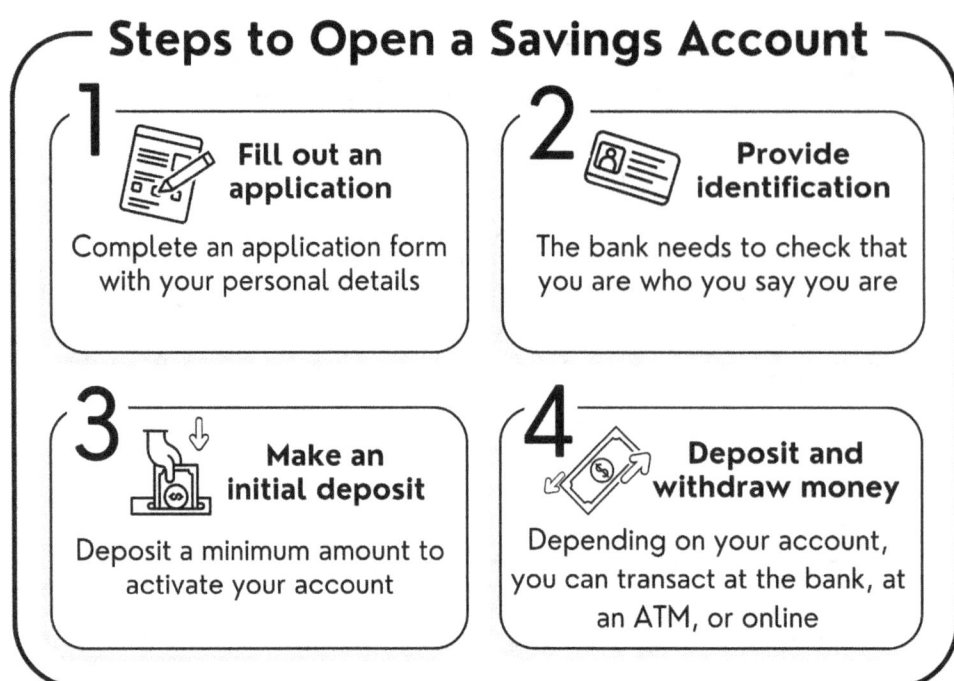

Step 1: Fill out an application.

The bank will first ask you to complete an application with your name, address, and other personal details. Once the application is filled out, you must sign it to show that you agree to their policies and that the information you gave them is correct. If you're under 18, you may also need a parent or guardian to sign.

Step 2: Provide identification.

Next, you may need to provide identification, such as your birth certificate, school ID, or passport, to prove your identity. This is a requirement, as the bank wants to be sure you are who you say you are.

Step 3: Make an initial deposit.

In most cases, you must deposit a minimum amount of money into your new savings account to activate the account. Remember, you may need to keep a minimum amount in your savings account to avoid a fee.

Step 4: Deposit and withdraw money.

Once the account is opened, you can deposit and withdraw money. There are three ways you can handle transactions that involve your account.

1. **In person at the bank:** Fill out a deposit or withdrawal slip at the bank. Hand it to the bank teller, and they will process your transaction.

2. **At an ATM:** Some banks issue bank cards with your name and account number. You can use these cards at ATMs. Set a PIN number for your card to ensure security. At the ATM, insert your bank card, enter your PIN number, select whether you want to make a deposit or withdrawal, and enter the amount. Once the transaction is complete, remove your card and keep the receipt for your records. Note that some banks may charge a fee for ATM transactions.

3. **Online:** Most banks offer online banking or mobile apps. Set up an online account with your bank. Once logged in, you can deposit and transfer money using the bank's website or app. You can even deposit checks by taking a picture using a phone.

THE SAVINGS GOAL THERMOMETER
ACTIVITY TIME!

INSTRUCTIONS

1 Think about what you want to save for:
This should be something you really want. It could be a toy, book, game, or even a fun day out. Remember, it should be something you'll need to save up for over a little while.

2 Write your goal at the top of the thermometer:
At the top of the thermometer, write down what you're saving for and how much it costs.

3 Break down your goals into smaller steps:
If you're saving $100, you could break it down into four $25 steps. Write down each step on the thermometer from bottom to top.

4 Track your progress:
Each time you save some money, color in your thermometer up to that level of your savings.

5 Keep going until you reach your goal:
It may take some time, but stick with it, and before you know it, you'll have your thermometer all colored in, and you'll have reached your goal.

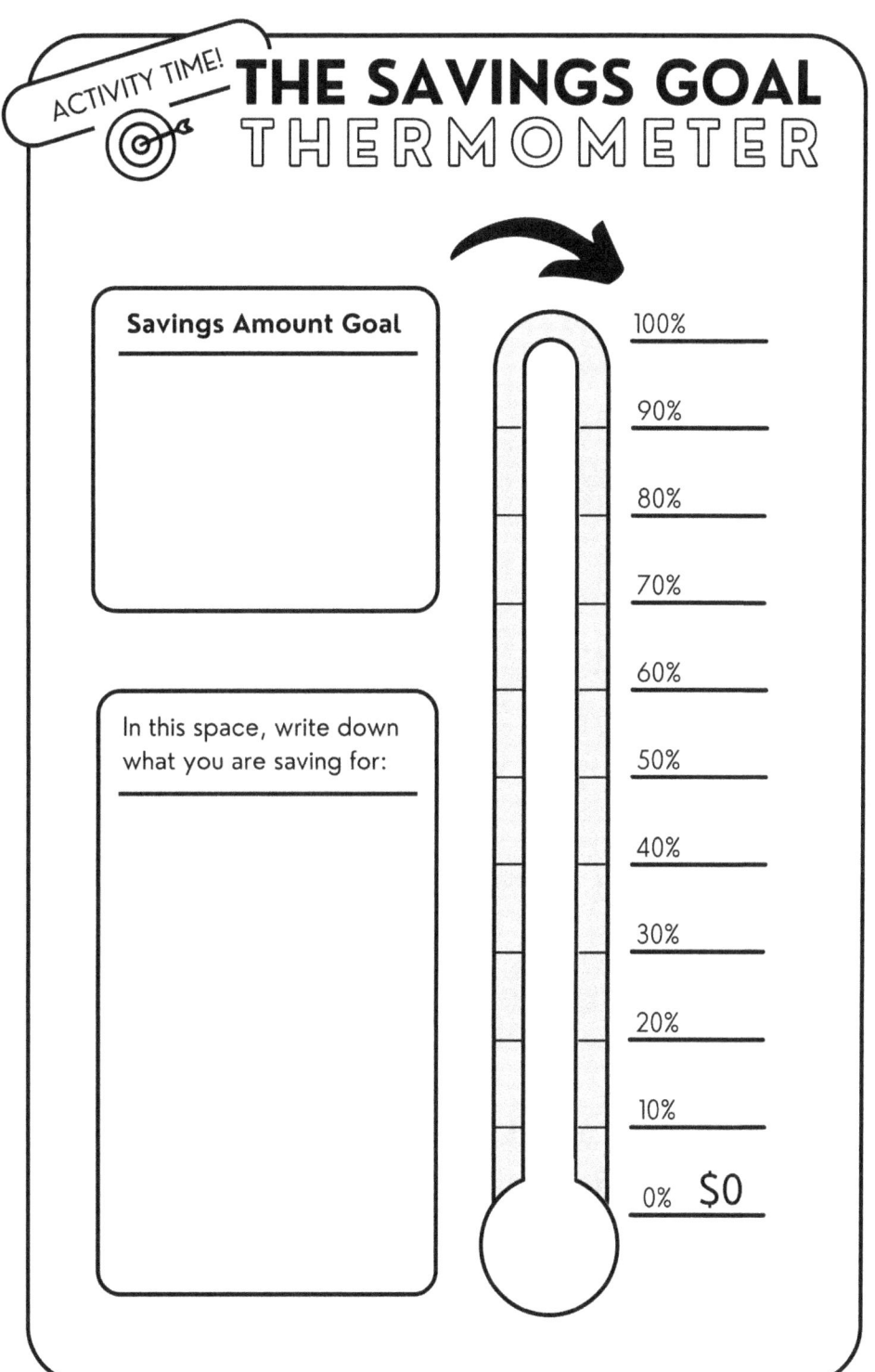

CHAPTER 4:

HOW TO SPEND MONEY WISELY

Now that you have a good idea about how to save money let's talk about spending money wisely.

Just because you have money doesn't mean you should go out and spend it all! It's essential to think carefully about what you are spending your money on and whether it is something you need. You might feel like you need a new game console, but is that a need? Or do you just want it because your friends have one? Let's look at needs and wants to help you make smart choices.

NEEDS VS. WANTS

- **Needs:** These are necessary for our survival and well-being, and we cannot live without them. Examples include food, clothes, water, and shelter.

- **Wants:** These are non-essential items and things we would like to have because they make life more enjoyable.

  For example, if your shoes are worn out and don't fit you properly anymore, you need a new pair to protect your feet and walk comfortably. However, wanting a new video game just because your friends have it is a want, not a necessity.

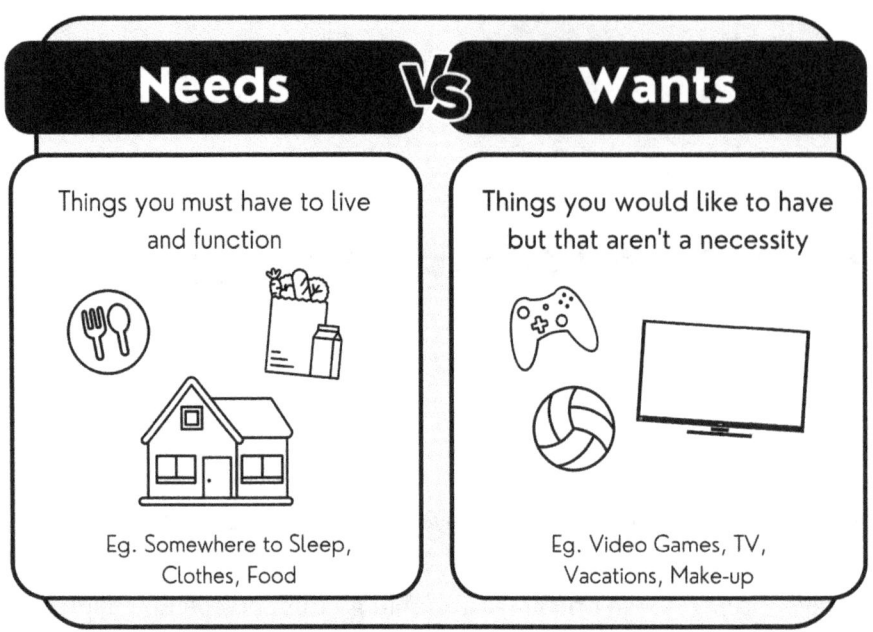

It's important to prioritize spending your money on needs before wants. Before you make a purchase, consider whether it's something you genuinely need. Ask yourself, "Is this something I really need to survive?" If the answer is no and you can wait a little while, it's not an immediate need, but more of a want.

Remember, it's okay to have wants—we all need fun and downtime. But it is important to make smart choices and spend money wisely.

HOW TO UNDERSTAND THE CONCEPT OF VALUE

Understanding the concept of value is essential when deciding how to spend your hard-earned money. Value refers to how much something is worth and what you get in return for what you pay.

When you think of value, there are a few things to consider:

1. **Utility:** How much use will you get from the item? Will it do its job or make you happy?

2. **Quality:** How long will the item last? Will it last a long time or wear out quickly?

3. **Price:** How much does it cost? Is it affordable?

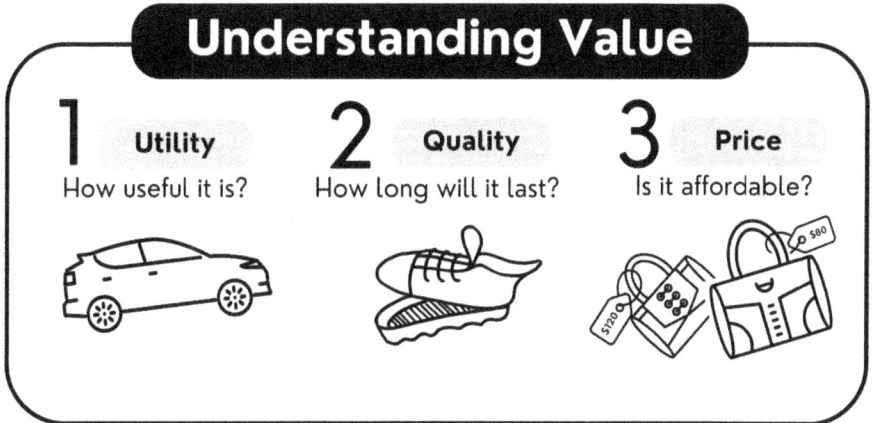

Considering these factors can help you decide whether something is worth buying. Remember, lower prices don't always represent better value.

For example, let's say you need a new pair of shoes. You find two options—one that costs $175 and another that costs $50. On the face of it, the $50 pair seems like a better deal because they are cheaper. But let's consider quality and cost per use.

The $175 shoes are made with superior materials and are built to last. On the other hand, the $50 pair uses low-quality materials that won't last as long.

Now let's consider the cost per use.

If the more expensive pair last for two years and you wear them daily, you've worn them around 730 times (365 days x 2 years). So the cost per use would be $175 divided by 730, which is approximately $0.24 per use.

In comparison, if the $50 shoes last only six months before wearing out and you wear them every day, that would be approximately 180 uses (30 days x 6 months). The cost per use would be $50 divided by 180, which is roughly $0.28 per use.

In this example, even though the $175 shoes are more expensive, they are better value in the long term, as they last longer and have a lower cost per use. Sometimes, buying higher-quality items that last longer can save you money.

Of course, once you have decided on the product you want to buy, it's always worth hunting for sales and discounts. You might be able to get those same shoes for $150 if you shop around.

Finally, it's also worth remembering that value is personal and can extend beyond how much something is worth. *For instance, a wooden toy made by your grandfather might not be worth anything on the market, but its sentimental value to you could be priceless.*

HOW TO MAKE WISE CHOICES WHEN SPENDING MONEY ONLINE

Spending money online can be convenient and easy. In just a few clicks, you can buy almost anything you want. However, just because you can buy something doesn't mean you should!

As with any purchase, when spending money online, it's essential to ensure you are only buying what you need and getting the best deal possible.

Here are a few tips to help you spend money online wisely:

- **Always ask your parents**: Before making a purchase, ask your parents or an adult if it is okay.

- **Do your research**: Before making a purchase, do your research to ensure the item does what you need.

- **Read reviews:** Read customer reviews to find out what others think and to get an idea of how the item performs. Look out for red flags or repeated problems. If there are many negative reviews, it may be worth considering a different option.

- **Compare prices:** Once you know the exact make and model of the item, compare prices to ensure you are getting the best deal.

- **Be aware of hidden costs:** Look out for delivery costs, taxes, and other fees that can add up.

- **Check the returns policy:** If the item doesn't meet your expectations, can you return it quickly without being charged?

- **Only buy from trustworthy websites:** This is the most important rule when buying anything online. Are you familiar with the site? Have you heard of it before? Before giving credit card information to any website, you should consider these things. If you're unsure, ask your parents or an adult for help.

- **Look out for sales:** Try to buy items on sale, since this is a great way to get something you want while spending less money.

- **Look for coupon codes:** You can often find discounts and coupons online. Be sure to check for these before you make a purchase.

- **Buy used:** Used items are often as good as new items, but cost less. There are often bargains to be found at garage sales and thrift stores. You can also find great deals on second-hand items on sites like eBay, Craigslist, and Facebook Marketplace.

- **Be patient:** If you can wait to buy something, you might be able to get it at a lower price or find a better deal.

Following these tips can teach you to spend money wisely online. If you take the time, you can find great deals and save money on the things you want to buy.

Remember, the best way to save money is to avoid spending it in the first place!

HOW TO PAY FOR THINGS ONLINE AND IN STORE

Once you've decided what you want to buy, you need to be able to pay for it using a digital payment method.

> **DID YOU KNOW?** In the United States, over 80% of adults make online payments for their purchases. That means the majority of people use digital methods like credit cards, mobile payment apps, or online banking to pay for goods and services.

Understanding Credit Cards, Debit Cards, and Buy Now Pay Later

When you make purchases online or in stores, you have the option to pay with a credit or debit card. What are these cards, and how do they work?

	👍 PROS	👎 CONS
CREDIT CARDS	• Useful for big purchases • Some cards give you rewards	• May encourage more spending • High interest rates if not paid back on time • Bad credit can hurt
DEBIT CARDS	• Can't go into debt • Don't have to carry lots of cash	• Easy to use, may encourage spending • Comes straight out of the account
BUY NOW PAY LATER	• Spreads payments over time • Easy to set up and use	• High interest if instalments are late • Encourages more spending

Credit Cards

Credit cards are a type of loan. This means that every time you use a credit card, you borrow money from the bank or card supplier. You will have to repay this money with interest.

Interest is the fee the bank or card supplier charges you for lending you the money to make your purchase.

> *For example, say you spend $100 using your credit card, and the bank charges 10% interest. This means you owe the bank $110.*
>
> $100 x 0.10 = $10
> $100 + $10 = $110
>
> *If you don't pay this back, the bank may charge you another 10% interest on the $110. Now, you owe the bank $121.*
>
> $110 x 0.10 = $11
> $110 + $11 = $121

As you can see, the interest can quickly add up, and you can owe a lot of money to the bank. This is why you must be careful if you use a credit card and always pay off the balance every month.

> **DID YOU KNOW?** The first consumer credit card was introduced in 1958 by Bank of America. It was called the "BankAmericard" and it revolutionized how people could make purchases by allowing them to use credit. BankAmericard became known as VISA in 1976, and it's still widely used for making payments worldwide!

Debit Cards

Debit cards are different from credit cards. When you use a debit card, the money is taken directly from your bank account.

This means you can only spend the money you have in your account. If you don't have the funds already deposited in your account, you won't be able to use your debit card. So, unlike a credit card, you cannot borrow money to make a purchase.

> *For example, say you have $100 in your bank account and use your debit card to make an online purchase of $50. The $50 is immediately taken from your account balance, leaving you with $50 in your account.*

If you try to spend more than you have in your account, the transaction will be declined.

Both credit and debit cards can be helpful for making purchases online. While they may look the same, they are very different and should be used with caution.

Here are a few things to keep in mind when using credit or debit cards:

- **Ask your parents:** Always ask your parent's permission before you use their cards.
- **Check your balance:** Check your balance regularly to know how much money you have in your account. This prevents you from spending more money than you have and helps you identify possible fraud on your account.
- **Stay on top of payments:** When you are older, if you get a credit card, ensure you understand the terms and conditions and stay on top of your monthly payments. Interest can quickly add up, and you can end up owing a lot of money to the bank if you're not careful.

- **Keep it safe:** Keep your credit or debit card in a safe place. This will help prevent someone from stealing and using it without your permission.

Many apps now allow parents to control their child's spending. This can be a great way to help teach young adults about money and how to spend it wisely.

Buy Now Pay Later

You may have heard of "buy now, pay later." This relatively new payment option allows you to buy something today and pay for it in smaller installments over time. A lot of online websites offer their customers this payment option.

> *For example, suppose you want to buy a new jacket for $200. The website offers you the option to pay for it over three months. This means you would pay $66.67 per month for three months.*
>
> *$200 ÷ 3 = $66.67*
>
> *At the end of the three months, you would have paid off the jacket in full.*

This may sound like a great idea at first, but there are some things you should know before you do this.

First, this is debt. This means you are borrowing money from the company to pay for the jacket.

Second, you will be charged interest if you don't pay on time. This means you will end up paying more than the original price.

> *For example, suppose you have three months to pay for your jacket. If you pay it all in those three months, there is no interest to pay. This is called "interest-free." But if you miss a payment and fail to pay it off in those three months and still owe $50, the company will charge you interest on the $50.*
>
> *If the interest rate is 20%, your $50 debt would turn into a $60 debt.*
>
> *$50 x 0.20 = $10*
> *$50 + $10 = $60*

So, while "buy now, pay later" might sound like a great idea, you should think carefully before using it. Be sure you can afford the monthly payments and that you will pay them off within the interest-free period.

 **Top Tip** If you need clarification on something, ask your parents or an adult you trust for help. They will be able to give you some good advice.

When shopping online, all it takes is a few clicks to make a purchase. Always review your purchase before confirming your order. Whether using a credit card, debit card, or cash, remember to think about what you are buying and why. By doing this, you can avoid making impulsive purchases that you may later regret.

AN INTRODUCTION TO BUDGETING

Budgeting is an important way to ensure you use your money wisely. It helps you plan and keep track of your spending so you can make smart decisions about your money in the future. This means looking at how much money you earn and determining how much you should save each month, as well as how much you can spend wisely.

> *For example, imagine you are saving up for a new pair of jeans that cost $100. You will need to work out how much money you have coming in each month and how much you can afford to put away until you have enough for the jeans.*

Remember, saving any amount is better than saving nothing at all. Even if it's a small amount, putting money into savings regularly adds up over time. It's always good to set aside some money for the future, just in case you need it.

By budgeting, you can avoid debt, save up for things you want in the future, and have peace of mind knowing that you have money saved up for unexpected expenses. It's a smart way to manage your money and plan for a better financial future.

DIFFERENT WAYS TO BUDGET

There are various methods to help you learn to budget your money. Here are a couple of popular ones if you're just starting out:

❶ **The Jar Method:** This method divides your money into different jars for different goals.

> *For example, you might have a "new shoes" jar and a "new pet" jar.*

Every time you receive money, you put a portion into your jars. This can be a fun way to save, and also helps you see how much you are saving for each goal.

❷ **The 50/30/20 Rule:** In this case, you divide your money into three categories: essentials, wants, and savings. You allocate 50% to essential expenses like food or clothes, 30% to things you want, like new toys or games, and 20% to savings.

> *For example, if you received $100 for your birthday, you would divide it up as follows:*
>
> *$50 for essentials, such as food or clothes*
>
> *$30 for wants, such as a new toy or video game*
>
> *$20 for savings, which goes into a savings account*

The 50/30/20 rule is a good starting point, but you can adjust it depending on your income and expenses.

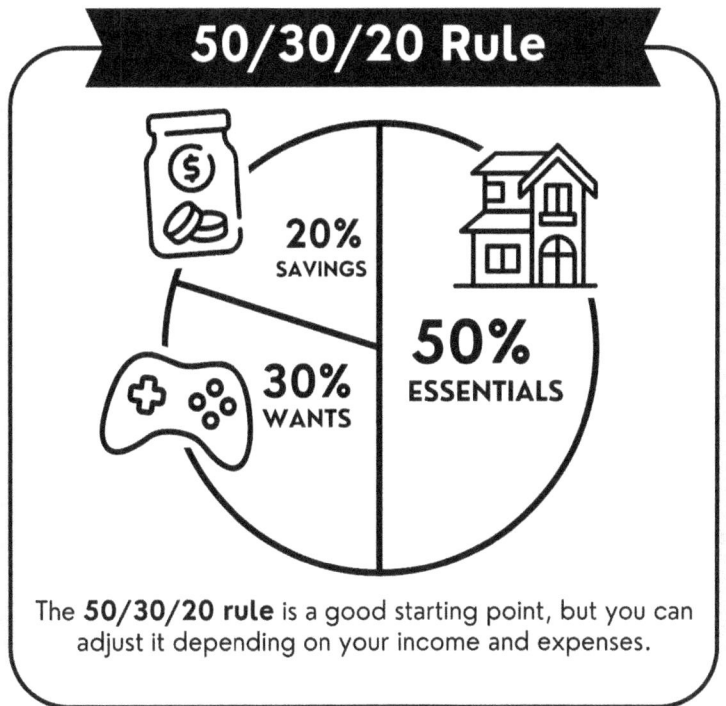

The **50/30/20 rule** is a good starting point, but you can adjust it depending on your income and expenses.

There are many ways to budget, and finding a system that works for you is crucial. Always be mindful of your spending and try to put some money away each month into savings.

HOW TO AVOID IMPULSE PURCHASES

Sometimes, you might see something and feel you need to buy it right away. This is called an "impulse purchase." Impulse purchases are purchases you make without much thought or planning. It's easily done, especially when shopping online. If you're not careful, impulse purchases can quickly lead to spending more money than you have. So, it's essential to think carefully before you buy something.

Here are a few tips to avoid impulse buying:

- **Wait 24 hours:** Have a waiting period of 24 hours before making a large purchase. This gives you time to consider how much use it would get and if it is worth buying.

- **Avoid shopping when emotional:** Sometimes, feelings of boredom, sadness, or even happiness can lead to impulse purchases. This is sometimes called "retail therapy," where people shop to improve their mood. But it's usually not a good way to spend money.

- **Create a shopping list:** By focusing on the list, you can avoid getting distracted by non-essential items.

ACTIVITY: THE SUPERMARKET BUDGETING CHALLENGE

Get ready to be a party planner! In this activity, you'll learn about budgeting while planning a fun party for your friends. The catch? You only have $25 to spend.

Here's what to do:

1. **Imagine your party:** Decide how many friends to invite, what snacks to serve, and if you want decorations or games.

2. **Make a shopping list:** List the items you need, like snacks, drinks, and decorations. Remember, you only have $25.

3. **Estimate costs:** Check online or think about the store prices to estimate the cost of each item.

4. **Use your budgeting template:** Fill out the template on the next page. Write each item, estimated price, quantity, and total cost (PRICE x QUANTITY).

5. **Calculate your total:** Add the costs. If it's over $25, adjust your plan until it fits the budget.

6. **Finalize:** Stick to your final party plan!

Remember, this activity is about making smart choices to have fun while staying within your budget.

THE SUPERMARKET BUDGETING CHALLENGE

ACTIVITY TIME!

PARTY DATE

BUDGET:
$ _____

ITEM	PRICE	QUANTITY	TOTAL COST
Example Mango	$2	2 pcs	$4
TOTAL SPENT			$

REMAINING BUDGET:
$ _____

MONEY SKILLS FOR KIDS

CHAPTER 5:

HOW TO GIVE AND SHARE

Now that we've talked about saving and spending wisely, let's explore another important aspect of handling money: giving and sharing. It's not all about keeping money for yourself. Sometimes, the most valuable thing you can do with your money is to help others.

Whether it's donating to a charity, supporting a friend in need, or contributing to a cause you care about, giving can have a significant impact. It's a wonderful way to make a difference and bring joy to others.

THE JOY OF GIVING AND HELPING OTHERS

There's nothing better than giving, sharing, or helping those in need. People often confuse giving with money, but you don't have to be rich to make a difference in someone's life. Even the smallest gestures, like giving up your seat on a bus or opening the door for a stranger, can brighten someone's day and make the world a better place.

There are many ways to give and share without involving money. Volunteering your time, donating items, or helping others costs nothing, but are all valuable ways to make a difference in people's lives.

When you give or help others, it brings a sense of satisfaction, fulfillment, and joy.

> *For example, think about when you made a special gift for your parents and saw their happiness when they received it. That feeling of joy and satisfaction is priceless.*

The same goes for helping others without expecting anything in return. It provides a warm and fulfilling feeling inside, knowing that you've positively impacted someone's life.

Here are some examples of ways you can help others:

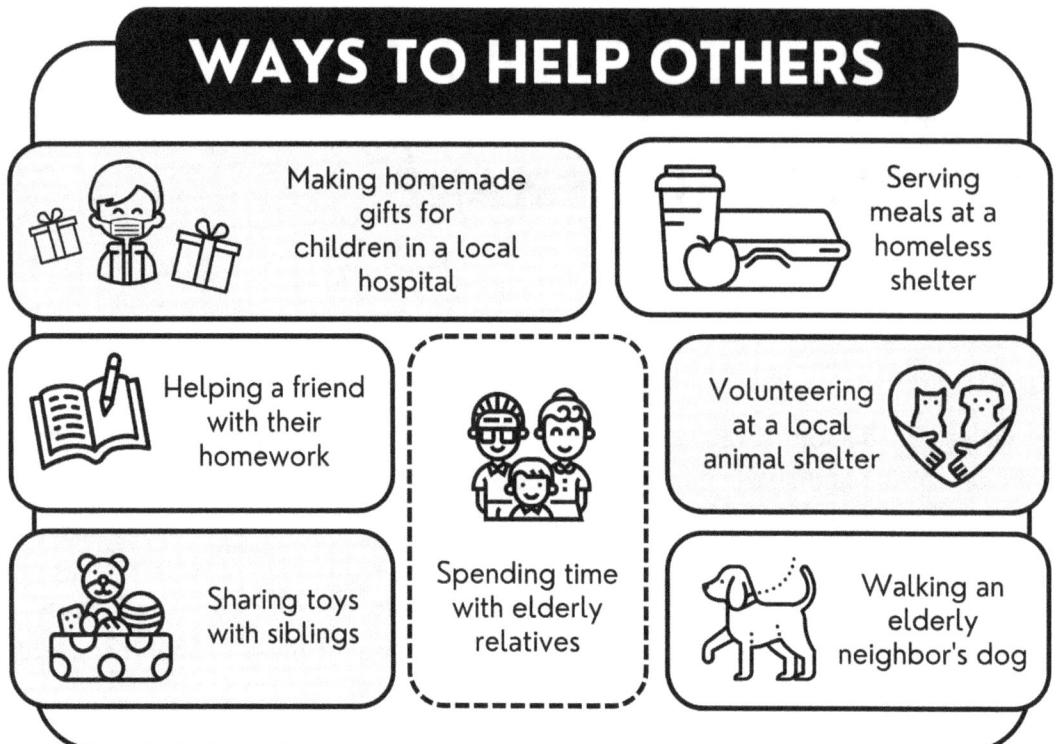

There are so many ways you can give and share. It's important to remember that even the smallest acts can bring joy to those on the receiving end and spread kindness and love.

UNDERSTANDING DONATIONS AND CHARITABLE GIVING

Giving can also involve making donations or giving to a charity.

Donations are a way of giving money, goods, or time to a cause or organization that helps others. It can be money, such as giving a portion of your monthly allowance, or it could be clothes, toys, or even food. You could also donate your time by volunteering at a charity or participating in community activities.

Charities are organizations that are set up to help and support different causes. They support diverse groups of people, animals, and communities, and rely on donations of money or items to do their work and help their causes. There are many charities that focus on many different areas. Some focus on local causes, such as building and maintaining playgrounds, while others focus on global initiatives, such as providing relief after international disasters like floods or earthquakes.

When you make a donation to a charity, whether you give money or items, you are helping the charity to make a difference. Your contribution might be used to help children displaced by wars, protect animals in the wild, or find a cure for diseases.

Here are some examples of charities and the vital work they do:

- **UNICEF:** UNICEF promotes the well-being and health of children around the world. They work to ensure children have access to clean water, sanitation, education, and health care.

- **Habitat for Humanity:** Habitat for Humanity brings people together to build homes for those in need.

- **United Way:** United Way supports programs that aim to improve communities' education, health, and financial stability.

- **SPCA:** The SPCA (Society for the Prevention of Cruelty to Animals) supports animal care and safety. Their work aims to protect animals by providing rescue services and vets and educating the public about pet ownership.

- **Wounded Warrior Project:** The Wounded Warrior Project supports service members and veterans wounded while serving in the military.

- **Special Olympics:** The Special Olympics supports athletes with disabilities.

- **American Red Cross:** The American Red Cross supports crisis intervention and disaster relief locally and worldwide. Their work includes blood donations, medical training, and supplies during emergencies or disasters.

When people donate to these charities, they help to support their activities or causes. These charities' donations help people, animals, and the community. The more donations they receive, the more significant impact they can have on the lives of others and the community.

> **DID YOU KNOW?** UNICEF helps children in over 190 countries. Through their programs, they provide lifesaving vaccines to around 45% of the world's children and help ensure that millions have access to education, clean water, and emergency assistance.

HOW TO FIND CHARITIES OR CAUSES YOU'RE PASSIONATE ABOUT

Finding a charity that you're passionate about can be an exciting journey.

Here are some steps to help you get started:

❶ Think about your interests.

The first thing you should do is think about what you're interested in. What do you enjoy doing? Who do you enjoy spending time with? The charity's work will mean much more if you can relate to it.

❷ Research charities online.

After you have thought about your interests, go online and do a search on "charities." You should come up with a list of relevant charities. Read about all the different ones to see if any do work related to your interests.

❸ Talk with an adult.

Talk with a parent or a trusted adult to see what knowledge or information they can share with you about their experience with charities.

❹ Volunteer at a local charity.

Find out which charities are local. Have an adult take you to visit some of these charities so you can experience them first-hand. While there, find out if you can volunteer at the charities that interest you.

❺ Follow your passions.

After gathering all the information you can about the various charities, revisit your interests and think about which ones you're passionate about. Then find the charity that is the closest match.

Remember, even a small act of kindness can have a big impact. By choosing to support a charity, you're not just giving money or time—you're helping to make the world a better place. Now, that's something to feel good about!

FINDING YOUR CHARITY

ACTIVITY TIME!

Making a difference in the world can be as simple as supporting a cause you believe in. Let's take a journey to find a charity that you really believe in.

1 **What matters to you:** What causes are you passionate about? Animals? Helping people in need? The environment? Write down a few causes that are important to you:

_____
_____

2 **Research charities:** Look up charities that work towards the causes that are important to you. Write them here:

_____
_____

3 **Evaluate the charities:** Look at how these charities use their money. Do they spend most of it on the cause they support, or do they spend it on other costs? Write down your findings:

_____
_____

4 **Pick your charity:** Based on your research, pick one charity you want to support:

_____

5 **Plan your support:** Think about how you could support this charity. Could you donate some of your allowance? Or volunteer your time? Write down your plan here:

_____
_____

6 **Take action:** Once you have a plan, it's time to put it into action!

CHAPTER 6:

HOW TO KEEP YOUR MONEY SAFE AND SECURE

You put a lot of effort into earning your money, so it's crucial that you keep it safe. This includes the money in your bank account, the cash you carry, and any cards you use to withdraw money.

HOW TO PROTECT YOUR MONEY AND PERSONAL INFORMATION

Here are some tips to protect your money and personal information:

1. **Keep your money in a bank account:** Putting it in a bank account is a smart way to keep it safe and organized. When you open an account, remember to keep your personal information private and only share it with people or organizations you trust.

2. **Carry less cash:** Carrying a lot of money can make you more likely to lose it or have it stolen. Try to only carry the cash you need for the day to keep your money safe.

3. **Stay safe when spending money online:** Be super careful when buying things online to protect your financial information. Look for secure websites with "https" at the beginning of the web address. Only share personal data like your name, address, or social security number if you trust the website.

4. **Avoid saving card details on shared computers:** If you use a computer other people also use, don't save your credit or debit card details. Other people might be able to access your personal information, which could be risky.

5. **Create strong passwords:** When you create passwords for your online accounts, make them strong and unique. A strong password has a mix of numbers, lowercase and uppercase letters,

and symbols. Remember not to use the same password for different accounts, and to change your passwords regularly to keep them extra secure.

6 **Don't share personal information online:** It's essential to keep your personal information private online. Avoid posting pictures of documents like your passport or bank statements with personal information. Keep your name, date of birth, address, and unique ID number to yourself to protect your identity.

7 **Keep your PINs private:** Your PINs are like secret codes, so never share them with anyone. Also, ensure no one can see you when you enter your PIN while making transactions. It's essential to keep your PINs safe and private.

By following these safety tips, you can keep your money and personal information secure. Remember, being cautious and protecting yourself from potential risks is always better.

> *DID YOU KNOW?* The most popular password is "123456." Using simple and predictable passwords like this can make it easy for hackers to access your accounts and steal your personal information. Choosing strong and unique passwords is vital for keeping your online accounts secure.

WHAT ARE SCAMS?

Always keep your eyes and ears open for scams. Scams are deceptive schemes designed to cheat people out of their money, and they usually sound too good to be true.

Scammers will pretend to be someone else or from a well-known company to gain your trust. They may contact you through email, text, or phone, offering you what seems like a fantastic deal. They might ask you to click on a link in an email or text, or request personal information over the phone to gain access to your bank accounts or credit cards. That's why it's super important to never give out your personal information to anyone.

Scammers are clever, and they use many different strategies to trick people into giving away their personal information so they can get their money. Here are a few examples you should watch out for:

1. **Phishing scams:** These scams involve fake emails or messages that look like they're from a genuine company or person you know. They might ask you to click a link or log into an account. Be careful! The link usually takes you to a fake website that wants to steal your personal information. They might even send you an email attachment that can harm your computer. Never click on links in suspicious emails or texts.

2. **Lottery and prize scams:** In these scams, scammers pretend that you've won a lottery, vacation, or prize. They might send you a letter or email, or call to congratulate you. But here's the catch: They'll ask you to pay fees up front or give them personal information to claim your prize. Be cautious and remember that real lotteries or prizes don't ask for money or personal information to receive your winnings.

3. **Online financial account scams:** Scammers might send you text messages or emails that seem to be from a bank or financial institution. They might claim there is a problem with your account and ask you to verify your information on a fake website. Remember, real banks will never ask you to provide personal details via email or text. If you receive such messages, don't click on any links. Instead, contact your bank directly.

4. **Card skimming:** This sneaky scam happens when scammers copy information from the magnetic strip of your debit, credit, or ATM card. They'll try to capture your PIN, bank, and credit card details to make unauthorized purchases. Be careful when using ATMs or card readers, and cover your hand while entering your PIN.

5. **Online shopping scams:** Beware of online sellers who promise great deals but deliver something that doesn't meet your expectations (or even nothing at all!). Some scammers use online shopping to collect your bank account or credit card information. Make sure to buy from trusted websites and read reviews from other customers before purchasing.

6. **Charity scams:** Unfortunately, even charity causes can be used by scammers. They might pretend to work for an actual charity and try to collect money from you. They often use recent crises or natural disasters to play with your emotions. If you want to donate, research the charity first and donate directly through their official website.

DID YOU KNOW? Scams and money fraud cost the global economy over $5 trillion annually. That's more money than the entire economy of a big country like the United Kingdom!

HOW TO RECOGNIZE SCAMS AND FRAUD

While scams may not be easy to spot, there are some things to look for that may indicate a possible fraud:

- They ask for money upfront.
- You receive offers that you didn't ask for.
- You receive a message from a number you don't recognize, asking you to click on a link.
- You receive a phone call, email, or text from someone claiming to be from an official department, like the government, fire department, or your bank, asking for money.
- You feel pressured to make a quick decision.
- They request that money be wired, sent by a courier, or transferred through a gift or prepaid card.
- They request access to your bank accounts, credit cards, or ATM cards.
- They offer you a deal that sounds too good to be true, but avoid answering any questions you may have.

If you come across any of these signs or feel unsure about a situation, talk to your parents or a trusted adult.

WHAT TO DO IF YOU SPOT A SCAM

If you come across something that seems like a scam, it's essential to take action to protect yourself. Here's what you should do:

1. **Trust your instincts:** If something doesn't feel right or seems too good to be true, it's better to be cautious.

2. **Stop communicating and don't share any information:** Stop communicating with them and don't provide them with any personal information.

3. **Tell your parents:** If something doesn't feel right, talk to your parents or a trusted adult. It's better to be safe than sorry.

4. **Report the scam:** You can report scams online or via phone to the Federal Trade Commission (FTC). They are a government agency that investigates scams and protects people from fraud.

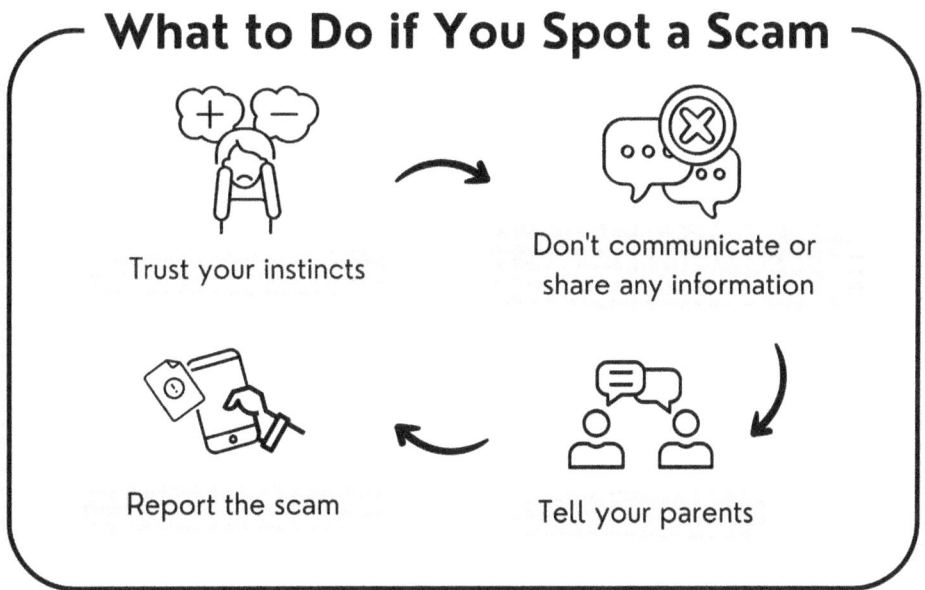

Unfortunately, scams are a regular part of everyday life. Still, by understanding how to spot them and being cautious, you can help to protect yourself.

Creating a strong password is one of the best ways to protect yourself and your financial information online. Here's a simple activity to help you create strong passwords that are easy for you to remember, but difficult for fraudsters to guess.

CREATING A STRONG PASSWORD

ACTIVITY TIME!

1 Start with a base word or phrase

Choose a word or phrase that is easy for you to remember. It could be something related to your interests or a favorite hobby.

For example, let's use the base word "guitar."

2 Mix in numbers

Add a series of numbers to your base word. You can choose numbers that are meaningful to you, such as your birthdate or a special number.

For our example, let's use the number "2023."

3 Incorporate special characters

Include special characters, like exclamation marks, question marks, or hashtags, to add complexity to your password. Pick a special character that you can easily remember.

For our example, we'll use the exclamation mark!

4 Use capitalization

Change the capitalization of some letters in your base word to make it even stronger. Mix uppercase and lowercase letters to make it harder to guess.

In our example, let's capitalize the letter "G" in "Guitar."

5 Combine and personalize

Put all the elements together to create your strong password. In our example, the final password would be "Guitar2023!" Remember, don't use this example as your password. Instead, create your unique combination based on your interests and the steps provided.

Now it's your turn

CREATING A STRONG PASSWORD

ACTIVITY TIME!

OVER TO YOU

1. Choose a base word or phrase:
   _____

2. Add a series of numbers:
   _____

3. Incorporate a special character:
   _____

4. Change the capitalization of some letters:
   _____

5. Combine all the elements to create your strong password:
   _____

Congratulations!
You've created a strong password by following these steps.

REMEMBER

- Always keep your password secure.
- Don't share it with anyone.
- Avoid using easily guessable information like your name, address, or common words.
- Use different passwords for different accounts to maximize security.

CHAPTER 7:

AN INTRODUCTION TO INVESTING

You've learned the importance of earning money, saving it, and spending it wisely. But what if there was a way to make your money work for you, even while you're not using it? Instead of simply setting your money aside, what if you could make it grow! Welcome to the world of investing. Let's explore how this process works and how it can help you achieve your financial goals!

WHAT IS INVESTING?

Imagine you have some money you earned from doing chores, or that you received as a gift. You can keep that money safe by putting it in a piggy bank, or earn interest by depositing it in a savings account. When you save money, you're setting it aside for a specific purpose at a later date, like buying a toy or saving up for something special. It's like keeping your money safe for later.

But what if you could make that money do more than just sit and wait for you? What if your money could work for you and even multiply? That's where investing comes in!

Investing is a way to use your money to make even more money over time. Instead of just keeping it in a piggy bank, you can grow your money by putting it into things that might increase in value. It's like planting a seed and watching it grow into a big tree.

> *For example, let's say you love playing video games and notice that a certain company that makes video games, like Nintendo or Sony, is doing well. You can buy a small part of that company by purchasing some of its stocks. Stocks are like tiny pieces of the company that you can own. When the company does well, the value of your stocks might go up, and you can sell them later at a higher price. This is how you can make money by investing!*

But if the company doesn't do so well and the stock value goes down, the value of your stocks may decrease. This means you could lose money if you decide to sell your shares at a lower price.

The main difference between saving and investing is the growth potential. When you save money, it usually stays the same or earns a small amount of interest. But when you invest, you take a calculated risk in the hopes that your money will grow even more.

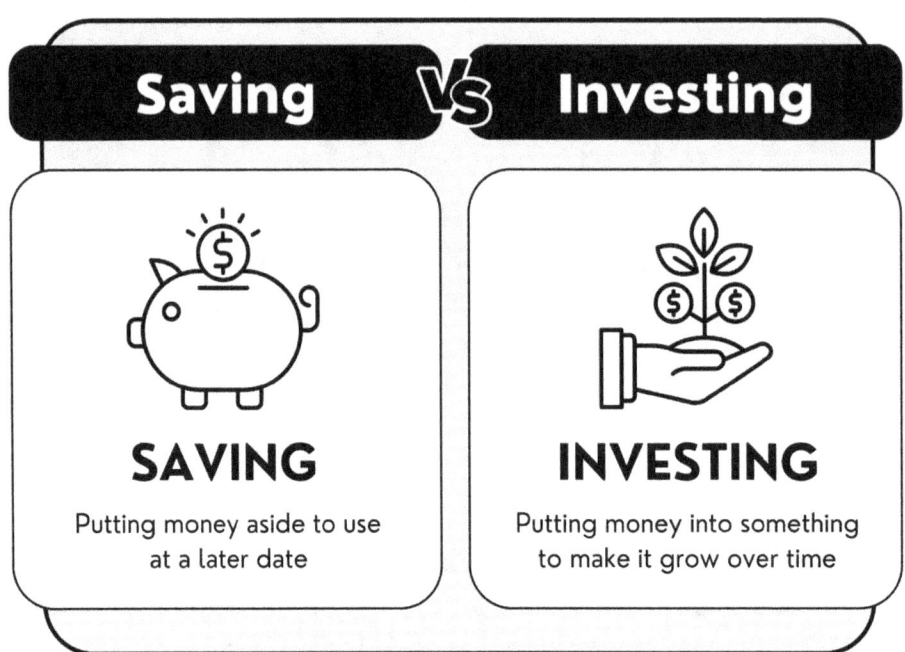

Saving is good for short-term goals, like buying a new toy or saving for a special occasion. On the other hand, investing is usually for long-term goals, like saving for college or retirement. It's about using your money to potentially make more money over a longer period of time.

> It's important to understand that investing always comes with some level of risk. The value of stocks can go up and down, and sometimes you may even lose money. It requires careful consideration and research, and is a long-term commitment. If you're interested in investing, it's a good idea to learn more and seek guidance from trusted adults or professionals who can help you make informed decisions.

Ways to Invest

Stocks
Stocks are small parts of a company. If the company does well, your part may grow. If they do badly, your part may be worth less.

Bonds
When you buy a bond, you are lending your money to a company or the government. Usually with a fixed interest rate.

Real Estate
Real estate involves investing in property. You make money by renting or selling the property for a profit.

Mutual Funds
Mutual funds include a bunch of different stocks, or other things like bonds or real estate, all in one package.

Exchange Traded Funds (ETFs)
An ETF is like a basket that holds a collection of different investments designed to track or follow the performance of a specific market index, like the S&P 500.

DIFFERENT WAYS TO INVEST MONEY

There are lots of different ways to invest money. Here are some of the most common:

- **Stocks:** When you invest in stocks, you buy a tiny share of a company. If the company does well, the stock may go up. If you sell your stocks at a higher price than what you paid for them, you make money.

  > *For example, let's say you buy a share of a company called ABC Toys for $10. You now own a small part of the company. If ABC Toys does well, the stock might go up. Let's say that, after a year, the stock is now worth $15 per share, and you decide to sell your share at a higher price. In that case, you'd make a profit of $5 ($15 – $10).*

- **Bonds:** Bonds are like loans. When you buy a bond, you are lending your money to a company or the government. They promise to pay you back the money you lent them, plus interest. Bonds are considered less risky than stocks, so the money you make from them is usually lower.

- **Real Estate:** Real estate involves investing in properties, like houses or apartments. When you invest in real estate, you can make money in two ways. First, by renting the property. Second, by selling the property for more money than you originally paid.

- **Mutual Funds:** Mutual funds are like a team of investments. Instead of buying just one stock, you can buy a fund that includes a bunch of different stocks, or other things like bonds or real estate, all in one package. This can help reduce your risk, because if one investment doesn't do well, others may do better and balance it out.

- **Exchange Traded Funds (ETFs):** Just like a mutual fund, an ETF is like a basket that holds a collection of different investments designed to track or follow the performance of a specific market index, like the S&P 500. ETFs are popular because they spread your money and reduce risk.

DID YOU KNOW? The most valuable company in the world in 2023 is Apple. With a market value of almost $3 trillion, Apple has become a technology giant known for its innovative products like iPhones, iPads, and Mac computers.

UNDERSTANDING RISK AND RETURNS

Risk involves the possibility of losing money. When you invest, there's a chance you might not get back all the money you put in.

Return, on the other hand, is the amount of money your investment can make. Some investments have the potential for higher returns, while others offer lower returns.

> *Imagine you've got $10. You have a choice: You could spend it on a cool toy car, which you know will keep some value over time. You can play with the car, and, when you're done, perhaps you can sell it to a friend for a little less than what you paid for. This is a type of low-risk investment. You're pretty sure you won't lose all your money, and you might even make a little bit of money if you find the right buyer.*
>
> *Now picture this: Instead of getting that toy car, you buy a trading card for the same $10. It's not just any card—it's a card that could become rare and valuable over time. There's a chance that other collectors might be willing to pay a lot more for it in a year or two. But if the card doesn't become as popular as you thought, you might not be able to sell it for what you paid. This is a riskier investment. The possibility of making more money is there, but so is the possibility of losing some.*

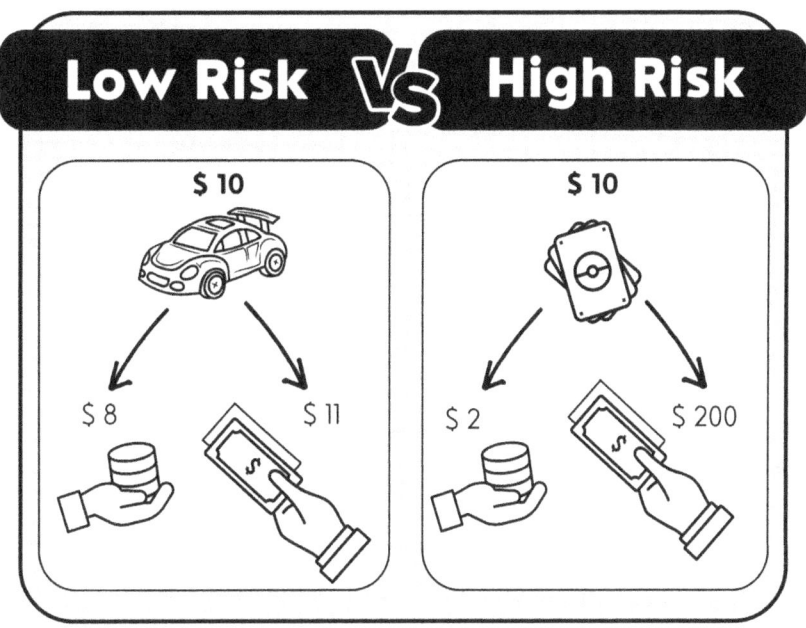

That's the essence of investing—using your money to make more money, but with the understanding that there are different levels of risk involved.

When you invest, you have to think about how much risk you're willing to take. If you take more risk, there's a chance for a higher return, which means you could make more money. If you take less risk, the potential return might not be as much, but you're also less likely to lose money.

Investing is like a game where you must make smart choices and consider possible risks and rewards. It's essential to do your research, ask for advice from grown-ups you trust, and remember that investing is a long-term plan.

UNDERSTANDING COMPOUND GROWTH

Remember when we discussed compound interest, where your money earns interest on the initial amount and the interest you've already made? The same idea applies to investing.

Let's imagine you start with $10 and your money doubles every day for 10 days. How much money would you have at the end?

Day 1: $10
Day 2: $20
Day 3: $40
Day 4: $80
Day 5: $160
Day 6: $320
Day 7: $640
Day 8: $1,280
Day 9: $2,560
Day 10: $5,120

As you can see, the amount of money you have is getting bigger and bigger each day. But something interesting happens as you go along. In the beginning, the growth might not seem very big.

For example, from $10 to $20 is a $10 increase. But, as you get closer to the end, the growth becomes much larger. Going from $2,560 to $5,120 is a $2,560 increase!

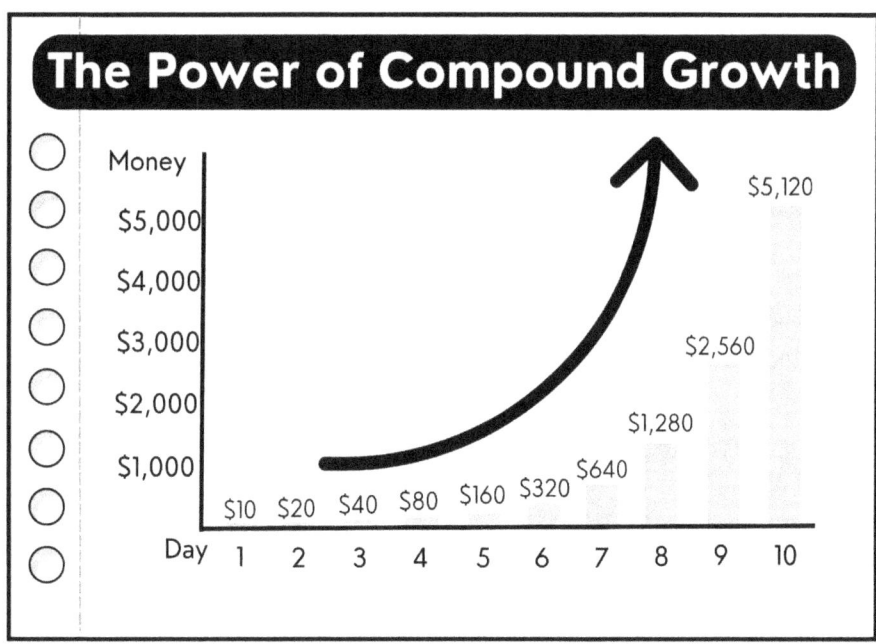

That's because compound growth makes your money grow faster over time. It's like a snowball rolling down a hill, getting bigger and faster as it goes. The more time your money stays invested, the more it can grow.

When you invest, it's essential to be patient and let your money work for you. Sometimes, the value might go down, but, if you give it time, it's likely to bounce back and grow even more.

Starting early is vital. The longer you leave your money invested, the more it can grow. Starting early gives you a better chance of achieving financial success and seeing your money grow bigger and bigger.

UNLOCKING THE POWER OF COMPOUND GROWTH IN EVERYDAY LIFE

This concept of compound growth applies not only to money, but to anything in life, such as learning to play a sport or a musical instrument. It's the idea that minor improvements or progress made over time can lead to significant results.

> *Imagine you're learning to play the guitar. If you practice for just a few minutes every day, you'll gradually get better. But, if you practice consistently for longer periods, over months and years, you'll become even more skilled. The more you practice, the more you'll learn and the better you'll become.*

MONEY SKILLS FOR KIDS

Like investing, where your money grows over time, your skills and abilities can also grow through consistent effort. The key is to be patient, keep practicing, and stay committed to your goals.

THE IMPORTANCE OF DIVERSIFICATION AND LONG-TERM INVESTING

Diversification is a smart strategy for reducing the risk of your investments by spreading your money across different types of things you invest in. These things are called assets, and you buy them with the hope that they'll increase in value over time.

> *Let's use a trading card collection as an example.*
>
> *Instead of just buying baseball cards, you might also buy Pokemon or Yu-gi-oh cards. That way, if the value of baseball cards doesn't go up, there's still a chance that the Pokemon or Yu-gi-oh cards will increase in value. Having different types of cards in your collection increases the chances of making money, even if one type doesn't do well.*

Buying a diverse collection of cards, spreads the risk.

Investing in a mix of assets means that even if some of your investments don't do so well, others might do better. It's like having a balance. Overall, diversification reduces the risk of losing money and gives you a better chance of earning more in the long run. It's a way to protect your investments and increase the possibility of making more money.

HOW CAN TEENS INVEST THEIR MONEY?

Investing can be exciting. While you may not be able to open your own investment account if you're under 18, you can still get started by partnering with an adult, like a parent or guardian, to open a custodial account.

A custodial account is a particular type of investment account where the adult manages the investments on your behalf until you reach the legal age to handle the account on your own. It's a great way to learn about investing and start growing your money, even at a young age.

Even though you may not be able to have your own investment account yet, you can still take advantage of the opportunity to invest and build wealth for your future. It's never too early to start learning about money and making smart financial decisions.

STEPS TO START INVESTING

Here are some steps to help you get started with investing:

1. **Learn about investing:** Take the time to read and learn about investing. You can find books, articles, and videos that explain the basics. Talk to an adult with investing experience and ask them to share their knowledge.

2. **Set your goals:** Consider what you want to achieve with your investments. Do you want to save for college, buy a car, or have money for the future? Setting clear goals will help you make investment decisions that align with your objectives.

3. **Choose your investments:** Research different investment options, such as stocks or mutual funds. Look for companies or funds you are interested in and that you believe have growth potential. Remember to consider the level of risk and potential returns.

4. **Open a custodial account:** Since you are under 18, you will need an adult to help you open a custodial account. This special type of account allows an adult to manage the investments on your behalf until you are old enough to handle it yourself.

5. **Invest your money:** Once you have chosen your investments, you can start putting your money into them. Use a trusted investment platform, like a bank or brokerage firm, to make your purchases. Always consult the adult managing your custodial account to ensure you use a legitimate platform.

6 **Start small and be cautious:** It's a good idea to start with a small amount of money that you can afford to invest. As you gain more experience and confidence, you can consider investing larger amounts. Remember, investing involves risks, so it's important to be cautious and only invest money you are potentially willing to lose.

By following these steps and seeking guidance from trusted adults, you can begin your investing journey and work towards achieving your financial goals.

ACTIVITY: DOUBLE THE PENNY CHALLENGE

Let's have some fun with the "Double Penny Challenge" to see just how powerful compound interest can be!

This simple challenge will help illustrate the concept of compound interest, when you earn interest on both the money you've saved and the interest you earned.

Once you've finished the exercise reflect: How does seeing this growth make you feel about saving money? Do you think it's a good idea to start saving as soon as possible?

Remember, this challenge is just an illustration of how compound interest can help grow your savings. In real life, money won't double daily, but over time, with regular savings and the power of compound interest, you can see your money grow in a similar way.

The lesson is: start saving early and save regularly! Even if it seems like a small amount, over time, it can grow into a substantial sum.

DOUBLE THE PENNY CHALLENGE

ACTIVITY TIME!

INSTRUCTIONS

Make Your Choice

Would you rather have a penny that doubles each day for a month or $1 million?

- ☐ A Penny that Doubles Every Day
- ☐ $1 million

- Write down your amounts for each day on the line provided inside the piggy banks. (You may need a calculator!)
- Start with a penny on the first day.
- On the following day, double the amount.
- Keep doubling the amount until you reach the 30th day.

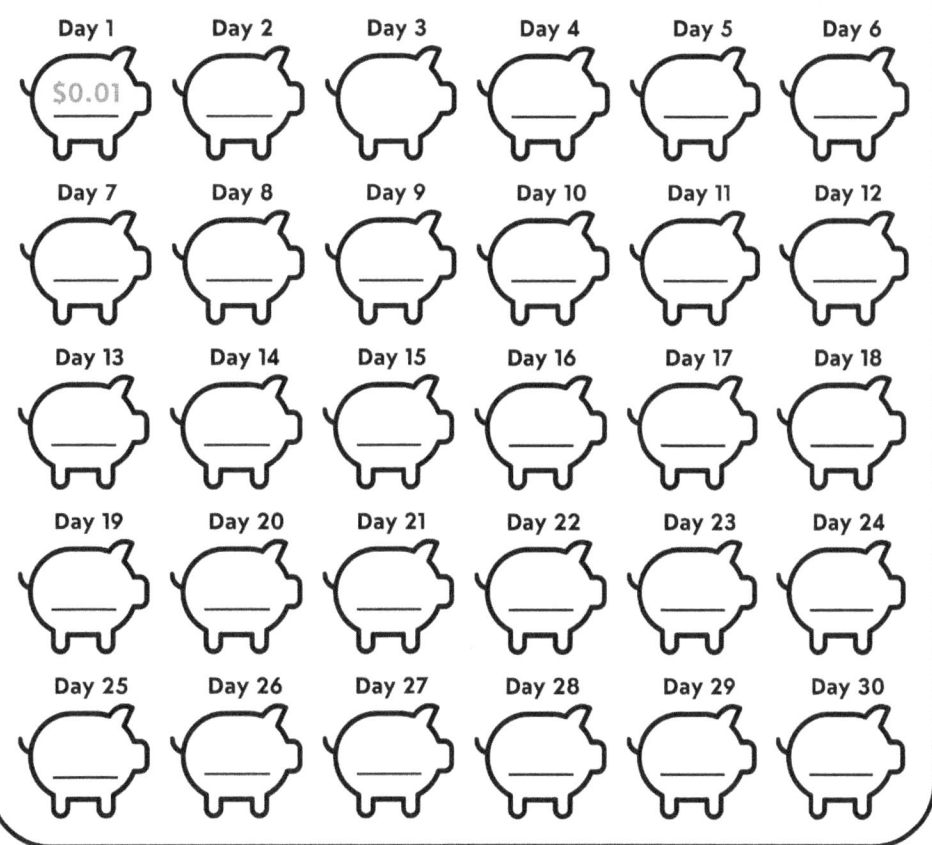

CHAPTER 8:

PLANNING FOR THE FUTURE

You've come a long way on your financial journey! From earning money to investing it wisely, you're already on the path to a bright financial future. But did you know that there's more you can do to ensure your future is even brighter?

Let's take a look at planning for the future and taking responsibility for your finances.

TAKING RESPONSIBILITY FOR YOUR FINANCES

Planning for your future is a crucial part of being financially successful. It's never too early to start planning. The sooner you begin, the better off you'll be.

As you grow older, you'll take on more financial responsibilities, like pursuing a career, buying a house, and getting a car. But there are other costs involved that you might not be aware of.

Let's take a look at some of these future financial responsibilities:

Future Financial Responsibilities

Taxes  Fees paid to fund public services and programs like schools and emergency services. The amount you pay is generally based on a percentage of your income.

Insurance  Protects you from paying a lot of money if something unexpected happens. There are different types of insurance, such as health insurance and insurance for your belongings.

Retirement  When you stop working and need money to support yourself. Before that time comes, you need to set aside or invest some money.

Taxes

Taxes are fees paid to the government to fund public services and programs like schools and emergency services. If you earn money, you'll likely have to pay taxes of some kind. The amount you pay is generally based on a percentage of your income. The higher your salary, the higher the rate of tax you have to pay.

> *For example, if you earn $25,000, you may only pay 10% tax, or $2,500. However, if you earn $100,000, you may pay a higher percentage (such as 37%) in taxes, which would amount to $37,000.*

If you work for a company, your employer will automatically take out a portion of your earnings to pay your taxes. They do this to make sure your taxes are paid throughout the year. This system is called tax withholding.

But if you're self-employed, like a freelancer or independent contractor, you are responsible for calculating and paying your taxes. This means you must figure out how much tax you owe and pay it yourself.

Insurance

Insurance is like a safety net that helps protect you from financial loss. It's important to know that insurance works differently in different countries. Not all countries have the same types of insurance, or even require you to have it.

> *For example, in some countries, like the United States, there is health insurance. Health insurance helps cover the cost of medical expenses, like going to the doctor or getting medicine.*
>
> *If you have health insurance, you pay a monthly or yearly amount called a premium to an insurance company. In return, the insurance company helps pay some of your medical costs when needed. Some companies may offer health insurance as part of their employee benefits.*

Another type of insurance is for your belongings, like your house or car. If something terrible happens, like a fire in your home or an accident with your vehicle, insurance can help cover the cost of repairing or replacing them. You pay a premium to the insurance company, and if something happens, they pay for losses or damages.

Having insurance is like having a backup plan. It helps protect you from paying a lot of money if something unexpected happens. Just like you wear a helmet while riding a bike to protect your head, insurance is there to protect your finances.

Retirement

Finally, there's planning for retirement. Retirement is when you stop working and need money to support yourself. It may seem like a long way off right now, but it's helpful to start thinking about it early in order to have a comfortable life when you're older.

Preparing for retirement means saving money for the future. The idea is to set aside and invest a portion of your income once you start earning so you have enough money to live on later when you're no longer working.

In most countries, there are specific retirement accounts, like a 401(k) or an individual retirement account (IRA) in the United States, that have rules and benefits to help your money grow.

Remember, the key is to start saving and investing for your retirement early. The more time your money has to grow and compound, the more you'll have when you retire.

> **DID YOU KNOW?** That the average retirement age in the United States has been gradually increasing over the years. As of 2021, the average age for retirement was around 66 years old.

PREPARING FOR YOUR FUTURE

It's never too early to start thinking about your future and how you want to live. Even before you finish school, you can begin to explore what excites you and what you're passionate about.

Finding the right job isn't just about making money. It's about finding something you enjoy and are good at. Explore your hobbies and skills, and ask yourself: What are you good at? What do you love to do? Learn about different careers and the education or training required, so you can make smart decisions for your future.

When you think about your future, it's essential to consider what makes you happy and excited. Talk to people in various professions and explore different options. Maybe you're interested in helping animals, creating artwork, or building things. No matter what your passion is, there are many paths you can take to turn it into a fulfilling career.

Your future is full of possibilities, and you have the power to shape it into something incredible. The choices you make now, like studying hard and exploring your interests, can help you create a life that reflects your passions and dreams. Remember, finding a job you love means you'll enjoy your work, and it won't feel like just a job. Your future is in your hands, so dream big and follow your passions!

THINKING ABOUT FUTURE EXPENSES: PLANNING AND SAVING

As you grow older, you'll have bigger dreams and plans. Maybe you'll want to go to college, start a business, or travel the world. It's a good idea to start thinking about these goals early and figure out how you can save up for them.

By setting aside a little bit of money regularly, you can build up your savings over time. This way, when the time comes to pay for your big plans, you'll have some money saved up to help you get started.

Remember, it's not just about having enough money for these goals. It's also about learning to plan ahead and being responsible with your finances. And the best part is, even if you're saving a small amount, it can add up over time and make a big difference.

So, start thinking about what you might want to do in the future and how you can save up for it. Every bit of planning and saving helps you get closer to achieving your dreams.

THE IMPORTANCE OF FINANCIAL INDEPENDENCE

As you grow older, you'll look forward to the time when you can move out of your parent's home and live on your own. This is when you'll need to support yourself using your own money to pay for everything you need. It's called financial independence.

Reaching the stage of financial independence is something to be proud of. It feels great to know that, when the time is right, you can take care of yourself without relying on others for financial help.

Here are the steps that lead to financial independence.

1. **Earning money:** Find a job and work hard to start making money. The earlier you start, the sooner you can work toward financial independence.

2. **Saving money:** Put a portion of your earnings into savings so that your money can grow over time through earned interest. This will also ensure you have money available for future expenses.

3. **Spending money wisely:** Use your money wisely, avoiding unnecessary expenses. Creating a budget will help you differentiate between what you need and what you want, keeping you on track toward financial independence.

4. **Investing money:** Once you have an emergency fund set aside and some extra money each month, you can think about investing. Investing is another way to potentially make your money grow over time.

5. **Planning for the future:** It's a good idea to start planning for future expenses before you become financially independent. By doing so, you'll have a head-start and already have some money set aside for those future needs.

Congratulations! You've reached financial independence! You've taken the necessary steps to earn, save, spend wisely, and plan for the future. Now, you have the confidence and freedom to care for yourself and live the life you've always dreamed of. Well done!

DISCOVER YOUR PERFECT CAREER

ACTIVITY TIME!

This activity is all about exploring your interests, passions, and aspirations. There are no right or wrong answers. Use your imagination and dream big about the possibilities for your future career!

1. Think about the things you enjoy doing and the subjects you find interesting.

    a) What are your favorite subjects in school?
    _____

    b) What topics or subjects do you enjoy learning about outside of school?
    _____

    c) What are your favorite hobbies or activities?
    _____

    d) Is there a cause or issue that you feel passionate about?
    _____

2. Look at your answers and consider how they relate to different career options. Write down any careers that come to mind based on your interests and passions.

    _____   _____
    _____   _____
    _____   _____

3. Now, consider what you want to achieve or contribute through your career.

    a) What are your favorite subjects in school?
    _____

    b) How would you like to help others or make a difference?
    _____

    c) What skills or talents do you have that could be valuable in a career?
    _____

4. Look at your answers and reflect on the careers that align with your interests, passions, and goals. Write down any additional jobs that you discover based on this reflection.

_____   _____

_____   _____

_____   _____

5. Take a moment to review your answers and consider the connections or patterns you notice. Write down any observations or thoughts about your ideal career path.

_____

_____

6. **Share and discuss:** If you feel comfortable, share your answers with a friend, family member, or teacher. Discuss your interests, passions, and the careers you discovered. Listen to their thoughts and feedback.

6. **Dream Big:** Imagine yourself in your perfect career. What does it look like? How does it make you feel? Write or draw your vision here.

CONCLUSION

Congratulations on starting your journey to learn about money skills! By understanding and applying the concepts we discussed, you are taking the first steps toward financial success. Remember, this is just the beginning of your lifelong journey of managing money responsibly.

When it comes to money, success means knowing how to take care of it from the very start. This begins from the moment you start earning an allowance, goes on to when you have your first part-time job, and continues throughout your entire life.

Once you start earning money, don't forget the power of saving. Consider opening a savings account where a portion of your earnings can stay safe and grow over time. Just like a tree needs time to grow from a seed, your savings also need time to grow.

Spending money wisely is another critical part of handling money responsibly. It's about making thoughtful decisions when you're about to buy something. Every time you spend money, ask yourself if you're spending it on something you need or just something you want. Make sure your needs are met that and you've put some of your money in savings before you spend money on things you just want. Before buying anything, do some detective work. Compare prices, read reviews, and consider the long-term costs and benefits.

When you buy something online or in a store, you may use a debit or credit card, or maybe even the "Buy Now Pay Later" option. Be aware that if you use a credit card or "Buy Now Pay Later," you could be charged interest, which means you may end up paying more for the item in the long run.

A smart way to keep track of your earnings and spending is by setting up a budget and sticking to it. Think of your budget like a roadmap for your money, helping you avoid the bumpy road of debt, meet your savings goals, and feel confident about managing your money.

Remember, money isn't just about earning, saving, and spending. It's also about giving. Whether it's your time, money, things, or just a kind word or smile, sharing with others can make a big difference and make someone's day a little brighter.

You'll also want to keep your money safe. This means not sharing your personal details, only shopping on secure websites, not carrying lots of cash, and always keeping an eye out for tricks or scams.

While keeping your money safe is crucial, you'll want it to grow, too. This is where investing comes into play. Do your research, start small, and always think long term. Investing isn't about getting rich quickly, it's about gradually building wealth over time.

Taking care of your money responsibly is key to being stable financially, making smart decisions, and reaching your long-term financial goals. It means developing a budget, saving regularly, investing wisely, spending smartly to avoid debt, and working towards being financially independent so that you can enjoy a secure financial future.

Remember, the journey doesn't end here. Continuously learning about handling money effectively will help you make smarter financial choices throughout your life. There are always new things to discover and ways to improve your money skills.

Keep exploring, keep learning, and keep growing. Your financial future is in your hands, and with the knowledge and skills you've gained, you have the power to shape it and achieve your dreams. Embrace the journey, and may it lead you to a lifetime of financial success!

Good luck!

GLOSSARY OF KEY FINANCIAL TERMS

1. **Cash:** Cash is what you probably think of when you hear the word "money." It's the paper bills and metal coins that you can use to buy things. You can also save it or even invest it to help it grow!

2. **Income:** Income is the money that you earn. This could come from doing chores, working at a part-time job, or even making a video that people pay to watch (like on YouTube).

3. **Expenses:** Expenses are what you spend your money on. This could be anything from a new video game to a meal at a restaurant, or even paying for a bus ride. Sometimes, you have to plan ahead for big expenses in the future, like saving for a bike or even thinking about college.

4. **Needs vs. wants:** "Needs" are things you must have to survive, like food and shelter. "Wants" are things that are nice to have, but that you don't absolutely need, like toys or video games. Knowing the difference can help you make good spending decisions.

5. **Budget:** A budget is like a map for your money. It helps you keep track of how much money you're earning (your income), how much you're spending (your expenses), and how much you're saving. It's a tool to help you manage your money and reach your goals.

6. **Saving:** Saving is when you put some of your money aside for later. It's like planting a seed that can grow over time. The sooner you start to save, the bigger your money "tree" can grow. This is thanks to something called interest, which can make your savings grow even when you're not adding more to it.

7. **Interest:** Interest can work in two ways. It's the money you earn from saving or investing over time, but it is also the extra money you pay when you borrow money. It's like a reward for saving and a cost for borrowing.

8 Compound interest: Compound interest is when your interest starts earning its own interest! It's like a snowball rolling down a hill, getting bigger and bigger. It's a powerful way to help your savings or investments grow over time.

9 Investing: Investing is a way to make your money work for you. It's like giving your money a job! For example, you could buy a small part of a company (that's called buying stocks), and if the company does well, your money could grow. Spreading your money into different types of investments is called diversification, and it can help protect your money from ups and downs in the market.

10 Debt: Debt is money you've borrowed and need to repay. This could be money you borrowed from a friend to buy lunch when you forgot your wallet, or it could be a significant amount, like a loan to buy a house when you're older. It's important to pay back debt quickly because the longer it takes to pay it back, the more it can cost you in fees or interest.

11 Credit card: A credit card is a plastic card issued by a bank or a financial institution. It allows you to buy things now and pay for them later. However, if you don't pay back the money by a specific date, you could be charged extra money called "interest."

12 Debit card: A debit card is another plastic card linked directly to your bank account. When you buy something with a debit card, the money is immediately taken out of your account. It's like digital cash!

13 Taxes: Taxes are payments that people make to the government. They help pay for things like schools, roads, and public services. You might not have to worry about these yet, but it's good to know about them for the future!

14 Financial independence: Financial independence is when you have enough money to take care of yourself without needing help from others. It's a big goal for when you're older, and being good with money now can help you reach it. Being financially responsible is a big part of this, and it starts with understanding these concepts!

ADVENTURE SKILLS FOR KIDS

The Ultimate Guide to Screen-Free Adventures

*How to Build Shelter, Make Fires,
and Master Survival Skills in the Great Outdoors*

FERNE BOWE

INTRODUCTION – SEARCHING FOR ADVENTURE

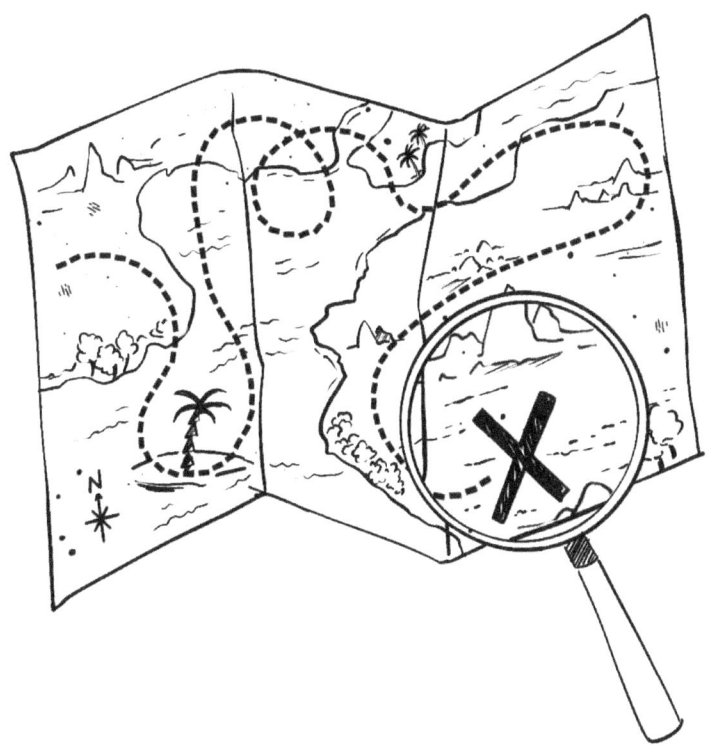

Adventure is everywhere, and it's easy to find—you just have to know where to look. Some adventures happen in the woods or the wilderness. Others happen around lakes or rivers. You can even find adventure in your own backyard.

Get ready to explore a whole host of new adventures. In this book, you'll learn about how to plan an adventure yourself, even if it's just a day-hike into the forest.

You'll also learn:

- How to build a shelter
- How to prepare for an overnight camping trip
- How to build a fire

What you'll discover is that every adventure is not only a learning experience, but also a fun way to discover nature.

Along the way, you'll discover:

- How to identify rocks and minerals
- How to recognize trees by their leaves and bark
- How to identify birds and wild animals
- How to cook over a campfire and make breakfast for the whole family

Mom and Dad can guide you on all of these adventures, and you can also teach them all about what you've learned.

Your Very Own Adventure Journal

Let's start with something exciting that you will use throughout your adventures: an adventure journal of your very own.

You can use this to:

- Plan your adventures.
- Take notes on where you go.
- Keep a record of what you do.
- Write down what you learn.

Get Creative

Your adventure journal is especially for you—and you can make it as unique as you are. Here are some ideas:

- Draw pictures in your journal of the shelter you build, the beautiful nature you see, the animals you encounter, or the interesting things you find.
- Add photos of your campsite and the amazing things you discover on your adventure.
- Press leaves and flowers in the pages of your journal to make it extra special.
- Write stories or poetry about your adventure.

Making Your Adventure Journal

Creating your very own adventure journal is easy and fun.

Here's what you'll need:

- A blank notebook
- Some pencils, markers, or pens

You might also want to try these extras:

- Some sticky tape and glue
- A pair of scissors
- Some fun stickers

This isn't just any notebook—it's where you'll write down all the fun places you want to go and keep track of what you discover when you get there.

Your life of adventure starts now, so get ready! There's no limit to the things you can discover and the places you can explore when you see each day as a new adventure.

 What you do with your journal is up to you! Make it your own, and remember that what we've listed here are just ideas and suggestions.

CHAPTER 1

PREPARING FOR ADVENTURE

Ready for an adventure? It all starts with an idea and some planning.

Think about what you want to do. Maybe there's a trail nearby you want to explore or a spot in the woods where you can watch the stars. Ask your parents for ideas, too. You can make a list of adventure spots you'd like to visit in your adventure journal, and when you find out about cool new places, add them to your list.

 **Top Tip** Check out local newspapers and magazines. They often talk about fun places close to home. You can also look online with your parents for more ideas.

MAKE IT HAPPEN

Once you've made your list, look for pictures or maps of those places. Talk with your family about how you'll get there and when you'll go.

PACKING FOR YOUR ADVENTURE

Getting ready for a trip, like camping or hiking, is part of the fun. Start by thinking about the most important things you'll need. What you take with you will depend on how long your trip is.

For instance, if you're just going for a day-hike, you'll need different things than if you're camping overnight. Here's an idea of what you might pack for a day-hike.

What to Bring on a Day Hike

When you're out and about, you'll need to bring some stuff with you. Think about what you might need if you can't just pop to the shops or get something from your fridge or your closet at home.

What things do you think it would be important to take with you on a camping trip?

Why not make a list in your adventure journal?

Here are some suggestions of things you are going to need for a day out in nature:

- **Small backpack:** To carry essentials like snacks, water, and personal items.
- **Water bottle:** A plastic water bottle or a canteen (a metal water bottle used by the military) so you can stay hydrated during the hike.
- **Snacks:** For energy on the trail.
- **Bug spray:** To keep pesky insects and bugs away.

- **Sunscreen:** To protect your skin from harmful UV rays.
- **First aid kit:** Just in case of any minor injuries.
- **Sunglasses and a hat:** To shield your eyes and face from the sun.
- **Camera:** To capture memorable moments.
- **Adventure journal and pen:** To keep a record of your thoughts and experiences.

Remember, you'll have to carry everything you pack—so don't pack too much! Luckily, since you're still young, you won't be going on adventures alone, so you should have some people you can share the load with. As a young person, you will always need to bring a parent or a trusted adult that your parents have arranged for you to go with. If you're old enough, your parents may let you go on an adventure with friends, but you would definitely need their permission!

TIME FOR A CAMPING ADVENTURE

If your adventure lasts for more than a day, then it's not just a hike anymore—it's a camping trip! When it comes to having an adventure away from the city, camping is part of the fun.

Be Prepared: Packing for Your Camping Trip

When you're setting out for an overnight camping adventure, you'll need to pack some extra gear. You'll need somewhere to sleep, a way to cook food, and a fire or some extra clothing to stay warm. Think of it as setting up a mini-home in the wild.

In your adventure journal, make a list of all the things you'll need for a night out in nature. Here are some ideas to get you started.

Camping Essentials

- **Tent:** Or, if you're feeling adventurous, maybe you could build your own shelter! We'll learn how later in this book.
- **Sleeping bag:** Also bring a comfy pillow, if you like.
- **Rain gear:** This will help you stay dry if it starts pouring!
- **Flashlight:** You'll need this for navigating in the dark.
- **Matches:** To start your campfire.
- **Water:** Don't forget a bottle for sipping, and some big jugs for your campsite.
- **Tasty drinks:** Like lemonade mix.
- **Water tablets:** Just in case you need to clean your water.
- **Cooking gear:** For all those camp meals.
- **Food:** Including all your meals and snacks.
- **Day-hike gear:** Don't forget the items from your day-hike list!

Camping Tools

The more prepared you are for your camping trip, the better it will be. You will need some tools to set up your tent, cut firewood, and do other things around camp. Remember, all of these tools should only be used if you have permission from an adult, or if there's an adult with you. Let's make a list in your adventure journal.

Top Tools

- **Folding shovel:** To dig fire pits or trenches and clear stuff out of the way.
- **Hatchet:** For chopping wood for the fire.
- **Saw:** To cut branches or logs for firewood or building.
- **Hammer:** To secure tent stakes and build makeshift structures.
- **Nails:** To use with the hammer for assembling or fixing things.
- **Rope:** To secure tents, create a clothesline, or for other tying needs.

Your Personal Hygiene Kit

You'll also want to feel comfortable while you're out in nature. Let's also write a list in your adventure journal of what to include in your personal hygiene kit, so you can keep clean while in camp.

Here's a start:

- **Soap:** For a clean body and hands.
- **Towel:** To dry off after washing, or if something gets wet.
- **Toothbrush and toothpaste:** Don't forget your teeth!
- **Toilet paper:** Essential for bathroom needs and spills.
- **Wet wipes:** To freshen up when a shower isn't available.
- **Hand sanitizer:** So you can keep clean without wasting water.

Dressing for an Outdoor Adventure

The clothes you wear when you're exploring are really important. You'll be outside most of the time, so be prepared for any weather! Depending on where you go and what time of year it is, you may need protection from rain, snow, wind, the cold, or the sun.

Time to make another adventure journal list! Let's think about the best things to wear and extra clothes to pack:

- **Hiking boots:** The shoes you wear are really important! Hiking boots do a great job of protecting your feet from sharp rocks, sticks, thorns, and other things you could step on. They also give you good traction in the mud so you don't slip.

- **Hiking socks:** Hiking socks are thick and will protect your feet from getting blisters. They can also keep you warm on cold days. Bring two pairs of socks for every day you are exploring. That way, you will always have dry socks.

- **Hiking shorts:** Shorts are great to wear on a hot day. Hiking shorts also have a lot of pockets, so you can carry all of the things you want to take on a hike or for exploring. It's a good idea to pack one pair of shorts for each day.

- **Long pants:** Long pants are important, too, especially if you're exploring the woods or fields, where thorns can scratch your legs. Long pants also protect you from bugs and keep you warm on cold days, or in the evening.

- **Long-sleeve and short-sleeve shirts**: It's a good idea to have both long- and short-sleeve shirts. Long-sleeve shirts can protect you from thorns while you are berry picking or walking through sharp branches and sticks. Short-sleeve shirts keep you cool on hot days.

- **Rain gear:** A rain suit with a jacket and pants will keep you dry on a rainy day. You could also pack a poncho with a hood.

- **A jacket, hat, and gloves:** It can get cold at any time of year. Make sure you have a jacket with a hood, a hat, and gloves in case the weather gets chilly at night, especially in winter.

- **A hoodie:** A sweatshirt with a hood can keep you warm on cold mornings. It can also help keep you warm in your sleeping bag on cold nights, or if you're hiking on a cold day.

- **Underwear:** This one is easy to forget, but you're going to need it! Make sure you have enough for each day of your trip!

Adventure Gear

An adventure in the great outdoors will be more enjoyable if you're well prepared with all the things you could need. This will allow you to go out into the wilderness with confidence, ready to explore and discover nature's wonders.

In this section, we'll introduce you to some essential gear that will make a big difference to your outdoor experience. It's a good idea to be prepared for any surprises nature may throw your way.

Here is a list of some things that could definitely come in handy on your adventure:

- **A small backpack or fanny pack:** Perfect for carrying essentials like water, snacks, extra clothing, or your adventure journal.

- **A compass:** To ensure you never lose your way in the wilderness.

- **A map:** To plan routes and find your way if you get lost.
- **A signal whistle:** An important tool to draw attention to yourself in an emergency.

- **A small flashlight:** To light your way in case you end up somewhere dark or need to find your way around your campsite at night.
- **Your adventure journal and a pencil:** To record your adventures and log anything interesting you discover.
- **A small pocket knife:** Useful for cutting rope or preparing food—though you will need to ask your parents if they feel you're old enough to carry one. You'll also need to learn how to use it safely.
- **Small binoculars:** To get a closer look at any wildlife you see on your adventures.
- **Plastic bags:** Ideal for protecting any items you collect on your adventures, like bugs, rocks, or flowers.
- **A small magnifying glass:** To get a better look at insects or plants.
- **Two walkie talkies:** To talk to your fellow hikers or campers over long distances—it's fun and great for safety.

Can you think of any other items that might be useful? Make a list in your adventure journal.

PLAN YOUR CAMPSITE

Let's imagine what the perfect campsite would look like.

When you arrive at your adventure destination, you'll need to set up a tent or build a shelter. You'll also want to build a fire pit or create the perfect place for your campfire.

Here are some things to look for if you're going to make a shelter you can live in comfortably overnight:

- **Flat ground for your tent, with no rocks or holes:** You want a nice, flat place to sleep and sit.

- **High ground that won't get wet if it rains:** You don't want a puddle of water under your sleeping bag in the middle of the night.

- **A place with lots of dead branches or fallen trees:** This will make it easy to find wood to make a campfire and keep it going. Remember, always make sure you build your fire safely, with help from an adult. Make sure your tent or shelter isn't under a tree with dead branches. You don't want a tree branch falling on your tent, especially in the middle of the night when you're sleeping!

- **A close water supply, like a creek, river, or lake:** If you make sure you take enough water with you, this won't be necessary. If you do decide to drink water from a natural source, you'll need to filter and purify it, but we'll learn more about that later.

Plan the Kind of Shelter You Will Build

Anytime you camp out, you'll need a shelter for the night. Here are some tips:

- **Take a tent:** If you're new to camping or want to keep things simple, a tent is your best bet.

- **Timing is important:** Setting your tent up during the day—and leaving yourself plenty of time to do it—is

246 ESSENTIAL SKILLS EVERY KID SHOULD KNOW

always best. Pitching a tent when you have enough time and don't have to worry about it getting dark is a lot more fun!

- **Practice makes perfect:** Even the best plans can go off track sometimes. There may be times when you reach your campsite after dark, or it could be raining or windy. This is why it's a good idea to practice at home first. Knowing how to set up your tent means you can get it up quickly and correctly, even in less-than-ideal conditions.

- **Build your own shelter:** If you want a challenge and have gone on a few adventures already, you could build your own shelter from branches, leaves, bark, or even snow. Later in the book, we'll explore all the ways to build a shelter.

Think About Your Campfire

There are many ways to build a campfire. Some fires are good for cooking, while other fires give off a lot of heat to keep you warm when it's cold.

Make sure you have extra firewood stacked up so you have enough to get through a cold, dark evening.

Remember, Fire Can Be Dangerous

When you're out camping, it's important to be smart about fire safety to keep your adventure nice and safe.

Here are some important fire safety tips:

- **Know the rules:** Make sure there's an adult around, or that your parents have decided you're old enough to make a fire on your own. You should also check and obey the local fire rules.

- **Choose your spot:** This means taking care of where you put your fire. If you're sleeping in a tent, you don't want the fire too close to the tent. If you're sleeping in a lean-to, you can build the fire closer so the heat reflects into the lean-to. A fire can also help light up your campsite at night.

- **Prepare properly:** Keep your fire away from things that can catch on fire easily, like tents or dry plants. Before starting a fire, clear the area and make a little fire pit with rocks.

- **Take precautions:** Have water nearby, and never leave the fire unattended.

- **When in doubt, put it out:** You will need to extinguish your fire completely before you turn in for the night or leave your campsite.

As long as you're responsible, you can enjoy a wonderful campfire without any problems.

Plan to Cook Over a Fire

One of the most exciting parts about camping is cooking your meals over your campfire. To do this, you'll need a camp cook-kit.

Here's a list of what you'll need to make some great meals out in nature:

- **A campfire grate:** So you can hold your pots and pans over the fire.
- **A frying pan:** To fry up delicious meals.
- **A big pot with a lid:** To cook food or boil water.
- **Utensils:** You'll need plates, cups, knives, forks, and spoons.
- **Campfire cooking tools:** A large wooden spoon, tongs, and forks are essential for hassle-free cooking. Hot pads or oven mitts are also useful for safely handling hot pots.
- **Don't forget the marshmallows, chocolate, and graham crackers**: S'mores are a must-have for any camping adventure.

 **Remember**: For your safety, always have an adult's help or permission when cooking. It's important to cook safely and be careful!

ADVENTURE FIRST AID KIT

It's very important to have a first aid kit whenever you go on an adventure, so you're ready for any unexpected injuries.

Why might you need it? You could get a cut or scrape when hiking, a burn when you are cooking over a fire, a bee sting, an insect bite, or a rash from touching the wrong plant. While your adventures will usually be problem-free, it's always best to be prepared. You can either buy a pre-made first aid kit or put your own personalized kit together.

Here are some of the first aid supplies you may need:

- **Bandages**: Useful for dressing cuts, sprains, or muscle strains.
- **Antiseptic cream/ointment:** Essential for keeping cuts clean and germ-free.
- **Wipes**: Handy for cleaning cuts or scrapes to prevent infection.
- **Tweezers**: Perfect for removing those pesky splinters.
- **Eye drops**: A relief if your eyes get irritated by dust or debris.
- **Burn cream**: A soothing relief for any minor burns.
- **Aftersun cream**: A big help when it comes to soothing sunburnt skin. Remember, it's always better to use plenty of sunscreen to avoid sunburn in the first place!

DON'T FORGET TO PACK YOUR ADVENTURE JOURNAL

Your adventure journal will not only let you record your memories from your adventures, but also help you to remember all the things you learned about and discovered.

Here is an example of how you could keep track of an adventure. Remember, this journal is all about your adventure, so fill it with your unique experiences and discoveries!

Adventure Journal Page: My Epic Journey

Weather & Temperature:
(Note down the weather – was it warm or cold?)

Date:

M T W Th F Sa Su

Adventure Companions:
(Names of the awesome people who joined you)

_____
_____
_____

Funniest Moments: (what made you laugh most?)

Most Interesting Sight: (what was the coolest thing you saw?)

Pressed Leaves/Flowers:
(Flatten and secure nature's treasures here)

Learned & Curious About:
(Jot down new things you learned and what you're curious to explore next)

_____
_____
_____
_____
_____

Memorable Pictures:
(Paste or tape your favourite photos)

250   ESSENTIAL SKILLS EVERY KID SHOULD KNOW

CHAPTER 2

BUILDING YOUR SHELTER

Think of the shelter you build in the wilderness as your home away from home. It's where you'll sleep, change clothes, and rest. You may even eat there if it's raining, windy, or cold. It's not a fancy hotel, but with the right setup, it can be comfortable enough for a great camping trip!

USING A TENT

For many adventurers, a tent is the go-to choice for shelter while camping or exploring. It's pretty straightforward to set up once you get the hang of it.

However, pitching a tent in the wild for the first time can be a bit tricky. That's why practicing beforehand is such a good idea.

> **Top Tip:** If you're going to try putting your tent up at home, why not make an event out of it? Set the tent up in your backyard with your family or friends. This way, you can learn the ropes in a familiar environment. You could even turn it into a fun backyard camping experience, complete with a barbeque and s'mores! Not only will this practice give you confidence, but it also makes for a great mini-adventure right at home.

Where to Set Up Your Tent

Here are some things to think about when it's time to set up your tent:

- **Keep it flat:** Make sure the ground is flat, and clear away any sticks or rocks, so you don't end up sleeping on something uncomfortable.

- **Stay dry:** Avoid low spots where rainwater might collect.

- **Watch out for wind:** When setting up your tent, find a spot behind things in nature that can act like windbreaks, such as bushes or trees. This provides extra protection from the wind, making your camping experience more comfortable.

Once you've got your spot ready, you can set up your tent and start to organize the rest of your campsite. But before we dive into that, let's explore some of the other shelters you can build from natural materials like logs, branches, bark, and leaves.

BUILDING YOUR OWN SHELTER

There are lots of ways to build a shelter in the wilderness. The key is to build something that protects you from the elements, like wind and rain. Let's explore some shelters that are easy to build, and that people who love the great outdoors have relied on for years.

Building a Lean-to Shelter

The lean-to is a classic and easy-to-build shelter. Its name comes from the way it uses branches, leaning them against a solid structure to form a roof-like shape.

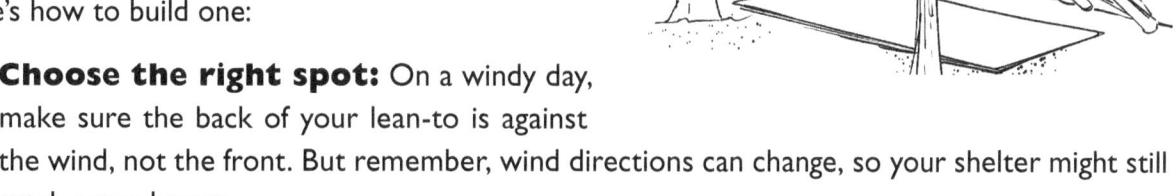

Here's how to build one:

1. **Choose the right spot:** On a windy day, make sure the back of your lean-to is against the wind, not the front. But remember, wind directions can change, so your shelter might still catch some breeze.

2. **Find anchor trees:** Look for two strong trees about 8 to 10 feet apart. These trees act as the anchors for your lean-to. They're the ones that will support the crossbeam—the backbone of your shelter.

3. **Create the structure:** Place a strong piece of wood between your two anchor trees. This is your crossbeam, and its job is to support the branches that make up the slanted roof of your shelter.

4. **Build the roof:** Lean branches against the crossbeam to form the roof. It's ok if there are some gaps.

5. **Waterproof it:** Cover the structure with bark, leaves, or pine branches for added protection against rain and wind. These natural materials help to fill in any gaps and make sure your shelter will be ok in any weather.

6. **Extra protection:** For even more shelter, stretch a space blanket (sometimes called a tarp) over the branch roof. This turns your lean-to into a waterproof and cozy camp. Secure the tarp well to make sure it stays in place in the rain or wind.

Another way to make a lean-to is with a rope. This is one of the easiest ways to build a shelter.

All you need is:

- A space blanket (or tarp).
- Some nice, strong rope.
- Some stakes (you can also use sturdy branches as your stakes).

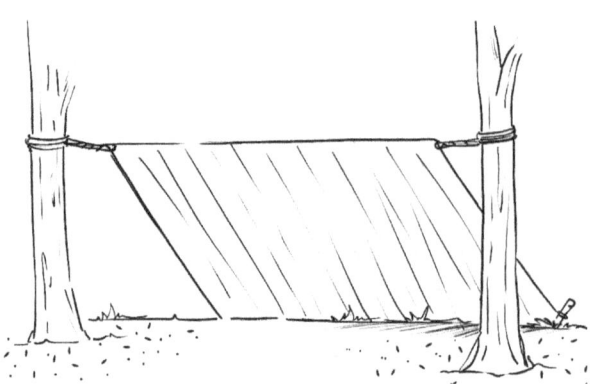

Here's how it's done:

1. **Find two trees:** Look for two strong trees that are a suitable distance apart for your lean-to.

2. **Stretch the rope:** Stretch a rope horizontally between the two trees. This will be the main support for your lean-to.

3. **Position the tarp:** Use the stretched rope as support for your tarp. Drape the tarp over the rope to form the top of the lean-to.

4. **Secure bottom corners:** Stake the bottom corners of the tarp into the ground to anchor the structure and serve as the slanted roof of the lean-to.

5. **Tie ropes to top corners:** If you want your lean-to to be extra strong and stable, tie ropes to the top corners of the tarp and attach them right onto the trees.

In the next chapter, we'll learn all about fires and how to build them. You'll also see how a lean-to can really keep you warm with a fire in front!

Building an A-Frame Shelter

The A-frame shelter gets its name because the front of the shelter looks like a capital A. It's a great shelter for colder days, and it's also very easy to build.

Here's how set up your own A-frame shelter:

1. **Find your branches:** You'll need two branches with a Y shape at one end, kind of like two arms stretching out.

② **Make the frame:** Lean these Y branches against a horizontal branch placed on the ground. Place them so that they look like a strong letter A. This will be the main support for the front of your shelter.

③ **Finish the shelter:** Lay more branches along the supporting branch to complete your A-shaped shelter. It's like solving a puzzle, fitting each branch to build a strong shelter.

④ **Make it warm and waterproof:** Once your frame is up, cover the top with leaves, pine branches, or bark. These materials act as a natural roof, shielding you from rain and wind.

 For extra warmth, build a fire in front to reflect heat into the shelter.

Building a Snow Shelter

Building a snow shelter can be as fun as making a snow fort or an igloo. Here's how to do it:

① **Build your framework:** Start by collecting sticks to become the skeleton or framework of your shelter. Arrange them in an A-Frame shape.

② **Cover it up:** Once your framework is ready, cover it with a space blanket (tarp) or some other kind of waterproof material. Make sure the material is securely attached to the framework and completely covers it.

③ **Insulate it:** Cover the outside of your snow structure with pine boughs or small branches. This adds an extra layer of insulation, helping to trap heat inside. Inside, cover the floor with more boughs to keep it warm and create a softer and more comfy surface to sit or lie on.

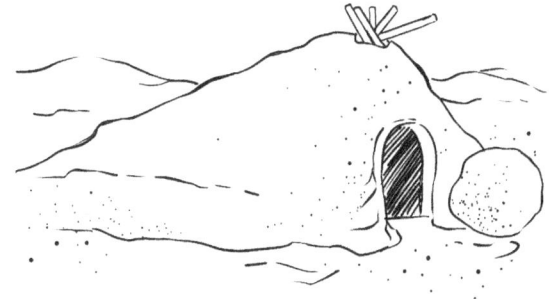

ADVENTURE SKILLS FOR KIDS

④ **Snow time:** Cover your shelter with a generous layer of snow. Pack it down firmly to create a thick, outer layer. This gives extra warmth and also helps protect your shelter against wind and cold temperatures. Don't forget to make a small entrance to serve as your door.

>  You can use extra snow to craft a door plug that can be easily removed or replaced, so you can seal off your shelter when you need to. But it is important to always make sure at least some air can flow in and out of your shelter so that carbon dioxide doesn't build up in your shelter.

By following these steps, you'll be able to create a sturdy and snug snow shelter for your outdoor adventures.

A well-built snow shelter shields you from snowstorms, keeping the inside dry and comfortable. You can even use snow to insulate the roof of your lean-to or A-frame! Stay warm and enjoy the unique experience of building and staying in your own snow fortress!

> ***DID YOU KNOW?*** In some parts of the world, people have been living in snow shelters for thousands of years. You might think that the snow would make the shelter cold. In reality, inside a snow shelter, it can be much warmer than the freezing temperatures outside.

Setting up a Tarp Tent

Setting up a tarp tent isn't too difficult, if you follow these steps:

① **Tie your rope:** Start by attaching a rope to each of the top two corners of the tarp. Each rope should be long enough to reach from the tarp to the trees you'll use as anchor points.

② **Find the right trees:** Look for two trees about 8 to 10 feet apart. These will be your anchor points.

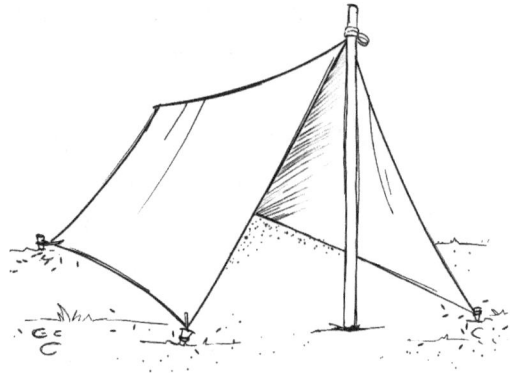

3. **Create your roof:** Attach the top corner ropes of the tarp to the trees. Tie them at a height of about three to four feet off the ground. This creates a slanted roof effect with your tarp.

4. **Attach your tarp:** Stretch the bottom corners of the tarp down to the ground and secure them with stakes. If you're unable to use stakes, use additional rope tied to the bottom corners, using nearby objects as anchors like large rocks or trees. Ensure your tarp is pulled tight and secure.

There you have it—your very own tarp tent, perfect for a camping adventure.

The Hammock Tent

Everyone loves lounging in a hammock, but did you know they can be transformed into a cozy tent for sleeping in the wilderness? Setting one up is simple:

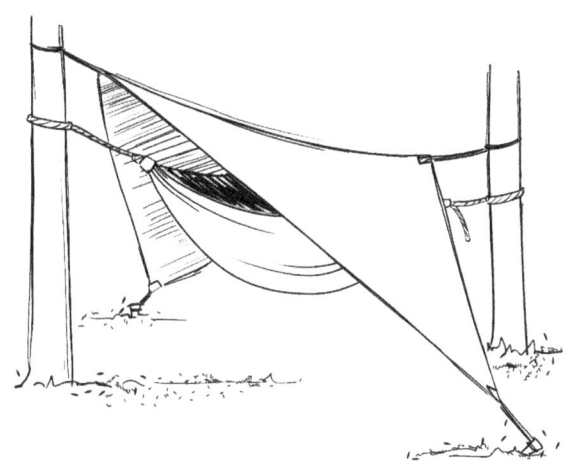

1. **Find the right trees:** Find two trees about 10 to 12 feet apart.

2. **Tie the support ropes:** Securely tie your hammock's support ropes to these two trees.

To convert your hammock into a tent, just follow these additional steps:

1. **Attach a rope:** It needs to be tied between the two trees above the hammock.

2. **Create a canopy:** Stretch a tarp over the top of the rope.

3. **Make a roof:** Secure the two corners of the tarp to the ground with stakes and rope. Now you have a roof to protect you from the rain!

The great thing about hammock tents is that they can be packed up nice and small, and they are light, making them easy to carry. Plus, they're pretty cheap and quick to set up. Some hammock tents even have mosquito netting so the bugs won't bite at night. And because you're off the ground, you won't get wet from muddy ground or bothered by creepy crawlies!

TOOLS NEEDED FOR SETTING UP SHELTERS

Whether you're building a lean-to or pitching a tent, having the right tools can make your job much easier and help make sure your shelter is sturdy and safe. Here's what you might need:

- **Hammer:** You'll need this for driving in stakes.

- **Long nails (three to four inches):** These are handy for joining poles and branches.

- **Extra rope:** This will be useful for securing tarps or lashing together logs and branches.

- **Knife:** You may need this for cutting rope and small branches. Make sure you have permission to use one, or ask an adult to help you.

- **Hatchet or axe:** This is great for chopping logs and branches.

- **Handsaw:** This is ideal for sawing wood and branches to the right size.

- **Space blanket (tarp):** These come in handy for covering firewood or adding extra protection from rain.

- **Extra tent stakes:** Important on windy days or as spares.

The number and type of tools you need depends on the shelter you're planning to build. For a hammock tent, you might not need much more than the hammock itself. But if you're building something more complicated, like a lean-to, you'll definitely need some good tools!

 Always remember to prioritize safety first. Build your shelter with an adult's help, and never use any tools without permission and proper guidance.

YOUR SHELTER: THE HEART OF YOUR CAMPGROUND

Your shelter isn't just a place to sleep—it's the centerpiece of your campground. It sets the tone for your entire camping experience. And no shelter is complete without a nice, roaring campfire....

CHAPTER 3

BUILDING CAMPFIRES

A campfire is a cozy spot for families and friends to gather, share stories, and enjoy meals. It's also essential for staying warm during cooler evenings under the stars. While there are many ways to build and start a campfire, the key is to always put safety first.

Making sure your campfire is well-managed and controlled is very important. Fires can spread quickly, so your number one job is to build a fire that's contained in one place and won't spread.

BUILDING A FIRE PIT

A fire pit is a safe area where you place your campfire. There are a few different ways to make your firepit. Let's take a look at some of them:

- **A ring of rocks:** Collect rocks and arrange them in a circle around the fire. The rocks contain the fire and prevent it from spreading.

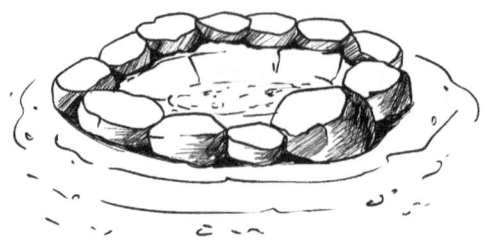

- **A hole:** Dig a hole in the ground for your fire. This is a simple way to make a great fire pit that also helps protect the fire from wind.

- **A log barrier:** Place large logs on either side of your fire area. This is a great option if you're planning on cooking on the fire, as the logs can support your cooking grate.

When it comes to choosing the location for your fire pit, safety should always come first! You don't want to accidentally start a forest fire.

Here are some crucial tips to ensure your campfire experience is not only fun, but also safe:

- **Choose your spot:** Make sure you set your fire up a safe distance from your tent and any other flammable materials.

- **Clear the area:** Before lighting your fire, clear the surrounding area of anything that could catch fire, like leaves, sticks, or dry grass.

- **Double check:** Always check with an adult to confirm you've chosen a safe spot for your fire pit.

Once you've created your fire pit, it's time to decide on the type of fire you're going to build.

There are lots of different types of fires, each with their own benefits and uses. We're going to learn how to make some different kinds, but first, let's learn about something you'll need for any fire.

Tinder and Kindling

The first step in any fire-building adventure is gathering tinder and kindling. You could also make something called a fuzz stick, which is a great homemade tool for starting a fire.

What's Tinder?

Tinder is stuff that people use to start fires, like small bits of grass, little sticks, small twigs, birch bark, pine needles, pine cones, and other things that will catch fire easily. Paper and small pieces of cloth can also be used as tinder to get your fire going. Or, try cattail fluff, small pieces of birch bark, a torn up piece of fabric, paper, or dry grass—basically anything that will light and burn easily.

No matter which one of the different methods you use to start a fire, you'll need tinder, as it catches fire easily and burns quickly, which is what you need to get your fire going.

What's Kindling?

Kindling are small sticks that burn easily, but not as quickly as tinder. You can find these sticks on the ground, or you can break them off bigger branches.

> **Top Tip** Make sure they're dry, dead sticks, which burn better and faster.

What's a Fuzz Stick?

A fuzz stick, also known as a feather stick, is a type of fire-starting tool that you can make by carving a dry stick into thin curls or shavings.

Here's how it's done:

1. **Select a stick:** Choose a dry stick from your surroundings, or that you have brought with you. It should be one that isn't too thick and has a smooth surface.

1. **Hold the stick in place:** Hold the stick firmly with one hand, to keep it safe and stable.

① **Make closely spaced cuts:** Using a knife, make some cuts in the stick, close together, along one side of it. The cuts don't have to be too deep, and should go all the way from one end of the stick to the other.

② **Leave curls attached at the base:** Make sure to leave the curls of wood attached at the base. The curls along the side of the stick are going to help you start your fire.

③ **Start your fire:** When you're ready, with the help of an adult, light a match or lighter and place the flame or sparks on the curls of the fuzz stick. They should catch fire easily.

Fuzz sticks are very useful when it's damp after some rain, as they are a great replacement for dry tinder if you can't find any. The curls quickly catch fire, making them a great fire-starting tool. And, instead of having to find lots of dry tinder and kindling, all you need is one dry stick.

Top Tip: Safety is always the most important thing, so make sure you are old enough to use a knife or have an adult around to help you!

Making a Tinder Nest

You can also put your tinder into a tinder nest. That way, you can start a little fire that you will later transfer to your bigger fire. Just make sure your big fire is ready to go before you start.

Here's how to make one:

① **Collect dry stuff:** Find dry grass, leaves, or plant bits. These should be easy to catch on fire.

② **Clear a spot:** Make a clean space on the ground where you want your fire.

③ **Make a pile:** Arrange your dry stuff in a pile on the ground. This is the start of your nest.

④ **Add twiggy things:** Put tiny twigs and dry branches on top of your pile. Make it like a little nest.

⑤ Make a hole: Use your hands to shape your nest. Leave a hole at the top so air can get in.

⑥ Get ready to light: Have your fire starter, matches, or lighter ready nearby.

⑦ Light the nest: Carefully use your fire starter or match to light the bottom of the nest. Watch it catch fire.

⑧ Blow gently: Blow gently on the flames to make them bigger. Add small sticks to keep the fire going.

Remember, always be careful with fire, and make sure you have an adult help you.

THE TEEPEE FIRE

Learning to build a teepee fire is a great skill for any outdoor adventure. It's a simple yet effective way to start a campfire, and is the base for many other fire types.

> **Top Tip**
> This fire is named after its shape. It looks like the teepee tents that many indigenous North American tribes used to sleep in.

Building Your Teepee

Once you've collected your tinder and kindling, put the tinder in the center of your fire pit. Then add some kindling.

Now it's time to build the teepee.

① Make your teepee: Lean larger sticks and branches against the tinder and kindling, creating the shape of a teepee. This structure allows air to circulate and feed your fire.

② Sustain your fire: To keep the fire going, continue adding larger branches and logs, carefully maintaining the structure of your teepee.

HOW TO BUILD A TEEPEE FIRE

1. Collect Tinder

(User dry leaves, pine cones, cotton lint and paper.)

2. Clear A Spot

(Dig a hole and put a ring of rocks around it to keep the fire contained.)

3. Place Tinder in the Spot

(Use your hands to shape your nest. Leave a hole at the top so air can get in.)

4. Add Kindling

(Arrange tiny twigs and dry branches on top of your pile.)

5. Make Your Teepee

(Lean bigger branches against the tinder and kindling, in the shape of a teepee.)

6. Light The Nest
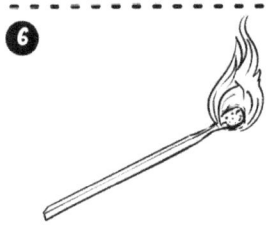
(Carefully use your fire starter or a match to light the bottom of the nest.)

7. Blow Gently

(Blow gently on the flames to make them bigger.)

8. Sustain Your Fire

(Continue adding larger branches and logs, maintaining the structure of your teepee.)

THE LOG CABIN FIRE

Just like its name suggests, the log cabin fire looks like a little log cabin. It's an excellent choice for those chillier days and nights, because it gives off plenty of heat and burns for a long time. Plus, it's pretty simple to build:

1. **Make a teepee fire:** Build a teepee fire as your base. If you're not sure how, just check the instructions above.

2. **Arrange your logs:** Next, place logs around your teepee fire, laying them out to form a square.

3. **Make your cabin:** Keep stacking the logs, building your "log cabin." With each layer you add, move the logs a bit closer to the center. This helps your fire burn steadily and warmly.

4. **Light your fire:** Once your log cabin structure is ready, it's time to carefully light it up, with help or permission from an adult, and enjoy the warmth. Remember, this type of fire is really hot, so it's not the best for cooking. But if you're looking to warm up quickly, the log cabin fire is perfect.

THE NORWEGIAN UPSIDE DOWN FIRE

True to its name, the Norwegian Upside Down Fire starts from the top and burns down. It's a popular method in Scandinavian countries, especially during the cold winters when the ground is often frozen or wet.

This fire design ensures that the flames don't directly touch the frozen or soggy ground, making it ideal for winter camping or wet conditions. Here's how to set it up:

1. **Make your base:** Put a layer of logs side by side in your fire pit. This will be the base of your fire.

2. **Stack your logs:** Next, stack another layer of logs on top, but this time, place them criss-cross over the first layer.

ADVENTURE SKILLS FOR KIDS

③ Build a teepee fire: On top of these crisscrossed logs, build a small teepee fire.

The teepee fire will slowly burn down into the gaps between the logs below, creating a long-lasting and efficient fire. Keep adding more logs on top as needed to keep the fire going.

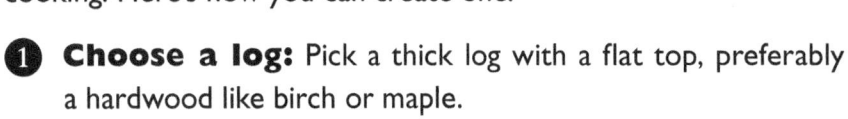

THE CANADIAN CANDLE

The Canadian candle (also known as a Swedish torch) offers a unique and efficient way to cook outdoors. It involves cutting grooves into a log and lighting a small fire on top.

As the fire gets going, the coals fall into the grooves and the fire burns steadily from within. The flat top design makes it excellent for cooking. Here's how you can create one:

① Choose a log: Pick a thick log with a flat top, preferably a hardwood like birch or maple.

② Make narrow grooves: Using a saw or another cutting tool, create narrow grooves on the flat top of the log. These grooves should run deep into the log, creating channels for the coals.

③ Build a tiny teepee fire: On the flat top above the grooves, build a small teepee fire using tinder and kindling. This small fire will produce coals that drop into the grooves to keep the log burning.

As the teepee fire at the top of your Canadian candle burns, make sure that it continues to produce coals that drop into the grooves. The production of coals will keep the fire going.

From time to time, you may need to add more kindling to keep the Canadian candle going. This layering process helps maintain a steady and controlled burn, ideal for cooking.

The Canadian candle doesn't give off a lot of heat, but you can always build a second fire for heat and have a Canadian candle off to the side for cooking.

THE KEYHOLE FIRE

The keyhole fire's shape gives you the best of both worlds—it keeps you warm and is great for cooking. The big, round end of the fire gives off a lot of heat, while the key section is a perfect space for cooking.

Here's how to build one:

❶ Set up a fire pit in the shape of a keyhole: You can do this by either digging a hole in the shape of a keyhole or using rocks to create the keyhole outline. If you're digging, make a large round pit for the main fire (the round end of the keyhole) and a long, narrower trench extending from it (the key part of the keyhole).

❷ Collect firewood, tinder, and kindling: Make sure the wood is dry so it can burn properly.

❸ Make a teepee fire: In the round part of the pit, assemble a standard teepee fire using tinder, kindling, and larger logs. This section is designed for warmth.

❹ Make your cooking section: In the long trench (the key part), place rocks or create a raised platform using soil to support a cooking surface. This section is for cooking.

❺ Light your fire: Now it's time to light the fire in the round section, making sure it burns steadily. If you're cooking, wait until you have a good bed of hot coals.

❻ Get cooking: Carefully move some coals from the round section into the trench. This will provide a steady heat source that is perfect for cooking your meals.

CAMPFIRE COOKING

Campfire Cooking Equipment

We've already touched on the basic cooking equipment for your camping adventure in chapter 1. Take another look for a refresher, but bear in mind that what you need might be a bit different. The more you plan your meals, the better you'll know what to bring.

Campfire Cooking on a Stick

One of the simplest and most fun ways of cooking outdoors is to roast food on a stick over a campfire. Whether it's marshmallows turning golden brown for s'mores or hot dogs crisping to perfection, cooking on a stick is a classic camping tradition.

All you need is a long, sturdy stick, and you're ready to skewer your favorite foods and hold them over the open flame. This is a social and delicious way to share meals with friends and family around the campfire.

Here's what to do:

1. **Find a safe spot:** Choose a safe area away from tents and trees to set up your campfire. Always have adult supervision.

2. **Gather cooking supplies:** Get a long, sturdy stick and any food you want to cook. Hot dogs, marshmallows, or even small chunks of veggies work well.

3. **Prepare the stick:** Ask an adult to help you sharpen the end of the stick, making it clean and pointy. This makes it easier to skewer your food.

4. **Skewer your food:** Slide your food onto the pointed end of the stick. Make sure it's secure so it won't fall off into the fire.

5. **Cook over the flames:** Hold your stick with the food over the flames of the campfire. Rotate it slowly to cook all sides evenly.

6. **Watch and smell:** Pay attention to the color and smell of your food. When it looks golden or smells yummy, it's probably done.

7. Let it cool: Be careful when taking your food off the stick—it's hot! Let it cool for a moment before taking a bite.

8. Enjoy your campfire treat: Sit by the campfire and savor your delicious, fire-cooked treat. Share the experience with friends or family!

Remember, always follow safety rules when spending time around a campfire, and have fun cooking over the flames!

Plates, Cups, and Forks from Nature

If you want the full camping experience, you can even bring nature into your dining setup. Instead of traditional plates, cups, and utensils, you could find some in nature.

Here are some ideas:

- **Large, flat leaves or flat stones:** These can become plates.
- **Gourds or hollowed-out pieces of wood:** These can become cups.
- **Sturdy twigs:** Can be used as forks.

 If you're allowed to use a knife, you could even carve your own wooden utensils.

This eco-friendly approach not only leads to less waste, but also makes you feel like you're a part of nature, creating an outdoors experience to remember!

HOW TO START A FIRE WITHOUT MATCHES

It's always a good idea to have matches and a lighter when you are camping. But if the matches get wet or the lighter doesn't work, don't worry—there are still ways to start a fire. Here, we'll explore various ways to start a fire. Some methods are straightforward, while others take more skill and patience. Always remember, it's best to have an adult around for safety.

Let's explore the different ways to start a fire without matches:

Magnifying Glass

Packing a magnifying glass in your explorer kit is a good idea for a lot of reasons. It not only lets you study small things like insects, flowers, and rocks, but you can also use it to start a fire.

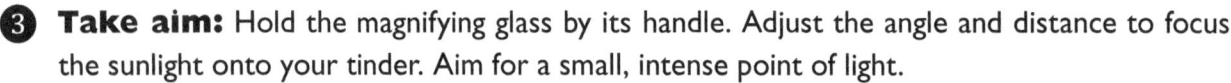

Here's how to harness the power of the sun to start a fire:

① Collect some tinder: Make sure it's dry!

② Find a spot in direct sunlight: The clearer and more focused the sunlight, the better.

③ Take aim: Hold the magnifying glass by its handle. Adjust the angle and distance to focus the sunlight onto your tinder. Aim for a small, intense point of light.

④ Focus the light: Keep the magnifying glass steady. Focus the sunlight into the most intense point possible.

⑤ Be patient: Soon, you'll notice the tinder begin to smoke. Continue focusing the light until the tinder ignites into flames.

⑥ Move your tinder: Carefully transfer the ignited tinder to a prepared fire pit or kindling. Gradually add larger sticks and logs to build your fire.

Remember to do this with the help of an adult, and to be extra careful during the process, ensuring you have full control over the fire at all times. This method is great for when it's sunny, and lets you explore the science of harnessing sunlight.

Magnesium Fire Stick

Magnesium fire sticks are a useful tool for starting a fire. These sticks contain magnesium, a metal known to produce sparks easily. Here's how to use one:

① Make a tinder nest: Collect some dry tinder and prepare a tinder nest.

② Get ready: Hold the magnesium fire stick by the handle. Make sure the striking surface is exposed and ready for use.

❸ **Get your magnesium:** Using a knife or the edge of the magnesium fire stick, scrape off some magnesium shavings. Be careful! The magnesium is highly flammable, which means it can catch fire very easily.

❹ **Let it fall:** Hold the magnesium fire stick at a slight angle above the tinder, allowing the magnesium shavings to fall onto the tinder.

❺ **Strike the fire stick:** You can use the built-in striker or another sparking tool. Aim the sparks at the magnesium shavings to ignite them.

❻ **Be patient:** Wait for the magnesium to catch fire. Once it ignites, the tinder will begin to burn.

❼ **Move your tinder:** Carefully transfer the burning tinder to a prepared fire pit. Gradually add larger sticks and logs to build and sustain your fire.

Remember to only use a fire stick under adult supervision, and handle it responsibly.

The Bow-and-Arrow Drill

The bow-and-arrow drill is a time-tested method that generates fire through friction. It's a technique that requires patience and practice, so make sure you have an adult's help when you're learning. Once you get the hang of it, you'll find it's a rewarding way to start a fire.

Here's what you'll need:

- A curved stick (the bow)
- A piece of leather or rope
- A dry, sturdy stick about 12 inches long (the arrow)
- A rock or tree knot to serve as a socket (to hold the top of the arrow)
- A large piece of wood for the base (the fireboard)

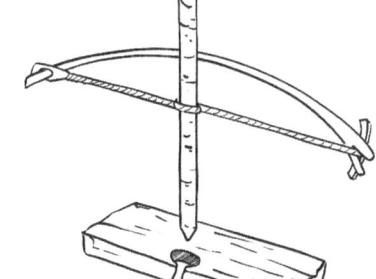

Here's how to do it:

❶ **Make a tinder nest:** Collect some dry tinder and prepare a tinder nest.

❷ **Create friction:** To do this, wrap the rope or leather around the arrow stick.

❸ **Place the arrow stick:** It can go into a small hole or notch in your fireboard. Use the rock or tree knot as a socket to hold the top of the arrow stick steady.

❹ **Hold and push:** Once everything is in place, hold the fireboard down with your foot and push down on the arrow stick with the socket.

❺ **Move the bow:** Start moving the bow back and forth. The arrow stick should rotate rapidly, creating friction against the fireboard.

❻ **Watch and blow:** Watch for glowing embers to form from the heat of the friction. Gently blow on the embers to encourage them to catch fire.

❼ **Move the embers:** Once you have a small flame, carefully transfer it to your tinder nest.

❽ **Build your fire:** Move the burning tinder to your main fire pit and build up your fire with larger sticks and logs.

Battery and Aluminum Foil

A battery from your flashlight and a small piece of aluminum foil can become a handy fire starter. This method is pretty creative and it works, but you do need to be careful and patient.

Here's how it's done:

❶ **Collect some tinder:** Make sure it's dry and arrange it into a nest.

❷ **Get some foil:** Cut a small piece of aluminum foil or a foil wrapper from a chewing gum packet. It should be large enough to hold and conduct heat.

❸ **Put your foil in place:** Carefully touch one end of the foil to the positive end of the battery and the other end to the negative. It will act as a conductor, creating heat as the electrical current passes through it.

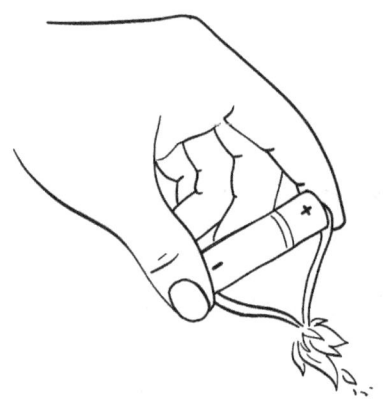

❹ **Wait patiently:** Be patient and wait for the foil to heat up. After a short while, It should eventually ignite.

5 **Move it carefully:** Using one of the tools you've brought with you, carefully move the burning foil to your tinder nest. Make sure it's in the right place to light up the rest of the fire.

6 **Build your fire:** Gradually add larger sticks and logs to build a sustainable fire.

REMEMBER TO ALWAYS BE CAREFUL WHEN MAKING A FIRE

Always remember the fire safety guidelines that we learned about a bit earlier. Starting a fire takes plenty of care. Make sure you have an adult with you, and always keep fire safety equipment like water or a fire extinguisher nearby.

CHAPTER 4

NAVIGATION AND EXPLORATION

The great thing about adventures in the wilderness is that you can escape the hustle and bustle of everyday life. Away from streets, road signs, and noisy machines, you'll find a world waiting to be explored. It's a place where you can swap the buzz of technology for the rustle of leaves and the song of birds. Even if you bring a phone, it might not find any signal—and that's part of the fun.

Taking this break from screens and gadgets is not just refreshing—it's also eye-opening. It reminds you that there's so much out there to see, feel, and explore. It's a chance to reconnect with yourself and nature, to enjoy the calm and the quiet, and to remember what life is like without the constant digital noise.

But here's the best part: Stepping away from technology means stepping into the role of an explorer. You'll learn to navigate the old-fashioned way, without a GPS or an app telling you where to go. This is your chance to learn the skills of adventurers from the past, to find your own way using a map and compass, and to make your own decisions out in the wild. It's all about you, the wilderness, and where you choose to go.

HOW TO USE A MAP AND COMPASS

The easiest way to find your way in the wilderness is with a map and compass. These tools have been helping people find their way for hundreds of years, and they're just as handy today as they ever were.

What Is a Compass?

A compass is a small tool used to find north, so that you can orient yourself and avoid getting lost.

It has a dial that spins around inside its case, and the big letters N, S, E, and W, which stand for north, south, east, and west.

The compass needle always points north, but here's a fun fact: It's not pointing to the true North Pole. It's actually lining up with a spot in the Arctic Ocean that's called magnetic north.

> **DID YOU KNOW?** Magnetic North exists because the Earth has something called a magnetosphere. This is a strong magnetic field that comes from the center of the Earth, where there's molten lava (called magma). This magma is melted or molten iron that creates the magnetic field that comes out at the top and the bottom of the Earth and creates magnetic north.

How to Use a Compass

A compass is made up of these parts:

- **Baseplate:** The flat, clear part with a ruler along its edge.

- **Rotating bezel:** The circular dial with degree markings.
- **Direction-of-travel arrow:** An arrow on the baseplate pointing out north on the compass.
- **Magnetic needle:** The red needle that always points towards magnetic north.

Here's how to use it:

① **Get oriented:** Hold the compass flat in your hand, with the baseplate level. Next, turn yourself and the compass until the magnetic needle aligns with the red arrow in the housing.

② **Find your direction:** Check where the direction-of-travel arrow points on the bezel. The degree markings indicate your compass direction.

③ **Navigate:** If you know the degree of your destination, rotate the bezel until that number aligns with the direction-of-travel arrow.

④ **Follow the arrow:** Head in the direction the arrow points. Keep the needle aligned with the arrow as you travel.

⑤ **Keep checking:** Regularly check your compass to make sure you're still heading in the right direction.

⑥ **Practice:** Practice using your compass in a safe and open area. Try finding your way to different locations.

⑦ **Have fun:** Using a compass is like a real-life treasure hunt! Enjoy the adventure.

Remember, the more you practice, the better you'll become at using a compass. Happy exploring!

- Keep the compass away from metal objects, as they can interfere with its accuracy.
- Stay oriented by paying attention to your surroundings.

How to Read a Map

Being able to read maps is an important skill for any adventurer. Like any skill, it takes practice, but once you get the hang of it, you'll find it incredibly rewarding. Here are some tips to help you get started:

- **Understanding the Symbols**

    Maps are full of symbols representing various features, like roads, lakes, forests, and more. Learn the basic symbols by studying the map key or legend. Once you know what these symbols mean, you can match them to the landmarks you find on your adventures.

    For example, lines of different thickness indicate different types of road or path.

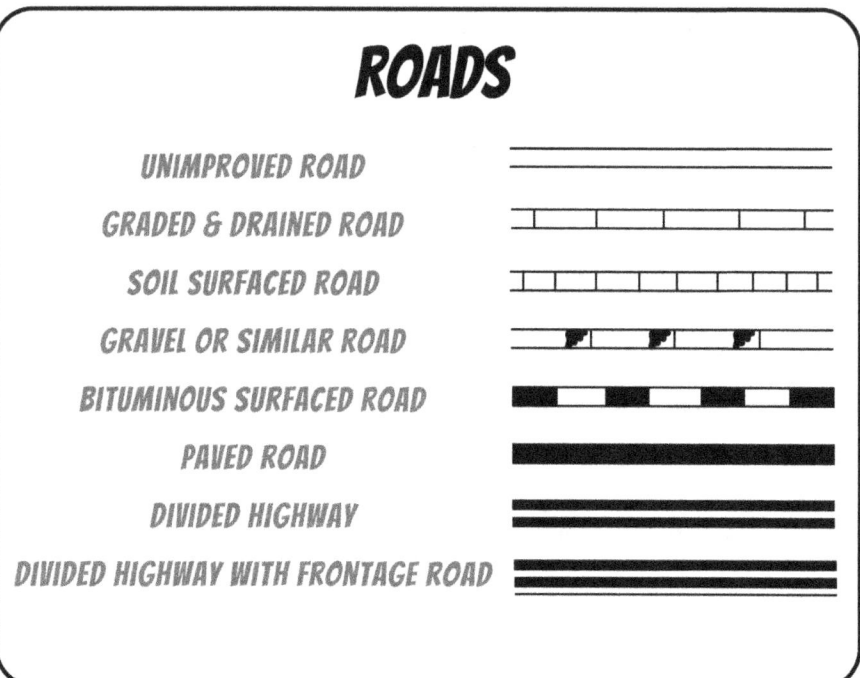

- **Map Scale Matters**

    Pay attention to the scale of the map to understand the actual distance between locations. Understanding the scale helps you estimate how far you'll be traveling and plan your time.

- **Use the Grid Lines:**

    Maps use a grid system of horizontal latitude and vertical longitude lines. A coordinate is where the line of latitude and the line of longitude connects. The point where these lines intersect gives you coordinates, which is a precise address on the map. If the grid seems confusing, refer to the legend—it will guide you on the scale and units used in the grid.

- **Finding Landmarks:**
Look for important landmarks on the map and match them up with the ones in your surroundings to help you find your way.

- **Plan a Route:**
Practice planning routes on the map. This can be a fun way to learn how to get from one point to another. You can start with maps of places you know well.

- **Orientation Is Key:**
Always check the map's orientation by matching your map up with a compass. Let's learn how this is done.

Orienteering

Orienteering is the skill of reading a map together with using a compass. It's something you should learn to do if you're planning an adventure, whether you're hiking, exploring, or traveling from your campsite. Orienteering allows you to figure out how to get somewhere, as well as how to get back.

It starts with your map. Remember, the top of the map is always pointing north, even if you don't see any markings on it.

Here's how you can begin orienteering:

1. **Align your map and compass:** Place your compass flat on the map. Turn the map and compass together until the north arrow on your compass lines up with the north arrow on your map. Most maps have a compass symbol or an "N" marking to show you where north is.

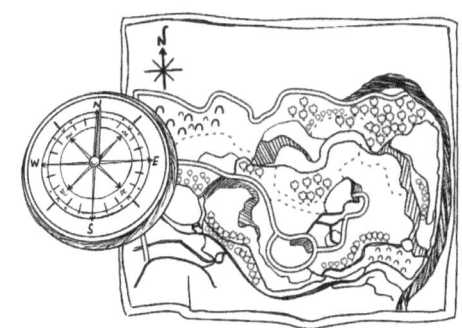

2. **Determine your location and destination:** Identify where you are on the map, and where you want to reach.

For instance, let's say you are at Little Goose Campground, and you want to hike to Bird Mountain:

1. **Draw an imaginary line:** It needs to go from your current location to your destination.

2. **Observe the compass direction of this line:** For example, if Bird Mountain is to the west of your campground, your line should point towards the west on your compass.

ADVENTURE SKILLS FOR KIDS   279

3 Check your compass: As you start your hike towards Bird Mountain, keep checking your compass to ensure you're maintaining your westward direction.

4 Go in the opposite direction: When it's time to go back, simply do the same route, but backwards. If you hiked west to reach Bird Mountain, you'll hike east to return to Little Goose Campground.

FINDING YOUR WAY WITHOUT A COMPASS

Even without a compass, you can find your way in the wilderness by working out which way faces north, south, east, and west.

One way of doing this is by using the stars to help you find north.

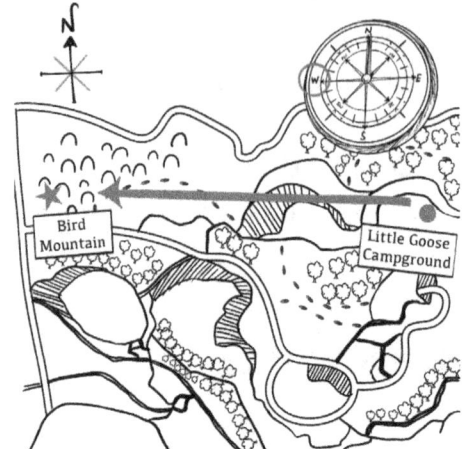

The red line is the direction you'll have to go to get to Bird Mountain

The North Star

The North Star, also known as Polaris, is a star in the sky that is almost always right above the North Pole, which makes it a helpful way of finding where north is.

Here's how to find the North Star.

1 Find the Big Dipper: The Big Dipper is one of the collections of stars that we call a constellation. It looks like a small pot, which was once known as a dipper.

2 Draw an imaginary line: After you find the Big Dipper, draw an imaginary line through the two stars at the end of the dipper.

3 Find the Little Dipper: This imaginary line points directly to the North Star, which is also the last star in the handle of the Little Dipper constellation.

Remember, you can only find the North Star at night, so you may need a way to remember which way was north in the morning.

Marking North at Night

- **Create a directional arrow:** Use branches or stones to create an arrow on the ground pointing towards the North Star. In the morning, you'll see your arrow and know that it's pointing north.

Once you know where north is, the other directions are easy to figure out:

- **South:** Directly opposite to north.
- **West:** To the left of north when facing the North Star.
- **East:** Opposite to west, or to the right of north when facing the North Star.

Well done! You've figured out where north, south, east, and west are without a compass!

Make Your Own Compass

Another way to find out where north, south, east, and west are if you don't have a compass is simply to make your own!

All you need is:

- A needle
- A dry leaf
- Water
- A small container (like a cup or bowl)

Here's how to create your own compass:

1. **Magnetize the needle:** Rub the needle through your hair as many times as possible—aim for about a hundred times. This friction actually magnetizes the needle, giving it a temporary north-south orientation.

ADVENTURE SKILLS FOR KIDS **281**

② **Prepare the water:** Fill the container with water and place a dry leaf on it, making sure it floats.

③ **Drop the needle on the leaf:** Carefully place the magnetized needle on the leaf. Watch as the needle slowly turns and stops. The needle is pointing north. But how do you know which end is north? Here's how:

④ **Determine north:** Look at your shadow. The sun always travels across the south side of the sky, so your shadow is pointing north. Now look at your leaf and figure out which end of the needle is pointing in the direction of your shadow.

That's north!

After finding north, if you imagine a criss-cross on the needle, you can figure out south, west, and east!

Using the Sunrise or the Sunset to Find Your Direction

One of the easiest ways to find your direction without a compass is simply by watching the sunrise or sunset.

- **Sunrise:** The sun always rises in the east. So, during sunrise, face the sun. East is in front of you, west is behind you, north is to your left, and south is to your right.

- **Sunset:** At sunset, the sun sets in the west. Face the setting sun. West is in front of you, east is behind you, south is to your left, and north is to your right.

It might seem like a lot to remember, but with a bit of practice and discussion with your fellow adventurers around the campfire, these methods will soon become second nature.

HOW TO TELL THE TIME WITHOUT A CLOCK

Just because you don't have a watch doesn't mean you won't be able to tell when the sun is going to go down. When you're camping, you'll often want to know when it's going to get dark. Luckily, there's an easy way to gauge the time until sunset:

① **Hand horizon measure:** Reach one arm out fully, keeping your fingers close together and flat.

② Align with the sun: Line up the bottom of your hand with the horizon, and measure the gap between the horizon and the sun using your fingers.

③ Calculate time: Each finger width is about the same as 15 minutes. So, if you can fit four fingers between the sun and the horizon, you have about an hour until sunset. Add or subtract 15 minutes for each finger above or below four.

④ Factor in twilight: After the sun dips below the horizon, there's normally about half an hour of light, called twilight. This means that if you measure six fingers from the sun to the horizon, you have about two hours before it's fully dark (six fingers x 15 minutes, plus 30 minutes of twilight).

This method doesn't tell you exactly what time it is, but it does tell you how much daylight you have left, helping you plan your activities and ensure you're ready for nightfall.

HOW TO PREDICT THE WEATHER BY READING THE SKIES

> **DID YOU KNOW?** Long before weather forecasts on TV or mobile apps, people used nature's cues to try and guess what weather would be coming. In ancient times, some people were able to read signs in nature to predict whether it was going to be sunny, rainy, or cloudy.
>
> They did this by taking a good look at the clouds in the sky, or by looking at smoke from a fire, how things smelled during the day, and how insects and animals behaved.

What they were figuring out was the difference between something called low and high barometric pressure.

High pressure usually brings nice weather, while low pressure often signals clouds and rain. If it helps you remember, you can remind yourself that the L in low pressure stands for *lousy*. The way the air pressure affects things in nature can tell you when the weather will be good or bad. Here are some signs to watch for:

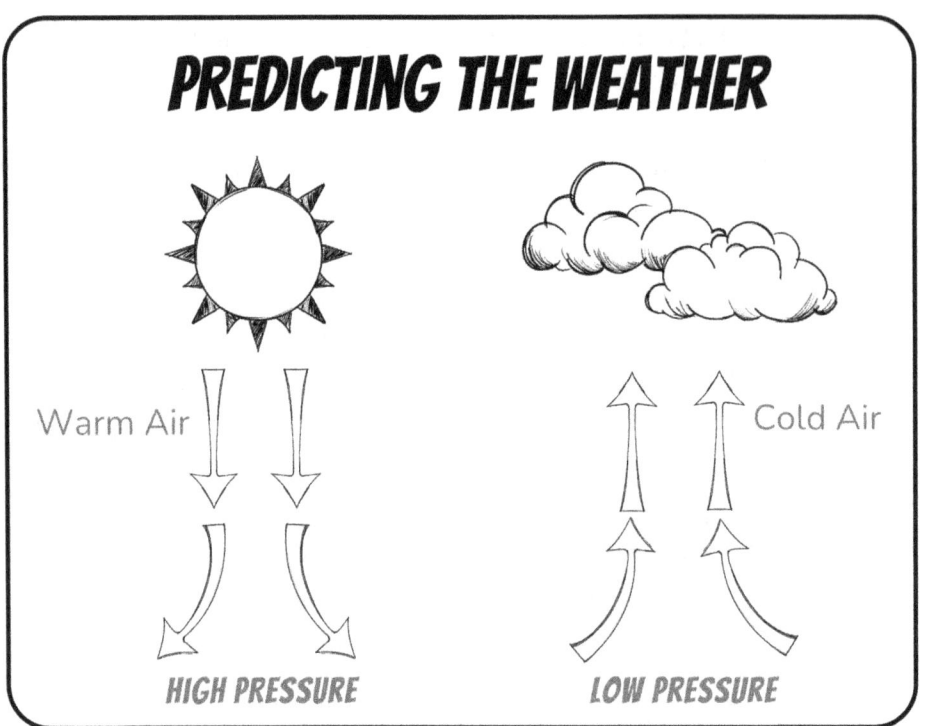

- **Campfire smoke:**
  Smoke that stays close to the ground means low pressure, so rain and cooler temperatures may be on the way.

  There's an old saying to help you remember this:

  "Campfire smoke descends, our nice weather ends."

- **Stronger smells near water:**
  Low pressure can make smells stronger, particularly around watery areas like ponds and swamps.

  There's another old saying which goes:

  "When ditch and pond offend the nose, look for rain and stormy blows."

- **Tall, puffy clouds:**
  Towering clouds, often called "thunderheads," may mean that a storm is approaching. These clouds can bring rain, thunder, and lightning.

  Another rhyme to remember:

  "When clouds appear like rocks and towers, the earth's refreshed by frequent showers."

- **Pillowy clouds:**
  Clouds that resemble hanging pillows can mean that dangerous weather is coming, like heavy rain, hail, or even tornadoes. If you see clouds like these, you want to make sure everything is picked up in camp and put in your tent. You might even want to pack up and go home.

  This one doesn't have a rhyme. Why not make up your own?

- **Halos around the sun or moon:**
  A halo around the sun or moon tells you that you're going to get high moisture and low pressure, which often means a storm is coming.

  Here's another old rhyme:

  "A ring around the sun or moon, means rain or snow coming soon."

- **Red sky:**
  The color of the sky at sunrise or sunset can also hint at weather changes.

  As the saying goes:

  "Red sky at night, sailor's delight; red sky in morning, sailors take warning."

It's fun to learn to read the sky, and you don't have to be camping or exploring to do it. Pay close attention to the sky when you walk to school or play in your backyard or at the park.

If you do this all the time, you'll soon become an expert at predicting the weather just by looking up.

CHAPTER 5

WILDERNESS SURVIVAL

Adventures in the great outdoors are great fun, but it's important to be prepared for unexpected situations, like getting lost. Whether you're drawn off the trail by something interesting or you simply lose your bearings, staying calm and knowing what to do is key.

Getting lost can make you feel worried, but with the right knowledge and equipment, you can find your way back. If you do get lost, try to relax and take a deep breath, because panicking never helps. The less you worry about it, the sooner you'll find your way back on track.

WHAT TO DO IF YOU GET LOST

Here's a step-by-step guide on what to do if you ever find yourself lost in the wilderness:

1) Stop
As soon as you realize you might be lost, stop moving.

2) Sit
Take a moment to catch your breath, so you can become less nervous, and gather your thoughts.

3) Look
Look at your surroundings carefully. Try to remember the direction you came from, and any landmarks you saw or turns you made. Don't rush to move just yet.

4) Make a plan
Based on what you see, decide which direction might lead you back. Walk about two hundred steps in that direction, then pause to look for anything you remember seeing before. If nothing seems right, go back to your original spot and try again.

5) Remember your starting point
Always try to remember the place where you first realized you were lost. That way, you can always return to a point you know if you aren't managing to get back on track.

6) Watch the time
Keep an eye on the time, especially as the day goes on. If it's one hour before sunset you might want to collect firewood for a fire and think about finding or making a shelter for the night.

7) Stay put at night
Finding your way in the dark can be very dangerous. If it's getting dark and you're still lost, chances are someone will start searching for you. In this case, it's safest to stay where you are until morning.

Of course, it's best not to get lost in the first place. That's why it's so important to keep checking your map and compass while you're hiking or exploring. And unless you're a seasoned explorer, always plan your adventures during daylight hours, and aim to be safely back at camp at least an hour before sunset.

No matter how hard you try, sometimes things won't go as planned. That's where having a survival kit comes in handy.

MAKING A SURVIVAL KIT

A survival kit has a few basic items you might need to help you spend an unplanned night in the wilderness. It has to be a small kit, so it's easy to carry, but also needs to have some really important things to get you through the night, or to signal to someone who might be looking for you. Here's what your need:

- **A case:** Pick something small but sturdy, like an empty Altoid tin, a fabric bag with a zipper, or a plastic box with a lid.

- **Matches and a lighter.** Pack both in case the matches get wet or the lighter doesn't work. Not only does a fire keep you warm, but the light at night and smoke in the day can also signal to anyone searching for you.

- **A small flashlight:** Conserve your batteries by using it sparingly. It's also handy for signaling.

- **A whistle:** This can help you get attention if you're lost or need help. In chapter 9, we're going to learn about how to send an emergency message called an SOS using a whistle.

- **A space blanket (tarp):** These are very thin, metallic blankets made out of a material called Mylar. They reflect heat to keep you warm, are waterproof, and can be used to make a lean-to.

- **A small knife:** This is an important tool for any adventurer.

- **Strong string:** To tie up your shelter, or for any other creative solutions you might need.

- **Water treatment tablets and resealable bags:** Safe drinking water is crucial. These tablets, along with bags for collecting and treating water, are a must.

- **Bandages and antiseptic wipes**: Clean and cover any cuts to prevent infection.

- **A small compass:** Even without a map, a compass can help you navigate your way back.

- **Fishing hooks and line**: Attach your fishing line to a stick, find some worms under a rock, and you might just catch your dinner!

Putting a survival kit together is a fun challenge, but it's important to remember it's more than just a collection of items—it could be your lifeline. That's why it's also a good idea to make sure everyone in your family or group has one before venturing out.

HOW TO FIND WATER IN THE WILDERNESS

If you're out in the wilderness and you get lost, knowing how to find and purify water becomes essential. While a canteen or water bottle is a must, what do you do if you run out of water?

Finding more water and ensuring it's safe to drink is a skill every adventurer should master. That's why we have included water treatment tablets in our survival kit essentials. But before you reach for those tablets, you need to find a water source, which can be a challenge on its own. Remember, turning water from the wild into something safe to drink takes both patience and practice.

Let's start by figuring out where the water might be, and then we'll look at all the different ways to purify it.

Drinking Water from a Natural Source

Heading out into the great outdoors means relying on what nature provides, including water sources. However, before you take a sip from a stream or lake, you need to make sure drinking this water is safe. Here are a few tips to help you find out if natural water is safe to drink.

- **Look around:** Check the area around the water. Look for signs of pollution, like objects or dead animals and insects floating in the water.

- **Smell and color:** Good water should be clear and free of any bad smells. If it's brown or stinky, it probably isn't safe.

- **Animals and plants:** Animals and plants around the water can be a good sign, because it means the animals have been drinking the water and the plants nearby are able to grow. But be careful—even clear water can have invisible bugs and bacteria in it, and will need to be purified.

- **Choose flowing water:** Whenever possible, choose flowing water sources like streams or rivers over stagnant water from ponds or lakes. Flowing water is less likely to harbor harmful bacteria and parasites compared to stagnant water, which can be a breeding ground for these organisms.

- **Ask locals or fellow adventurers:** Speak with any local people who are around, or other adventurers you meet. They might be able to tell you if the water is safe to drink.

- **Follow the rules:** Check if there are any rules about water safety. Some areas have strict rules to make sure the water is okay.

Remember, it's important to be careful with water from nature because even if it looks clean, there might be things you can't see that could make you sick. Unless you have been told otherwise by an adult, you should always purify and filter natural water before you drink it.

Now let's look at where you might be able to find drinkable water in the wilderness:

Springs and Creeks

Imagine a small trickle of water popping up from the ground or the side of a hill—that's a spring! Spring water is usually crystal clear, but remember that all water in the wild needs purifying before it's safe to drink.

Now, picture a larger flow of water—that's a creek, formed by several springs coming together. Creeks are great for water collection, as they're usually cleaner than other sources. Even so, the golden rule is to always purify the water before drinking, no matter how clean it seems.

Ponds and Lakes

Collecting water from a pond or lake can be a good option, but it's important to do so safely and effectively. When using your canteen or bottle, try to collect water from deeper areas, away from the shore, where water is often cleaner. However, be careful and avoid wading into deep or murky water where there could be hidden hazards.

Collecting Water from the Deep

1. **Preparation**: Before you start, make sure your water bottle or canteen is empty and the cap is tightly secured.

2. **Reach deep**: Carefully extend your arms, holding the canteen or bottle as deep into the water as possible, ideally up to your shoulders.

3. **Filling up**: Gently open the cap underwater. You'll notice bubbles as the bottle fills up.

4. **Tips for Sealing**: Once the bubbling stops, indicating a full bottle, quickly screw the cap back on to avoid capturing any surface debris.

5. **Retrieving**: Carefully lift the now filled canteen or bottle out of the water.

You now have a canteen full of water, without anything that might have been floating on the surface.

Remember, water in ponds and lakes is often stagnant, which means it can harbor bacteria and algae, especially during warmer weather. It's better to find flowing water. And no matter what, always filter and purify this water before drinking.

Rivers

Rivers can be another good water source, but you have to look out for pollution. Rivers often carry pollutants from farming, animals, or urban areas that enter the water. If you spot a creek or a spring flowing into the river, that might be a better place to collect your water.

If a river is your only option, aim to collect water from the deepest point you can safely reach, which is often a bit away from the shoreline. But be careful with rivers. If there's a strong current or deep water, it's best to collect your water from the shoreline. And, of course, it's essential to purify all collected water.

Rain

Rainwater is one of the purest natural water sources, and can easily be collected using a space blanket, poncho, or even by wringing out your wet clothes.

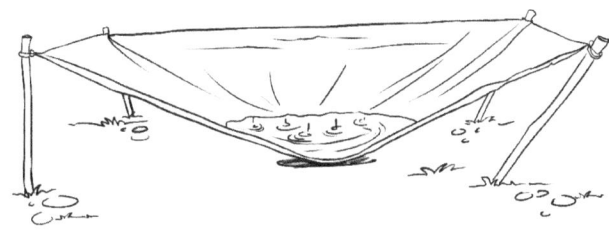

To collect rain, tie a space blanket or poncho to trees and use a small rock to weigh it down in the center. Once the rain has collected, dip your bottle into the water to collect it.

While rainwater is relatively pure, it can pick up dirt from leaves and pollutants from the air, especially in towns and cities, so purifying it is still a good idea.

Snow and Ice

If it's winter and there's snow on the ground, you have a ready-made water source right at your feet. Both snow and ice can easily be melted and transformed into drinkable water with a little effort.

Here's how to melt snow or ice:

- **Using a metal canteen:** If you have a metal canteen, fill it with snow or ice. Then, place it near a fire, but not so close that it could melt the canteen itself. The heat will slowly turn the snow or ice into water.

- **Using a plastic bag:** If you have a plastic bag, you can fill it with snow or ice. Seal the bag tightly and place it inside your coat pocket. Your body heat will slowly melt the contents. It takes a bit longer, but if there's no fire around, it works.

Once you've melted the snow or ice, purify it by adding a water treatment tablet. While freshly fallen snow is generally clean, it's always safer to purify it.

FILTERING AND PURIFYING WATER

When you're out in the wilderness, finding water is only half the battle. The next steps—filtering and purifying—are crucial to ensure the water is safe to drink. Even the clearest stream can harbor unseen germs or bacteria. Here's how you can turn wild water into drinking water.

Filtering Wild Water

The first step is to filter your water. This is to remove any of the visible debris that can be found in natural water sources, like leaves, twigs, bugs, and anything else that might fall into the water.

If you don't have a water filter, you can make your own simple funnel filter.

Here's what you need:

- A cloth (like a t-shirt or towel) to collect the debris.
- A stick shaped like a Y to hold the fabric.

Here's how it's done:

❶ **Tie the cloth:** Attach the cloth to the two ends of the Y-shaped stick, creating a funnel.

❷ **Position the filter:** Hold the filter over a container.

❸ **Pour the water:** Gently pour the collected water through the cloth into the container.

❹ **Repeat:** If necessary, pour the water through the filter again for extra clarity.

Making a Plastic Bottle Water Filter

If you have a plastic bottle you can make a really effective water filter.

Here's what you'll need:

- A plastic water bottle
- A piece of fabric cut from a t-shirt or other piece of clothing
- Charcoal from your fire
- Some sand and gravel

Here's how it's done:

1. **Prepare the bottle:** With the help or supervision of an adult, carefully cut the bottom of the water bottle and cover the open end with fabric.

2. **Add charcoal:** Collect some small pieces of cold charcoal from your fire, and fill one third of the bottle.

3. **Add sand:** Add sand over the charcoal to fill another third.

4. **Add gravel:** Top the sand with some gravel.

5. **Filter:** Pour the water into the top. It will filter through the layers of charcoal, sand, and gravel and come out clearer at the bottom, free of the visible debris. However, it's still not ready to drink.

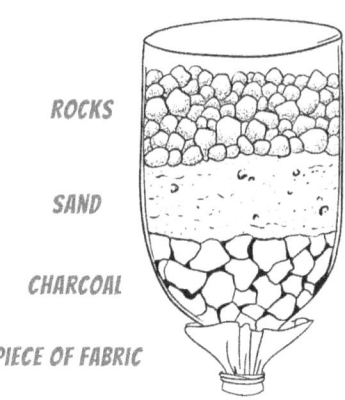

Purifying the Water

After filtering your water, the next crucial step is purification. This process is essential to remove any bacteria or microorganisms that might be invisible to the eye but harmful if consumed.

There are two effective methods to purify water in the wilderness to make it safe to drink.

- **Boiling**: Boil the filtered water for at least three minutes. This process and the boiling time is sufficient to kill most germs or bacteria. Once boiled, let the water cool down before you drink it or pour it into your water bottle.

- **Water treatment tablets**: These are a practical option when boiling isn't possible. To use, follow the package instructions carefully. The effectiveness of these tablets depends on using the correct amount for the volume of water and allowing enough time for the tablets to act. Typically, it takes about 30 minutes for the tablets to purify the water effectively, though this duration can vary depending on the type and brand of tablet.

Regardless of the method you choose, ensuring that your water is safe to drink is a vital aspect of wilderness preparedness. Never underestimate the importance of clean, purified water during your outdoor adventures.

CHAPTER 6

INTERACTING WITH NATURE

Exploring the wilderness is a chance to get away from the hustle and bustle of everyday life and surround yourself in nature—something we don't always get to experience in our everyday lives. It's also an opportunity to have new experiences and discover the beauty of the natural world, including trees, plants, and animals.

The plants and animals you see will depend on where you live and where you explore. But no matter where your adventures take you, it's fun to take some time to learn more about nature and take in everything around you.

Your Adventure Journal: Remember, your adventure journal is perfect for jotting down your thoughts about what you see, sketching the plants and animals you discover, or sharing your thoughts about nature.

LEARNING ABOUT TREES

Learning to identify trees can be a fun part of your adventure. Let's explore some common types you might come across.

Maple Trees

Maple leaves have a special five-point shape that is easy to recognize. In the fall, these leaves turn beautiful colors like orange, red, and yellow. In winter, it's harder to tell trees apart because the leaves are gone, but you can still identify a tree by looking at its bark.

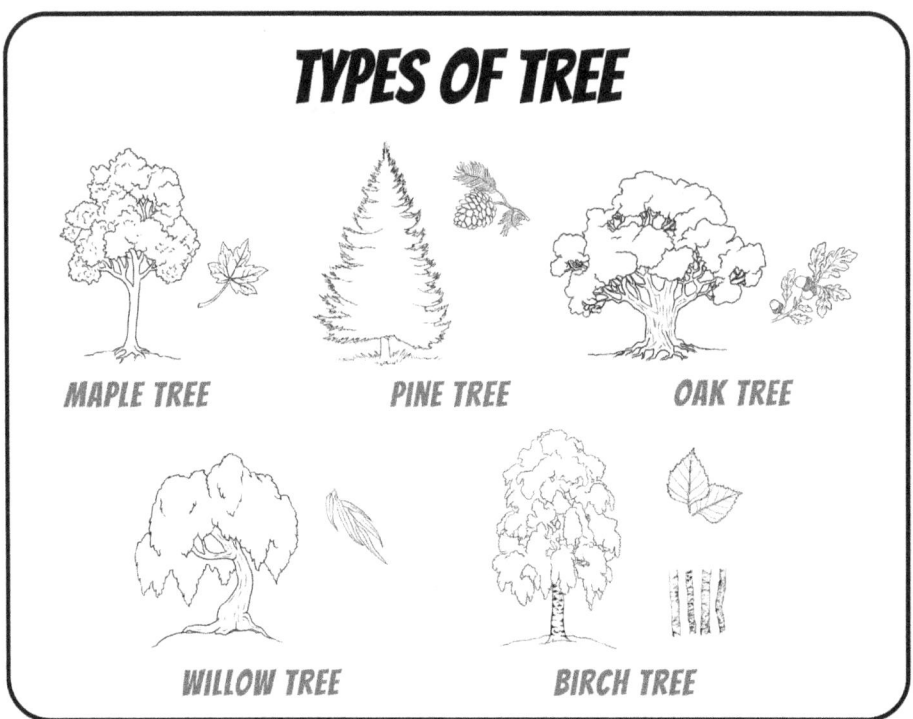

Young maple trees have smooth bark. As they get older, the bark develops grooves up and down the trunk. Maple trees also have special seeds that look like propellers. When these seeds fall, they spin in the air like a top because of the wind. You can have fun tossing one in the air and watching it spin!

Pine Trees

Pine trees are green all year round, which is why they're part of the group of trees called evergreens. Their needles come in different sizes, and seeds grow on them called pine cones, which are great for starting campfires.

Pine cones can also be used in some crafts you can make, which we'll learn more about in a later chapter.

Oak Trees

Oak trees are among the largest in the woods. Their leaves are special because they have round parts called lobes. In certain species, like the black oak, the leaves don't fall off in winter, but instead turn brown and stay on the tree. Acorns are the seeds of oak trees. They have a unique cap on top that you might recognize.

Willow Trees

Willow trees are known for their long, drooping branches, which is why they're sometimes called "weeping willows."

Both their leaves and their branches are long and thin. The bark of willow trees has an unusual texture, with long, angled grooves in it.

Birch Trees

Birch trees stand out with their bright white, peeling bark, which is excellent for starting fires and even crafting torches (we'll get to that in chapter 10).

Birch leaves have saw-tooth edges and straight-line veins. Look out for their soft, hanging seed pods in late summer and early fall.

Telling the Age of a Tree from its Rings

If you ever come across a tree stump that has been cut down, you'll see that the top of it has rings. Each of these rings represents one year of the tree's life. By counting them, you can work out the tree's age at the time it was cut down.

Try counting the rings of this tree and see if you can figure out how old it was when it was felled.

> **DID YOU KNOW?** The oldest tree we know about had over 5,000 rings! That means it was five thousand years old—dating back to the time of the ancient Egyptians.

OBSERVING WILDLIFE

When you're out in nature, there's a good chance you'll come across some of the creatures that live there. Sometimes you'll see them at a distance, and other times they'll wander close to your camp.

However, seeing animals isn't the only way to enjoy wildlife. You can also look for animal tracks. Each species leaves behind its own set of prints. Recognizing these footprints can be an exciting and useful skill, helping you identify the animals sharing the wilderness with you.

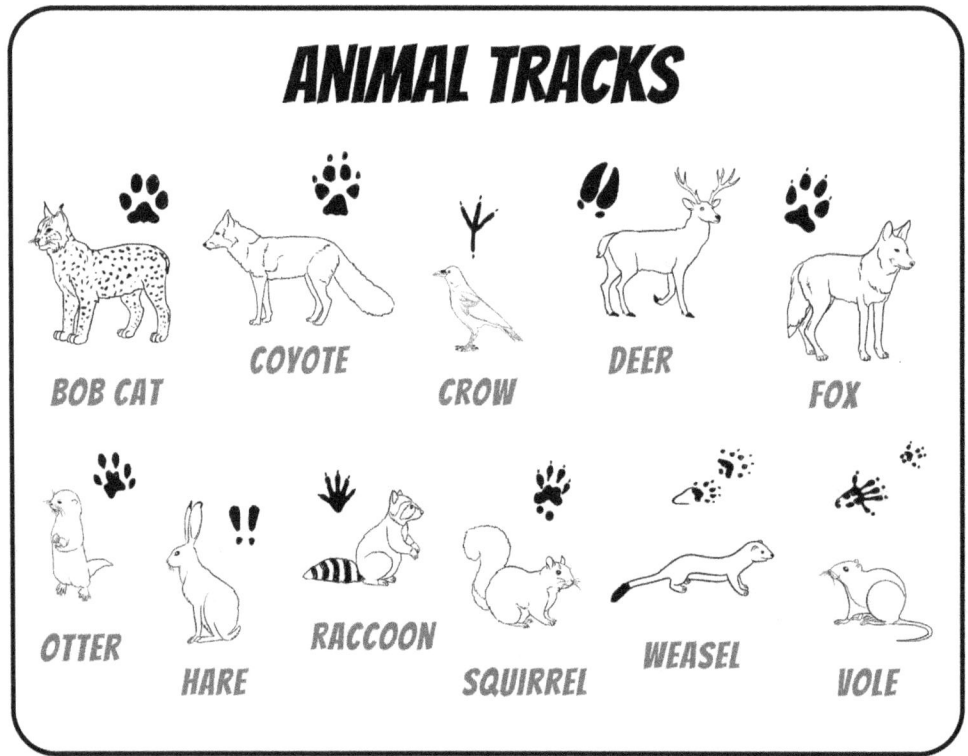

When you spot animal tracks, try to take a photo or sketch them in your adventure journal. This is a great way to remember your adventure and keep a record of the wildlife in the area.

PROTECTING YOUR CAMPSITE FROM WILDLIFE

In the wilderness, encountering wildlife is part of the adventure. However, it's important to take precautions to keep both you and the animals safe, especially around your campsite.

Safeguarding Food and Garbage

- **Hang food high**: Use a rope to hang your food from a high tree branch. This prevents animals, like raccoons or foxes, from accessing it.

- **Securing your garbage:** After meals, dispose of leftovers in a sealed plastic bag. Hang this bag high in a tree, especially if there aren't any trash facilities nearby.

- **No food in the tent:** Never keep food inside your tent, especially at night. The scent can attract animals, which could lead to unwanted visitors!

By following these steps, you can help make sure that wild animals are less likely to come near your campsite, scavenging for food.

Respecting Wildlife

When you are away from your campsite on an adventure, there may be times when you'll come face to face with a wild animal. This can be an exciting encounter, but you do have to be careful.

Here are some things to remember:

- **Do not approach:** Keep a safe distance from wild animals. Sudden movements or getting too close can startle them, potentially leading to a defensive reaction.

- **Beware of rabies:** Rabies is a very dangerous disease. If a wild animal bites you, you'll have to get a rabies shot from the doctor. There is no definite way to know if an animal has rabies or not just from looking at it, but animals with rabies often exhibit strange behaviors, such as aggression or overt friendliness. It's best not to go too close to wild animals, just in case.

- **No feeding:** Feeding a wild animal may seem kind, but it can make animals overly reliant on humans and lead to future problems.

- **Stay together:** If you encounter a wild animal, stay with your group. There's safety in numbers, and most animals will avoid a group.

Encountering Potentially Dangerous Animals

It's rare that you'll come across dangerous animals like wolves, bears, or snakes in the wilderness, but it can happen. If you do:

- **Stay calm and walk away**: If you spot a potentially dangerous animal, calmly and slowly walk in the opposite direction. Running might trigger a chase.

- **Give them space**: Many large animals will naturally avoid human interaction. If you see one, give it plenty of room and do not attempt to get closer.

- **Be aware of their behavior**: Animals often show signs of agitation or discomfort. If you notice these signs, increase your distance from the animal immediately.

In most cases, even large animals that could be dangerous will move away from you when they see you. It's usually only when they feel threatened or are protecting their young that they will attack humans. If you see a large wild animal on your adventure, you should move away and avoid it. Here are some large animals you should avoid in the wild.

Wolves

Wolves look like very large dogs, and often roam in packs or alone. It's better if you spot them before they see you, and steer clear. Usually, wolves avoid people, but if you see one that doesn't run away, stay still. Raising your arms and shouting can sometimes scare them off. If that doesn't work, back away slowly, keeping an eye on them. Remember, the key is to avoid sudden movements or running, as this could trigger a chase.

Snakes

Snakes are another animal that will usually shy away from humans, but it's important to be careful. Most snakes are not poisonous, but all snakes can bite and potentially cause infections or carry diseases, so it's always best to try to avoid them.

If a snake coils up, that means it's feeling threatened and might strike. The best thing to do is to slowly back away, giving it space. If you aren't sure if a snake is poisonous or not, you can sometimes tell by the shape of its head.

Safe snakes usually have slim heads, but some, like the coral snake, can be venomous even with a slender head. Venomous snakes usually have wider heads with bulges.

If someone gets bitten by a snake and you're not sure if it's safe or not, get help from a grown-up or call for medical help right away.

Bears

If you're hiking in a place with bears, it means you're in a wild and natural area. There are different kinds of bears, but the most common are black bears and brown bears.

Bears usually stay away from people, but sometimes you might surprise one. If that happens, it's important to stay calm and not run, because running might make the bear chase you.

If the bear is alone and you're with others, make a lot of noise and raise your hands to look big. Don't go near the bear. If it doesn't leave, back away slowly.

If the bear has babies, be extra careful. Don't make loud noises or sudden movements. Back away slowly, keeping an eye on the bear. Mama bears are protective, and they might think you're a threat to their babies if you get too close or make loud sounds.

Other Wildlife

When you're in the wild, you'll see many different animals, and most of them are safe. Birds are one example, and they're everywhere. You can take cool pictures of them to remember your adventure and add them to your adventure journal.

When you're out exploring nature, meeting dangerous animals is uncommon, but it's smart to be prepared. When you get to a new place, talk to local rangers or people who live there. They can tell you about the animals in the area and give you safety tips.

And don't forget, when you're in the wild, you're like a guest in the animals' homes and nature's beauty. It's important to keep this beauty for others, and to take care of the environment. That's why low-impact camping is so important.

LOW-IMPACT CAMPING: LEAVING NO TRACE

Whenever you make a campsite, the time will eventually come to break camp and go home. The way you leave your campsite is very important. Here are some key things to ensure you're camping with minimal impact:

- **Garbage cleanup:** Pack up all your trash. Leaving food or garbage behind can attract wildlife, altering their natural behavior and potentially creating issues for future campers. Dispose of your waste in designated bins or take it home with you.

- **Make sure your fire is out:** Ensure your campfire is fully extinguished. Douse it with water, stir the ashes, and then douse it again. Many wildfires are caused by unattended or improperly extinguished campfires.

- **Leave no trace:** Strive to leave your campsite as you found it, or even better. While this is more challenging in established campgrounds, minimizing your impact is still important. The goal is for others to hardly notice that you were there.

Always remember, it's your job to take care of the natural places you visit, for the sake of the animals and plants that live there, as well as any adventurers who come after you.

CHAPTER 7

CREATIVE ADVENTURE PROJECTS FOR YOUR JOURNAL

Engaging in creative activities like drawing and photography is a wonderful way to connect with nature. Whether you're sketching the intricate details of a leaf, capturing the wonders of a landscape, or using charcoal from your campfire, these artistic pursuits enhance your appreciation of the outdoors. Here's a simple guide to help you get started on your creative journey, focusing on easily accessible subjects like trees, leaves, and flowers.

HOW TO DRAW A TREE

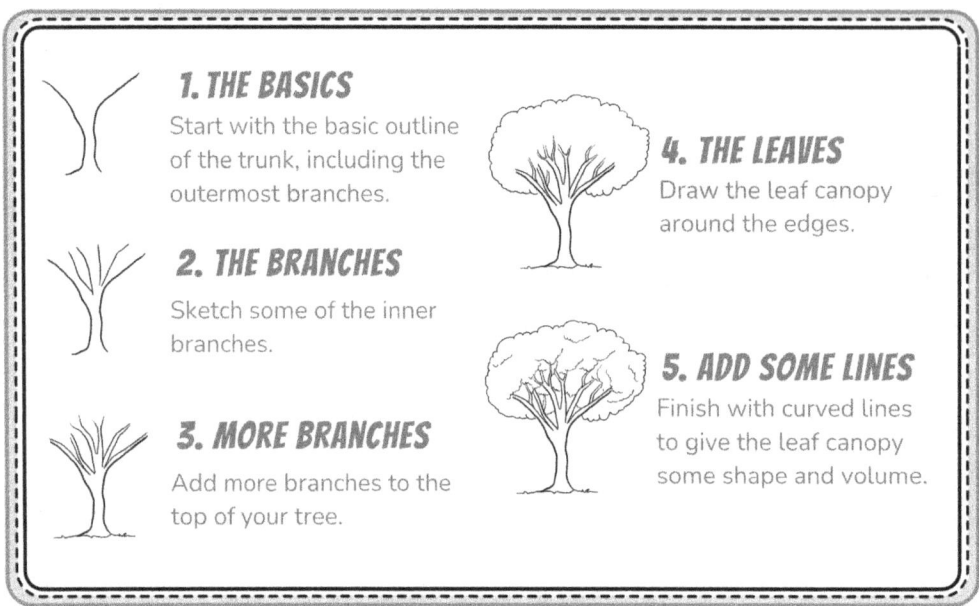

1. **The basics:** Start with the basic outline of the trunk, including the outermost branches.

2. **The branches:** Sketch some of the inner branches.

3. **More branches:** Add more branches to the top of your tree.

4. **The leaves:** Draw the leaf canopy around the edges.

5. **Add some lines:** Finish with curved lines to give the leaf canopy some shape and volume.

HOW TO DRAW A LEAF

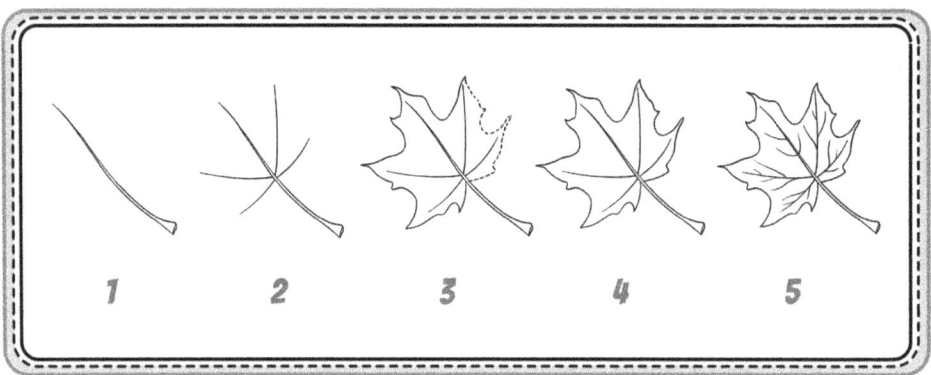

Leaves come in different shapes and sizes, but they have a lot of things in common. Most leaves have a stem, central veins, and side veins. Their shapes can vary from pointy to rounded. Start by drawing the stem and the main vein, then add the side veins. Next sketch, the overall shape, then finally add in more side veins.

HOW TO DRAW ROCKS

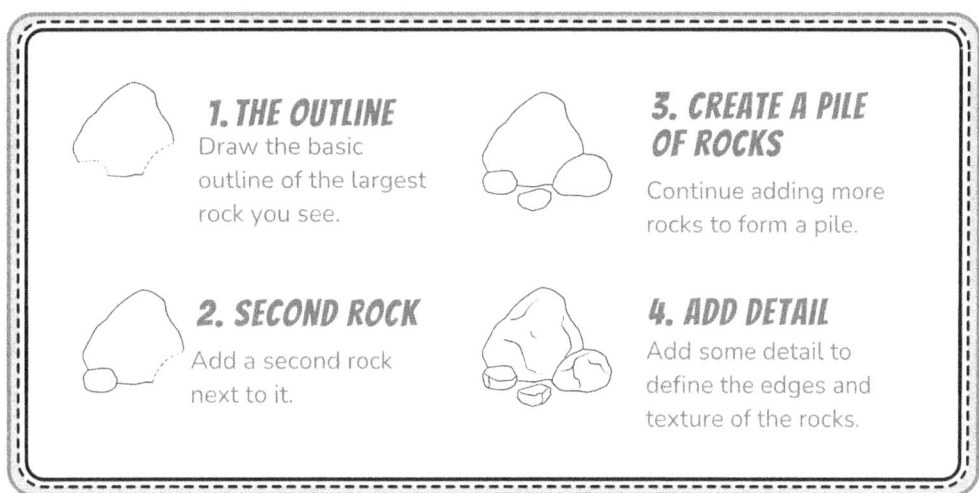

Rocks also come in different shapes and sizes, and some of them have different textures and colors.

1. **The outline:** Draw the basic outline of the largest rock you see.

2. **Second rock:** Add a second rock next to it.

3. **Create a pile of rocks:** Continue adding more rocks to form a pile.

4. **Add detail:** Add some detail to define the edges and texture of the rocks.

HOW TO DRAW FLOWERS

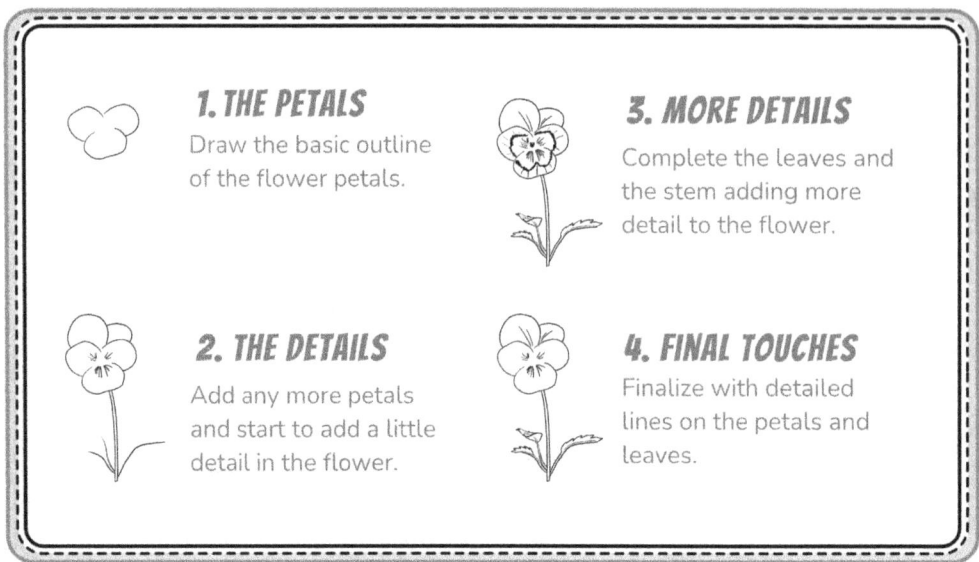

You'll see plenty of flowers on most adventures, and they're easy to draw if you take it step by step.

❶ **The petals:** Draw the basic outline of the flower petals.

❷ **The details:** Add more petals, and start to add a little detail in the flower.

❸ **More details:** Complete the leaves and the stem, adding more detail to the flower.

❹ **Final touches:** Finalize with detailed lines on the petals and leaves.

Drawing what you see is a great way to add memories to your adventure journal, or to simply learn more about the leaves, trees, and rocks you find. Try to identify each one. After you draw it, you'll remember its name and what it looks like forever.

As time goes on, your journal will have more and more information from the observations and drawings you made when you explored the wilderness, or even the wonders of nature in your own backyard.

PRESSING FLOWERS AND LEAVES

Another way to record the flowers and leaves you find is to press them between the pages of your adventure journal. This simple but fun activity preserves the natural beauty and adds a colorful personal touch to your journal.

Here's what you need:

- Fresh flowers or leaves
- Heavy books or a flower press
- Absorbent paper
- Parchment paper
- Your adventure journal or craft paper (optional)
- Spray adhesive (optional, for fixing in your journal)

Here's what to do:

- **Selection:** Choose fresh, vibrant flowers or leaves.
- **Preparation:** Lay the absorbent paper on a flat surface.
- **Placement:** Carefully place your flower or leaf on the absorbent paper.
- **Press down:** Cover it with parchment paper, then use a heavy book or a flower press over it to press it down.
- **Let it dry:** Let it sit under the weight for about one to three weeks, until it is dry and papery.
- **Check and remove:** Once your pressed flower or leaf is dry, gently remove it from the paper. If you wish to add it to your adventure journal, lightly spray the back with adhesive and carefully place it on the page of your choice.

Avoid using regular glue, as it might stick the pages of your journal together.

CHARCOAL LEAF RUBBINGS

Many artists use charcoal for drawing, but you can also use cold charcoal from your campfire to create unique rubbings of leaves, capturing their unique shape and their intricate details.

Here's what you need:

- A leaf (or several different leaves)
- Plain paper
- Cold charcoal from your campfire

Here's how to do it:

1. **Collect charcoal:** Ensure your campfire is completely out. If you need to extract charcoal while the fire is still warm, use a shovel or bark to safely remove the charcoal pieces. Let them cool for a few hours.

2. **Prepare your leaf:** Place your chosen leaf under a sheet of paper.

3. **Rub:** Gently rub over the paper with your piece of charcoal. The leaf's shape, along with its veins and textures, will be transferred onto the paper.

4. **Journaling:** If you'd like, spray some adhesive on the back of your rubbing and carefully place it in your adventure journal.

INK LEAF PRINTS

Ink leaf prints are another creative method to capture the intricate details of leaves.

Here's what you'll need:

- Ink (preferably with an eye-dropper)
- Paintbrush
- Plain paper
- A roller (for even pressure)
- Protective plastic sheet (to prevent mess)

Here's what to do:

1. **Place the leaf:** Place the leaf on a table covered with a plastic sheet.

2. **Spread the ink:** Drop ink onto the leaf. Use a paintbrush to evenly spread the ink across the leaf.

3. **Place the paper:** Gently lay a sheet of paper over the inked leaf.

4. **Rolling:** Roll over the paper once with the roller, applying firm but gentle pressure.

5. **Peel it off:** Lift up the paper and carefully peel the leaf off of it.

You should now have a beautiful ink print of the leaf, perfect for adding to your adventure journal or displaying as a piece of natural art.

ADVENTURE PHOTOGRAPHY

Photography is a fantastic way to capture the memories of your adventures. Whether you have your own camera or you're borrowing one, capturing the beauty of nature can be incredibly rewarding. It could be anything—a rainbow arcing over your backyard, a butterfly perched on a flower, or a breathtaking sunset.

Getting to Know Your Camera

Before you start snapping photos, get familiar with your camera. Understand its features and how they work. Many modern cameras have auto-focus and light adjustment settings to help make your photos look great. But knowing how to manually use these controls can elevate your photography, giving you more creative freedom.

Photo Composition

Photo composition is like the magic ingredient that turns an ordinary snapshot into a captivating image. It's all about framing your shot, choosing your subject, and finding the best angle.

Here are some tips for better photo composition:

- **Framing:** Decide what your main subject is. Do you want a close-up using a zoom lens or a broad view with a wide-angle lens? Your choice here sets the stage for your photo.

- **Horizon placement:** Avoid putting the horizon right in the middle of your shot. Try positioning it either above or below the center to add interest to your composition, like a low horizon for a dramatic sunset.

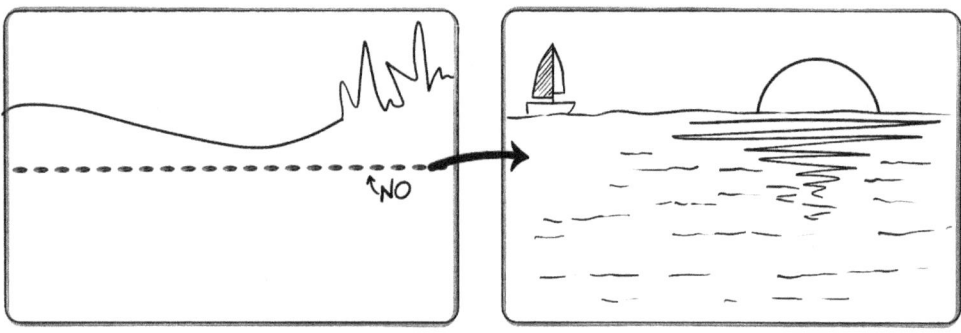

- **The rule of thirds:** Imagine your image is divided into nine equal parts by two horizontal and two vertical lines. Position important elements along these lines or at their intersections for a more balanced composition.

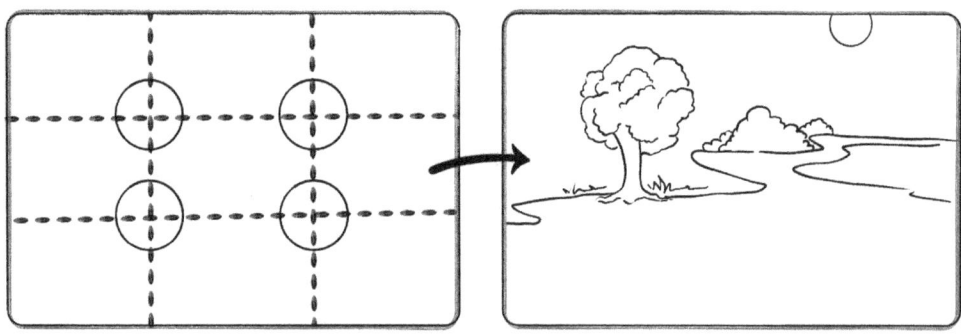

312   Essential Skills Every Kid Should Know

- **Visual paths:** Use natural lines—like paths, branches, or river edges—to guide the viewer's eye towards your main subject. These lines create a journey within your photo.

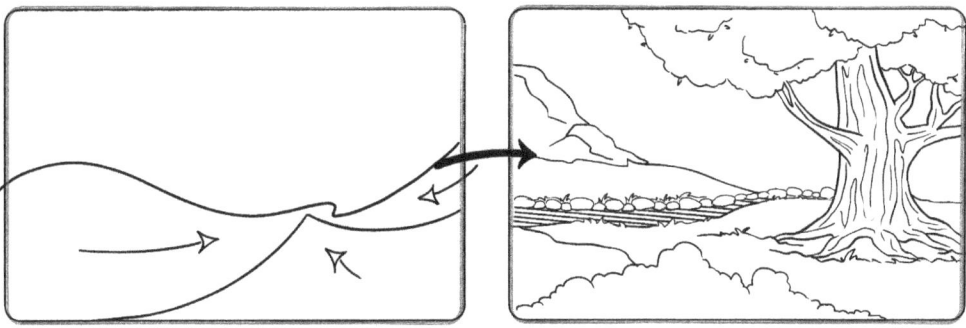

- **Color focus:** The subject of your photo should have the strongest color. This draws the viewer's eye directly to the main point of interest.

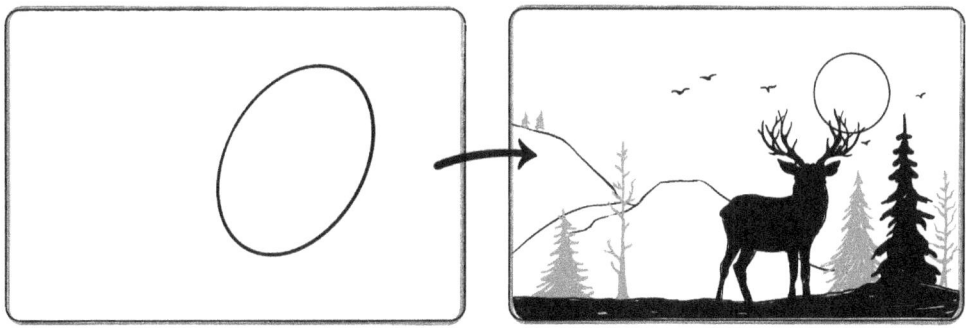

- **Mix it up:** Make your photos interesting with horizontal, vertical, and diagonal elements. For example, combine vertical pine trees, a horizontal horizon, and the diagonal shape of mountains.

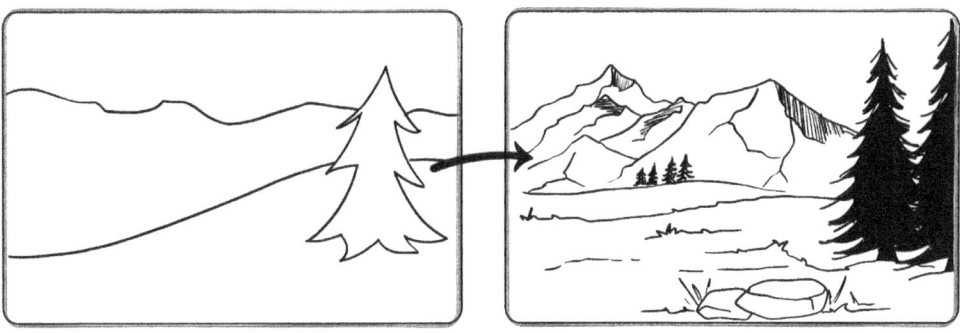

- **Use curves:** Nature is full of curves, like winding trails and river bends. Curves add an element of grace and fluidity to your photos. They can also lead the eye and add depth to your image.

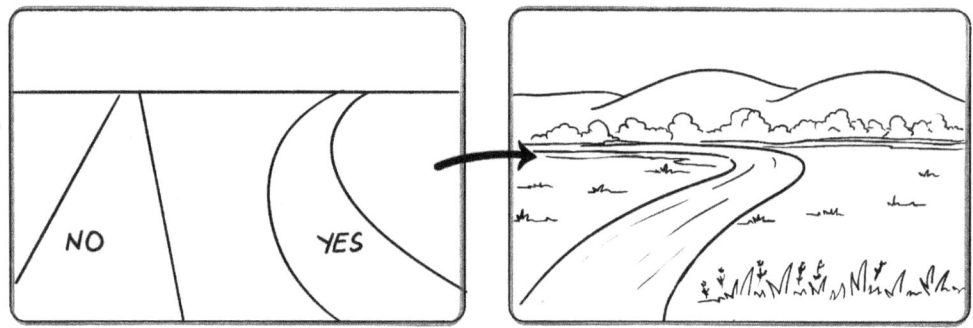

- **Be your own critic:** After each photography session, take time to review your images. Analyze what works and what doesn't, learning from each shot.

Photography is not just about capturing what you see; it's also about sharing how you see the world. Each photo you take is part of your unique story. Keep experimenting with these composition techniques, and remember to include your best shots in your adventure journal to share your journey and progress.

CHAPTER 8

THE GREAT INDOORS – BRINGING ADVENTURE HOME

Just because you can't head out into the wilderness doesn't mean you can't have an adventure. Adventures can happen right at home. Whether you're planning your next outdoor trip or finding ways to bring a touch of the wild into your living room, there's plenty of fun to be had indoors.

Here are some fun, creative projects to keep the spirit of adventure alive.

BUILDING A MINIATURE CAMPSITE DIORAMA

A diorama is a miniature representation of a scene, capturing its essence on a small scale. Let's craft a tiny version of a campsite, using everyday items to mimic a wilderness setting.

What you'll need:

- A flat board as your base
- Sticks and twigs for structure
- Stones and pebbles for detailing
- White glue for assembly
- Sand and dirt for texture
- A hand drill (for adult use)

Here's how to create your tiny campsite:

- **Prepare the board:** Start with a board as the platform for your campsite.

- **Groundwork:** Spread white glue evenly over the board. Sprinkle sand and dirt over the glue to mimic natural ground. Allow it to dry for an hour.

- **Make your shelter:** Once it's dry, shake off any loose sand. With adult supervision, drill two holes for inserting Y-shaped sticks. These will be the supports for your lean-to shelter. Secure a horizontal stick across the Ys to act as the ridgepole. Lean smaller sticks against this ridgepole to create the lean-to structure.

- **Build a fire pit:** Put a circle of glue on the ground in front of the lean-to, then arrange small stones in a ring on the glue to create the fire pit.

- **Adding details:**
    - Surround your campsite with larger rocks for a natural look.
    - Stack miniature firewood by gluing small sticks together.
    - Place larger logs (created from bigger sticks) around the fire pit to serve as seats.
    - For an extra touch of realism, use a tealight candle as your campfire.

Your diorama is finished. Now you can have some fun, imagining and enjoying the activities of your next adventure in your miniature campsite.

MAKING A MAP OF YOUR HOUSE, YARD, AND NEIGHBORHOOD

Learning to read maps is an essential skill for any adventurer, and a fun way to start is by creating a map of your own house, yard, and neighborhood. Using Google Maps, enter your home address and see if you can find an aerial view of your house and neighborhood.

Once you find your house, you're ready to start making your own map.

What you'll need:

- Paper or a sketch pad
- A pencil and a ruler
- Colored pencils or markers
- Access to Google Maps (or a similar mapping service)

Here's how to create your map:

① **Explore Google Maps:** Begin by opening Google Maps on a computer or device. Enter your home address in the search bar and switch to the aerial view to see a bird's-eye perspective of your house and neighborhood.

② **Sketch your house:** Using the aerial view as a reference, start by drawing the outline of your house on your paper or sketch pad.

③ **Add nearby features:** Include surrounding elements visible from the aerial view, like roads, parks, and significant buildings in your neighborhood.

④ **Incorporate landmarks:** Don't forget to draw important local features such as trees, driveways, or any unique landmarks near your home.

Here are some tips to make your map even better:

- **Use scale and proportions:** Use a ruler to make sure there are accurate proportions and scale on your map.

- **Label street names and landmarks:** If possible, add street names to your map to make it even more complete.

- **Detail with colors:** Use colored pencils or markers to add details and differentiate between different areas, like streets, parks, and buildings.

- **Color-coding:** Consider using different colors for streets, parks, and landmarks.

- **Add directions:** Include north, south, east, and west.

Once your map is complete, you can use it to practice your map-reading skills. You could even challenge yourself or family members to find the quickest route from one point to another.

PLANNING A TREASURE HUNT AT HOME

Once you have a map of the neighborhood, you can plan a treasure hunt. You can do it in your own backyard, or hide the treasure in the yard of a friend's house. If it's raining outside, you can even do a treasure hunt inside the house.

Here's how to organize your treasure hunt:

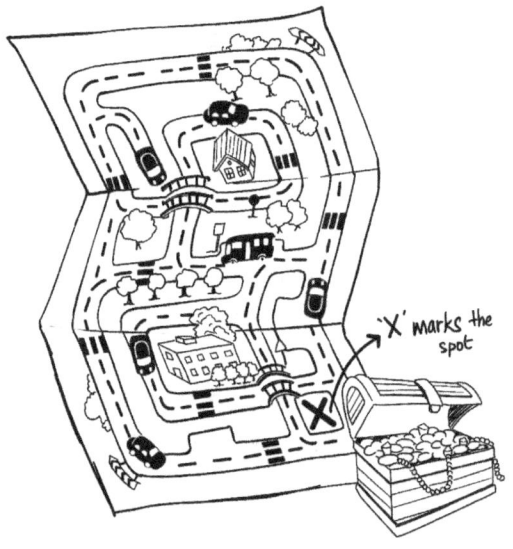

'X' marks the spot

❶ **Hide the treasure:** Find a secret spot to hide your treasure. This could be anywhere from a hidden corner in your backyard to a hiding spot indoors. Once it's hidden, you're ready to start writing clues.

❷ **Create a trail of clues:** Each discovered clue should lead to the next, creating a chain of discoveries. Hide these clues in various locations, guiding participants through the hunt.

❸ **Continue the adventure:** As each clue is found, it points to the next location, keeping the excitement alive.

❹ **Final discovery:** The final clue leads to the grand discovery of the treasure.

 **Top Tip:** Choose places around the house that will keep the hunters moving to different locations.

Ideas for Treasure: It can be anything that sparks a sense of adventure or discovery, like a miniature compass, a unique rock, or even a homemade certificate for the winner. Of course, a bar of chocolate will be equally welcome, too!

ORGANIZING A NATURE SCAVENGER HUNT

A nature scavenger hunt is a fantastic way to explore the outdoors while engaging in a fun challenge. This can be set up in a variety of locations, like your backyard, a nearby park, or even around your neighborhood.

Here's what you'll need:

- A list of natural items or clues
- Pens or pencils to record the finds
- Containers or bags for collecting items
- Optional: Prizes for the winners

Here's how to organize the hunt:

1. **Plan the hunt:** Decide on the location for the scavenger hunt (e.g., house, backyard, neighborhood, park).

2. **Create your clues:** Make a list of items to find or create clues leading to each item's location. Tailor the list or clues to the theme or purpose of the scavenger hunt.

3. **Start the hunt:** Begin the scavenger hunt and let participants search for the items or solve the clues. It's all about creativity and teamwork!

4. **Meet at the end:** Set up a meeting point or designated area for everyone to gather at the end of the scavenger hunt.

5 **Find a winner:** Check the collected items or solved clues against the list. Declare the winning person who collected the most stuff in the least amount of time. If you have prizes, now is the time to dish them out!

BUILDING AN INDOOR FORT

It's not always possible to go camping, but creating your own indoor camping experience can be just as fun as being outdoors.

Here are some creative ideas to build a fort at home:

- **Broomstick fort:** Gather some broomsticks, drape sheets over them, and cushion the floor with pillows to create a cozy fort in your bedroom.

- **Table fort:** Throw some blankets over a table and imagine you're sleeping under the stars. Bring your adventure journal into your camp and write down the things you want to do on your next adventure.

- **Make your own wilderness:** Pick a room in the house and pretend you're out in the woods. You could place blankets and sheets over furniture to make rocks and cliffs. Make a roof with a blanket and sheets over an umbrella or table, and line the floor of your tent with pillows.

- **Light up your tent:** Light up your fort with flashlights or a small lamp. Remember, never use candles indoors, to avoid fire hazards.

Your home fort is not just a fun hideaway, but also a perfect spot for learning and practicing new skills. You can try tying different types of knots, learn basic first aid, or engage in adventure-related games and activities.

PLAY THE "BLINDFOLD NATURE CHALLENGE"

This game is a great indoor activity that you can play with a friend or sibling. It's a fun way to explore nature through touch.

Here's what you'll need:

- A variety of natural objects, like pine cones, feathers, fir branches, bark, acorns, flowers, and sand.
- A blindfold (a cloth or piece of clothing works well).
- A box to hold your nature items.

Here's how to play the game:

1. **Tie the blindfold:** Blindfold your friend or sibling so they can't see.

2. **Bring out the box:** Place all the interesting objects you've collected in the box.

3. **Time to guess:** Hand an object from the box to your blindfolded partner. They should feel it and guess what it is.

4. **Take turns:** Now it's your turn to be blindfolded and guess an object.

This can be a really fun game to play in your home fort.

LEARNING HOW TO TIE KNOTS

Knowing how to tie various knots is a must-have skill for any outdoor adventure. Knots can be useful for setting up tents, tying things together, and in emergency situations. Here are six essential knots every young explorer should learn. Grab some different colored ropes and practice each knot until you master them!

How to Tie a Half-Hitch Knot

This is a simple knot for attaching a rope to a pole or a tree.

1. **Hold the end** of the rope.

2. **Wrap the rope** around the pole or tree.

3. **Pass the end** of the rope through the loop you've made.

4. **Pull tight** to secure the half hitch.

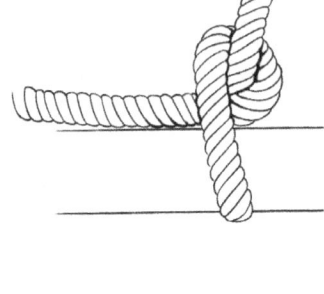

How to Tie Two Half-Hitches

This knot is stronger than a single half hitch and easy to untie.

1. **Wrap the rope** around a pole or tree.

2. **Make the first half hitch** by passing the end of the rope through the loop.

3. **Wrap again** for the second half hitch.

4. **Create the second half hitch** in the same way as the first.

5. **Pull tight** to secure the knot.

How to Tie a Square Knot

A well-tied square knot has two loops and is great for securing two rope ends together!

1. **Cross one rope end** over the other, right to left.

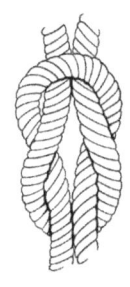

② **Pass it underneath** the other rope.

③ **Reverse direction** and cross the second rope over the first, left to right.

④ **Pass it underneath** the first rope.

⑤ **Pull tight** on both ends.

How to Tie a Figure Eight Knot

A figure eight knot, also known as a Flemish bend, is a reliable and secure knot often used for rock climbing and sailing.

Here's how to make one:

① **Form a loop** with the rope.

② **Go under and around** the rope, following its path.

③ **Pass the end** through the loop.

④ **Tighten** the knot securely.

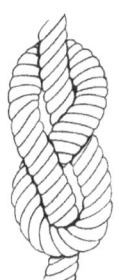

How to Tie a Clove Hitch

A clove hitch is a great knot for securing a rope to a tree or pole. It's easy to untie, but very strong when in use.

① **Wrap the rope** around the object.

② **Make a loop** and place it over the object.

③ **Form a second loop** with the free end of the rope, passing it over the first.

④ **Pull the end** of the rope to tighten the hitch.

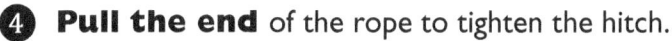

Remember, the more you practice, the better you'll get at tying these knots. They could come in handy in a variety of situations, so it's worth taking the time to learn them well.

CHAPTER 9

ADVANCED OUTDOOR SKILLS

As you continue to find new adventures, your outdoor skills will grow and you will learn more and more about how to survive in the wilderness. In this chapter, we'll look at some of the more advanced skills you can learn. They're fun to practice with your family and friends and will make you a true master of adventure.

HOW TO SIGNAL FOR HELP IN EMERGENCIES

If you ever get lost or need emergency help, one of the oldest and most effective ways to signal for help is by using something called Morse Code.

Morse Code is a combination of dots and dashes, symbolizing letters of the alphabet.

> **DID YOU KNOW?** Morse Code was invented by a man named Samuel Morse in 1838. He invented it so people could communicate using a telegraph, which was the first form of electronic communication.

Here's what Morse Code looks like:

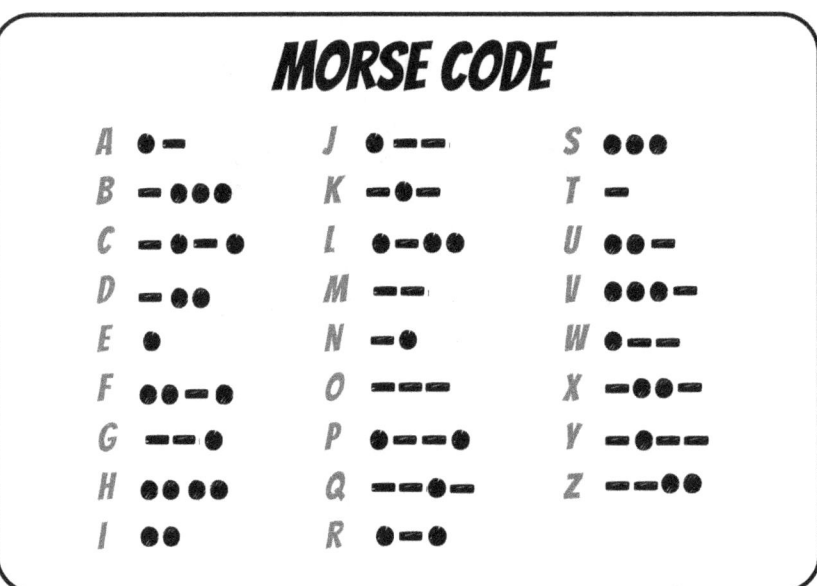

Here's how to read Morse Code:

- **Understand dots and dashes:** When it's written down, Morse Code uses a combination of two symbols—dots (•) and dashes (-)—to represent each letter of the alphabet.
- **Listen and watch:** Morse Code can be translated into sound, where dots are a short beep and dashes are longer beeps. It can also be signaled visually using a flashlight or a signal mirror. In this instance, a dot is a quick and short burst of light and a dash is a longer flash of light.

- **Practice with a cheat sheet:** Morse Code is like a secret language that has to be learned. Keep a sheet with the Morse Code for each letter until you remember them.

Spaces and Pauses in Morse Code

When sending a morse code using sound, the time between the sounds is important. Here are the different types of pauses:

- **Dot (•) and dash (-) breaks:** A brief pause between dots and dashes forms a letter. For example, the letter "A" is a dot followed by a dash, with a short pause in between.
- **Letter breaks:** When you hear a slightly longer pause, it means the end of one letter and the beginning of the next.
- **Word breaks:** Longer pauses act like a space between words. They tell you that one word has ended and the next is starting.

Morse Code is like listening to a rhythm: short breaks for letters, a bit longer for the end of a letter and start of the next, and even longer for the spaces between words.

Sending an SOS Signal

If you're lost or in real trouble, you may need to send out an SOS signal. SOS is a universally recognized distress signal in Morse Code that is easy to remember and send.

The sequence for SOS is three dots followed by three dashes followed by three more dots.

SOS = •••−−−•••

Anytime you signal: **dot-dot-dot/dash-dash-dash/dot-dot-dot**, you are telling someone you need help.

> ***DID YOU KNOW?*** SOS was first chosen because it was an easy combination of letters to send using Morse Code. Later, some people made up a phrase for it, saying it meant Save Our Souls or Save Our Ship.

Let's look at all of the ways you can signal an SOS and other messages using Morse Code:

Signal Mirror

A simple handheld mirror can be used to send Morse Code messages by reflecting sunlight.

Here's how to send a Morse Code message with a signal mirror:

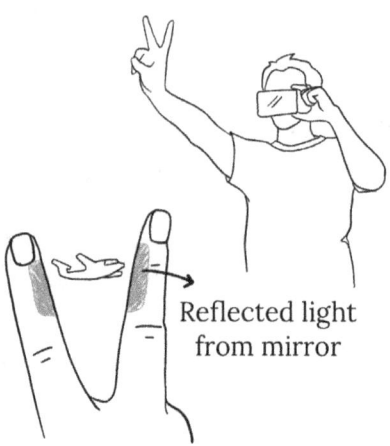
Reflected light from mirror

❶ **Find the sun:** Stand where the sun is shining bright. Hold your mirror in place to catch the sunlight.

❷ **Use the two finger trick:** Form a V with your fingers and place the mirror in the middle to aim the reflection.

❸ **Aim at someone:** Point the mirror's reflection at someone (or something). Imagine drawing a line from your fingers to them.

❹ **Move the mirror:** To send Morse Code, move the mirror slightly to create dots (quick movements) and dashes (longer movements).

❺ **Repeat the movement:** Keep adjusting the mirror's angle to maintain the reflection towards your target.

❻ **Practice:** Test your skills with friends on sunny days using your Morse Code cheat sheet as a guide.

Using a Flashlight to Signal

Turning a flashlight off and on is an easy and effective way to send Morse Code, especially at night.

❶ **Find a dark spot:** Go to a dark or dimly lit area, like your backyard at night or inside the house with the lights turned off.

❷ **Turn it on and off:** Practice turning your flashlight on and off.

③ **Practice SOS:** Practice sending an SOS signal: three short flashes (dots), three long flashes (dashes), followed by three short flashes.

④ **Try your name in lights:** Now, try spelling your name in Morse Code. Make short flashes for dots and longer ones for dashes. For example, if your name is Sam, it's "▨▨▨ ▨ - - -".

⑤ **Learn more letters:** Keep practicing with different letters and words.

Signaling with a Whistle

You may remember that we included a whistle in our survival kit in an earlier chapter. That's because the sound of a whistle travels a long way. It can help you signal that you have an emergency using Morse Code, by sending out an SOS. If you ever hear a whistle in the woods, listen to see if someone needs help.

Here's how to use a whistle to send a message using Morse Code:

- **Blow the whistle:** You can use short or long breaths to create dots and dashes. A short blow is for dots, and longer ones for dashes.

- **Practice SOS:** An SOS using a whistle is three short blasts, three long blasts, and three more short blasts in succession.

- **Practice other words or messages:** Using the Morse Code alphabet code, try signaling other words or messages.

> *DID YOU KNOW?* Any sound-producing device can be used to send Morse Code. There's an old story about a man whose car ran off the road. No one could see it, and he was hurt, so he used his car horn to send an SOS. Someone heard it and knew what he was saying, and he was soon rescued.

PREPARE FOR THE WEATHER

Weather can be unpredictable and changeable, so it's always best to be prepared for any eventuality. Always take a look at the weather forecast before you set out, as this will give you an idea of the conditions and what to take on your trip.

How to Stay Warm Outside

It's always cold in winter, but even nights in the spring and fall can get chilly when you're outdoors. That's why it's a good idea to learn how to stay warm when you're on an adventure.

Here are some ways to keep warm outdoors:

1. Dressing Right for Cold Weather

Clothing is your first line of defense against the cold. Pack these essentials for your adventure:

- A long-sleeve shirt
- A sweater or hoodie
- A warm jacket or coat
- Hat, scarf, and gloves

Top Tip: Wearing layers of clothing can help keep you warm in cold weather. For example, you can wear your long-sleeve shirt plus a sweater or hoodie and a warm jacket or coat. If you are active and start to overheat, you can always remove a layer.

2. Warming Up with Hot Drinks

A hot drink can provide internal warmth.

Here are some favorites:

- Hot chocolate
- Apple cider
- Tea
- Warm milk
- Ovaltine or a similar malt drink

Not only will a hot drink help you get warmer, but the hot cup also helps warm your hands. A little added sugar or the natural sugar in the drink can also help you generate some body heat.

3. Snacks and Meals

Eating is another good way to keep warm, because it lets your body generate heat. So, don't forget to have some snacks or eat regular meals when it's cold outside.

4. Build a Reflector Fire

A fire is always a great way to stay warm when it's cold outside. We've covered some of the basic types of fires in an earlier chapter, but on a cold evening, you may want to try out a reflector fire.

A reflector fire has a layer of logs propped up against two branches pounded into the ground on an angle behind the fire. The layer of logs reflects the heat from the fire so you get more heat.

How to make a reflector fire:

1. **Collect what you need:** Get dry sticks and logs for your fire. Also, find two strong branches to stick into the ground.

2. **Clear the space:** Make a clean area for your fire, without any twigs or leaves around. Look up and make sure there are no branches above you. Also make sure your tents, camping chairs, and other camping equipment are far enough away.

3. **Stick in the branches:** Push the two branches into the ground at an angle, like sticks in a tent, to support your log reflector wall.

4. **Make a log wall:** Arrange the logs on top of the angled branches to make a wall behind your fire. This wall will bounce the heat towards you.

Now you can go ahead and make your fire using one of the methods from chapter 3. Remember, always have a grown-up with you when making a fire, and be super careful!

Building a Self-Feeding Fire

On a cold winter's night, it's always hard to get up and put another log on the fire. But there's a way to build a fire so it feeds itself and the logs keep rolling onto the fire as it burns. It's called a self-feeding fire. Here's how to build one:

❶ **Base logs:** Roll some logs to either side of your fire pit. These will support the logs you're going to arrange at an incline for your self-feeding fire.

❷ **Supporting logs:** Set two smooth, straight logs against the base logs on both sides at an incline and cover them at the bottom with sand or soil.

❸ **Tinder and kindling:** Fill the center of the fire pit with tinder and kindling.

❹ **Get stacking:** Stack some dry logs in a row in the pit on either side of the incline.

❺ **Light your fire:** As each log burns, one of the next ones will roll down and take its place.

 **Top Tip** You can even leave this kind of fire overnight, and, with any luck, it will still be burning in the morning. You can then just add more logs to keep it going.

Remember, you'll need to take your self-feeding fire apart when you're ready to go home, in order to leave the campground the way you found it.

Staying Cool on an Adventure

Now that you know how to stay warm outside when it's cold, it's time to learn how to stay cool on hot, summer days.

There are two things that will keep you feeling hot and sweaty on summer days: the heat and the humidity. The way our bodies try to keep us cool is by sweating, but as we sweat, we lose water and start to get thirsty. When you get thirsty, your body is telling you that you're getting dehydrated. This means your body is losing too much water, and you could get sick. Listen to your body when you're thirsty and stop to take a drink of water.

There's more to surviving in hot weather than just drinking water. Here are some things you should always do when you know it's going to be a hot day.

1. Choose the Right Clothes for Warm Weather

Here are some clothes that you should pack if you're going on an adventure and are expecting warm weather:

- Short-sleeve shirts
- Shorts
- Light, white hiking socks
- A hat
- Sunglasses

Don't forget to wear sunscreen, and make sure you take lots of sips from that water bottle!

2. Stay in the Shade

The temperature difference between hiking/sitting in the sun and the shade can be as much as 10 to 20 degrees Fahrenheit (or 5 to 10 degrees Celsius). That's why you should try to take frequent breaks in a shady spot when hiking on a hot day.

If there's no comfortable place in the shade, you can make your own shade with a space blanket or tarp. Here's how:

1. **Find a nice spot:** Choose a good spot outside where you want some shade (maybe in the backyard or at the park).

2. **Tie it up:** Use ropes to tie one corner of the tarp to a tree, pole, or anything tall. We recommend using the half-hitch, or, even better, the two half-hitches knot we learned to tie in chapter 8. Once you've tied the tarp to one corner, do the same with the opposite corner.

3. **Pull it tight:** Make the tarp tight by pulling it. This way, it'll give you good shade.

4. **Watch the sun:** Pay attention to where the sun is. If it moves, adjust the tarp so you always have shade.

5. **Enjoy your shady space:** Once your tarp is up and giving you shade, you've made your own cool space to play or relax on a scorching hot day!

Remember to have fun and be careful with ropes. Always ask a grown-up for help if you need it!

CHAPTER 10

CRAFTING TOOLS IN THE WILDERNESS

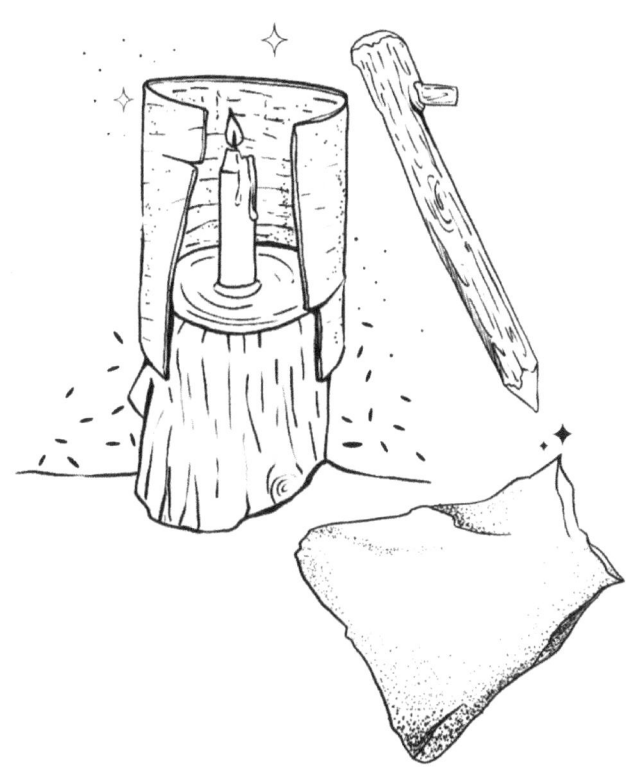

Sometimes, you need tools that you don't have. For instance, what if you go camping or exploring and you forget something like a hammer to pound in tent stakes, or you find that the tent stakes aren't in the bag with the tent? That's when you have to get creative. If you look around in nature, you can often find or make something to take the place of the tools you need.

Here are some of the tools you can make from natural and found materials if you find yourself on an adventure without the tools you need.

A ROCK HAMMER

No hammer? No problem. You can find a rock and use it as a hammer to pound in tent stakes.

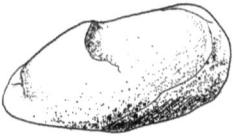

Here's how:

1. **Find the right rock:** Look for a small, heavy rock. It should be just the right size for you to hold comfortably. Rocks with round edges are ideal for pounding in things like tent stakes.

2. **Hold it tight:** Grab the rock with your hand, and make sure you can hold it tight. Ask a grown-up for help if the rock is too heavy.

3. **Pound those stakes:** Use your rock to hammer those tent stakes into the ground. Nice, firm movements are fine. Don't try to hit the stake too hard, or you might hurt yourself or damage the stake.

4. **Keep the rock handy:** After using your rock, keep it in your camping area. You never know when you might need it again.

There you go! Your rock hammer is ready to help you with your camping adventures. Always be careful with rocks, and ask a grown-up for help if you need it.

A LOG HAMMER

A log from your firewood pile could be used as a hammer in camp.

Here's how to make a log hammer:

1. **Find a log:** Look for a log in your firewood pile or in the woods. It should be a sturdy piece that's not too big for you to handle.

2. **Trim the log:** If you have a saw and a hatchet, you can make a handle for your log hammer by trimming part of the log. It should be smooth and comfortable for you to hold. Remember to be careful! Ask a grown-up, like Mom or Dad, for help with the saw and hatchet, especially if it's your first time using them.

③ Use it when needed: Your log hammer is now ready for you to hold firmly and use for jobs around the campsite, like driving in tent stakes.

④ Keep the log hammer handy: Keep your new hammer in a safe place for the next time you need it.

A CUTTING TOOL

If you need to cut some rope and can't find your knife, you could look for a rock with sharp edges. Remember, cutting rope can be dangerous, and it's best to put safety first when you use a cutting tool.

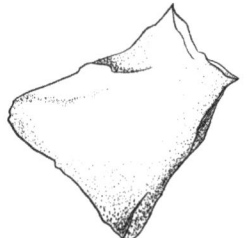

Here's how to cut a rope by using a rock as a cutting tool:

① Find a sharp-edged rock: Start by going on a rock hunt and looking for rocks with edges that are a bit sharp. Choose one with a flat, sharp edge, but that isn't sharp all over (so you can still pick it up). Be careful not to pick up anything too heavy or sharp.

② Hold it safely: Hold the rock carefully, making sure your fingers are away from the sharp part.

③ Cut the rope: Use your rock cutting tool to carefully cut the rope. It might take a bit of effort and time, but, with a bit of patience, it can be done. Remember to be careful and ask an adult for help if you need it!

It's always fun to collect rocks on any adventure. The next time you're out in a rocky area, see what kind of rocks you can find that you could use as tools.

TENT STAKES

Tent stakes are easy to make. Here's how:

① Find a branch: Look for a branch that's about a foot long and about as thick as your thumb.

2. **Sharpen with your cutting tool:** Pick one end of the branch and sharpen it into a pencil point. A knife would be best to use, as this will be difficult to do with your sharp rock. This can be very dangerous, so it may be best to ask an adult to do it for you (or to do it with them, if you're old enough).

3. **Trim your stake:** If there's any extra stuff sticking out on your stake, trim it off so it doesn't get in the way of the tent loops.

4. **Use your stake:** Now, your sharpened branch is a tent stake. Use your rock hammer to pound it into the ground to help keep your tent in place.

Top Tip: If you find a branch with a smaller branch sticking out, that's cool! You can use it to grab onto the loops on your tent. Simply sharpen the long part and trim off the smaller branch.

MAKING CAMP TOOLS FROM BARK

The bark from trees can be used to make a surprising number of tools, but you do need to respect nature when you search for your bark. You should only collect bark from dead trees. If you take too much bark from a living tree, the tree could die.

Removing all the bark around a green, living tree is called "girdling," and it's how ancient people used to kill trees so they were easier to cut down the following season. Only take bark from trees that have died or have fallen to the ground.

Start with Birch Bark

If you can find a dead birch tree, you're in luck. Birch bark is some of the easiest bark to work with because it's thin and flexible. Here are some of the things you can make.

Remember, these can help if you have nothing to protect your eyes from the sun, but they can't take the place of real sunglasses. You should never look directly at the sun, even if you do have a pair of real sunglasses on.

BIRCH BARK SUNGLASSES

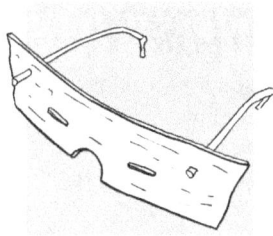

If you want to protect your eyes from the sun but don't have any sunglasses, you can make your own pair from birch bark.

Here's how:

1 Carefully cut your bark
You'll need a piece about six inches long and two inches wide .

2 Make a place for your nose:
Cut a half circle at the bottom of the piece of birch bark so the sunglasses will fit over your nose.

3 Measure your eye slits:
Hold two fingers up to our eyes and then move your hand to the birch bark without moving your fingers. This will tell you where to cut the slits in the birch bark so you can see.

4 Make your eye slits:
Use your knife to cut criss cross slits in the birch bark at the point where your fingers marked the distance for your eyes.

5 Cut some small branches:
These will make supports for your birch bark sunglasses so they'll fit over your ears.

6 Cut holes in the glasses:
These should be on either of the top corners of the glasses. Now you can carefully push the support sticks through the birch bark holes you made.

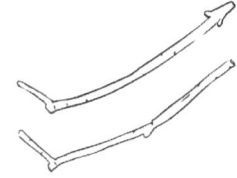
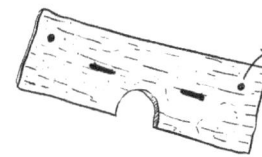

There you have it! The slits in the birch bark allow you to see, but they cut down the brightness of the sunlight - acting like sunglasses.

DID YOU KNOW? This way of making sunglasses was discovered by ancient people who lived in the Arctic. They often found that the sun reflecting off snow was blinding. But since it was long ago and there was no such thing as sunglasses, they figured out how to make their own from birch bark.

ADVENTURE SKILLS FOR KIDS

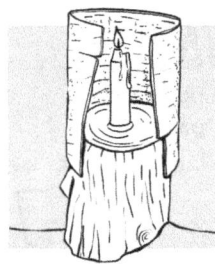

A BIRCH BARK CANDLE LANTERN

When birch bark is removed from a dead tree trunk it has a natural curl. The curl in the bark curls in towards the dark, inner bark. For a candle lantern you want a curl in the bark but you want the white, outer bark on the inside of the curl. The white bark reflects more light and will make your candle seem brighter.

1. Find your bark and stick: Look for birch bark with the white inside. Curl it and place it between two logs in your wood pile.

2. Wait until evening: Leave the curled bark in the wood pile all day. When it's evening, take it out.

3. Make a lantern shape: Cut the birch bark about twelve inches high. Bend the curled bark around a stump or a piece of log to make the right shape.

4. Light the candle: Light a candle. Let the wax drip onto the stump or log. Put the candle on the melted wax to stick it.

You now have your candle lantern but be careful with it and don't bring it close to anything that could catch on fire.

A BIRCH BARK TORCH

If your flashlight batteries are dead or you forgot to bring it, you can make a torch to light your way. Always be very careful with this kind of torch so you don't start a fire

Here's how:

1. Collect what you need: To make a birch bark torch you'll need some strips of birch bark cut about two feet long. You'll also need a 3-foot solid tree branch. A green branch is best so it won't burn as easily as a dead branch and break off.

2. Make some slots: Cut two slots into the end of your branch.

3. Insert the strips: Fold the strips of birch bark so they'll fit into the slots, and insert them.

You now have a birch bark torch that should burn for ten to fifteen minutes.

A BIRCH BARK LADLE

If you didn't bring a ladle for serving warm drinks, soup, or meals, you can make one with the help of some birch bark.

Here's what to do:

1 **Find your bark and stick:**
You'll need a large piece of birch bark (eight to ten square inches) and a foot-long stick.

2 **Make a cone shape:**
Cut the birch bark into a circle and carefully fold it into a cone shape.

3 **Make the handle:**
Split a branch at one end to hold the birch bark together and create a handle.

4 **Put it together:**
Insert the cone part into the handle as shown in the picture.

That's it! Your very own birch bark ladle.

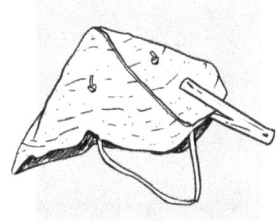

A BIRCH BARK HAT

You can even make a hat out of birch bark.

Here's how:

1 **Cut out your hat:**
Cut a big circle of birch bark, about twelve to sixteen inches across. Then, cut a slit from the edge to the center of the circle.

2 **Shape your hat:**
Pull the bark together, just like making a bark ladle. Hold it in place with a stick that has a slit cut into it. Voila! You've got a birch bark hat.

3 **Keep it secure:**
To keep your hat on in the wind, put a string or a piece of leather lacing through two holes at the top of the hat with a slip knot. This makes a lanyard to hold your hat snug.

You now have a stylish birch bark hat. You can wear it to stay shaded from the sun or dry in the rain. It's your nature-friendly accessory!

ADVENTURE SKILLS FOR KIDS

HOW TO MAKE AN ANCIENT DIGGING STICK

Before shovels were invented, ancient civilizations used a digging stick to dig into the ground. You might need it in camp, because most of us don't think to pack a shovel.

> **DID YOU KNOW?** Archeologists think a digging stick was the first tool ever made.

Reasons you might have to dig a hole is to make a fire pit, dig a latrine, or just flatten bumps in the ground where you're going to set up your tent. You could also use it to help you become a rock hound, something we'll learn more about in the next chapter.

Here's how to do it:

1 Find a sturdy stick: Look for a strong and straight stick. It should be about as tall as your chest. This stick is going to be your ancient digging tool!

2 Sharpen both ends: Using a safe tool, or with adult help, sharpen one end of the stick to a point. This will be your digging end. On the other end, shave it so it's flat but has a sharp edge. This will be your scraping and scooping end.

3 Digging time: When you need to dig a hole for a fire pit, latrine, or just to flatten the ground for your tent, grab your digging stick.

4 Loosen the ground: Use the pointy end to loosen the ground. Push it into the soil and wiggle it around to make the dirt softer.

5 Scrape and scoop: Turn the stick around and use the flat, sharp end to scrape away and scoop out the loosened dirt.

Top Tip

- **Hands-on digging:** Sometimes, you might need to use your hands to scoop out more dirt. Be gentle and take your time.

- **Creative play:** Why not pretend you're an archaeologist on a mission to uncover ancient treasures buried in the soil? Your digging stick can be your magical tool for exploration!

- **Clean up with bark:** After digging, use a large slab of bark as a makeshift shovel to tidy up. Nature is full of handy tools!

Remember to be careful with your digging stick, always have adult supervision, and always respect nature! Enjoy your outdoor adventures and let your imagination soar as you uncover the mysteries of the earth!

CHAPTER 11

CREATING YOUR OWN ADVENTURES

You don't always have to travel long distances to find adventure. Adventure is everywhere, if you know how to find it. There are activities you can do with your family and friends that can make every day an adventure. One of those adventures is rockhounding.

A rockhound is someone who likes to look for and collect rocks. It's fun and it's easy to do. Perhaps you have already done it. Here's how to prepare for a rockhounding adventure.

ROCKHOUNDING ADVENTURES

To start, you need to put together your rockhound kit. These are all the things you'll need to look for rocks and minerals.

Rockhound Kit

- **Small backpack or side pack:** To hold everything you need.
- **Hammer or pick:** This is what geologists use to dig for rocks and minerals.
- **Small chisel:** To help you clean up the interesting rocks you find.
- **Goggles:** To protect your eyes from bits of rock while you're using your hammer, pick, or chisel.
- **Gloves:** To protect your hands from sharp rocks.

- **Magnifying glass:** For a closer look at the amazing rocks and minerals you find.
- **Magnet**: Some rocks are magnetic. A small magnet will allow you to test the ones you find.
- **Small satchel or bag:** To keep your rocks and minerals in.
- **Hat and sunscreen:** To protect yourself from the sun.

- **Water bottle:** It's important to stay hydrated while you're finding rocks.
- **Snacks:** So you don't go hungry while having fun as a rockhound.
- **Insect repellent:** So bugs don't ruin your fun.
- **Your adventure journal:** To make notes about your rockhound discoveries.
- **A field guide to rocks and minerals:** This should be a small book that's able to fit in your pocket or bag.

If you don't have all of these things, that's okay. You can look for rocks anytime, but it helps to have some equipment.

Where to Look for Rocks and Minerals

Rocks and minerals can show up anywhere, but there are specific places where you'll find lots of them. Here are some prime spots to start your search:

- **Rock outcrops and hillsides:** Where the earth's crust is exposed.
- **River banks and lake shores:** Flowing water can uncover a variety of rocks and minerals.
- **Open fields:** Early in spring, before the plants have grown to cover them up.

What to Look for When You're Rockhounding

When you're out rockhounding, there are several types of rocks and minerals to look out for. Here's what to keep an eye on:

- **Colorful and patterned rocks:** Rocks that feature a variety of colors or intriguing patterns are always worth a closer look. These rocks can teach you a lot about how rocks were formed over millions of years. Start by looking for colorful rocks that stand out.
- **Crystals:** These are always fun to find, but sometimes you have to turn a rock over in your hands to find one. If a rock looks interesting, pick it up and turn it over so you can see all sides of it. Sometimes, a crystal will be hiding underneath.
- **Dull-colored rocks:** Don't overlook dull looking rocks. Some of these rocks can reveal surprising textures, layers, or even fossils inside.

Here are some examples of a few dull-looking rocks that may be hiding something:

- **Geodes**

    Geodes look like a tan clump of cauliflower, but when you pick one up, they sometimes feel lighter than you would expect. That's because geodes are hollow and filled with crystals. They're usually a lump of limestone that captured some water inside. Over millions of years, the water dissolved the limestone and crystals formed. Whenever you see a round rock that looks like a cauliflower, make sure you pick it up to see if it's lighter than you would expect.

    You can even shake a geode, and sometimes you'll hear bits of crystal inside, shaking around. Just be careful when you crack a geode open. Take them back to camp and gently tap them with a chisel and a hammer, and put on your goggles first.

- **Meteorites**

    Meteorites are chunks of rock that have fallen to Earth from space. They have been bombarding the Earth for billions of years. Most people ignore meteorites when they see them because they're usually a dull grey or black color. Sometimes they look a little rusty. That's because a lot of meteorites have iron inside of them.

    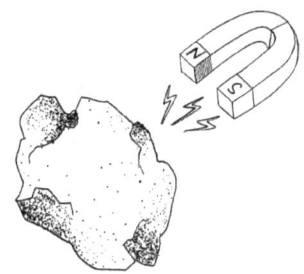

    Any time you see a dull rock that you think might be a meteorite, hold a magnet next to it. If it sticks to the magnet, it might be a meteorite!

- **Fossils**

    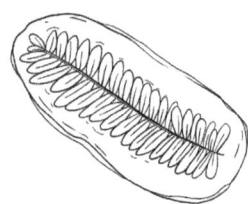

    Fossils are ancient plants and animals that have been captured in stone. Many of them are millions of years old!

How to Display Your Rocks

A simple but effective way to display your rocks is to organize them in a compartmentalized plastic box, the kind typically used for nuts and bolts found in hardware stores. Once you've identified them, label each compartment so you always remember what they are. After a while, you'll be able to identify them just by looking at them.

FOSSIL HUNTING ADVENTURES

Fossil hunting is an exciting journey into the Earth's distant past. Fossils are the remains of animals and plants from millions of years ago that have been transformed into rock. It's amazing to think that there's still something around today from so long ago—thousands of centuries before human beings first walked the earth.

> **DID YOU KNOW?** Fossils are typically formed when a plant or animal settles to the bottom of a lake or ocean. Over time, sediment layers accumulate and the organic matter gradually turns into stone, preserving the shape of the original organism.

Here's how to hunt for fossils:

1. **Tools of the trade:** Use the same tools you use for rock hunting to find fossils. Remember, some of these tools can be dangerous to use, and it's best to ask an adult for help.

2. **Choose the right location:** Look for areas with lots of sedimentary rocks. Fossils love to hide in these rocks. Coastal regions and places with ancient lake beds are fantastic fossil hunting grounds.

3. **Eagle eyes on:** Train your eyes to spot things that look out of the ordinary. Fossils often have unique shapes, so keep an eye out for curves, circles, or anything that doesn't quite fit with the rocks around it.

4. **Flip some rocks:** Gently turn over rocks, especially in areas where the rock layers are exposed. Fossils might be hiding on the undersides of rocks.

5. **Try some digging:** With adult supervision and permission, try gentle digging. Use a small trowel or your hands to explore layers of sedimentary rocks. Be patient and gentle to avoid damaging any potential finds.

6. **Color clues:** Keep an eye out for rocks with unique colors, like brownish or reddish tones. Fossils often form in sandy environments, and the sand turns into distinctive-colored rocks like sandstone.

How to Identify Fossils

Fossils are a little easier to identify than rocks because they often retain shapes of the organisms they once were. For example, a fossil of a leaf looks like a leaf. Similarly, a fossil of a seashell looks like a seashell. However, identifying exactly what animal or plant the fossils are can be challenging, especially when they belong to extinct species unfamiliar to us.

In this case, you'll need to search on the Internet, buy a guide book, or visit a local museum to identify the fossil.

LEARNING MORE ABOUT TREES

A fun way to learn more about nature and the world around you is to go on a leaf-hunting adventure. You can do this anywhere from forests to your neighborhood. Learning how to identify trees is fun and easy, and leaves are the easiest way to get to know trees.

You could dedicate a section of your journal to your tree leaf collection, or start a separate notebook.

The leaves you find are all different, and it's fun to walk through the woods or even to school and be able to identify every tree you see.

You could also collect the nuts and seeds from trees along with their leaves to learn even more about tree identification.

The next time you see a tree that you can't identify, see if you can take one of the leaves and bring it home to identify it.

GEOCACHING – A MODERN TREASURE HUNT

Geocaching is a modern-day treasure hunt combining outdoor adventure with the wonders of GPS technology. This activity involves navigating to specific coordinates to find hidden treasures, or "geocaches," placed by fellow adventurers. It's a great way to build your navigation skills, learn about GPS technology, and embark on exciting explorations.

> ***DID YOU KNOW?*** GPS stands for global positioning system. These satellites orbit Earth, providing location data to devices like smartphones and GPS devices. They're like magical guides on your smartphone, showing maps, compass directions, and latitude and longitude coordinates.

Getting Started with Geocaching

To begin geocaching, you'll need a phone or a tablet with GPS. If you don't have one of your own, you might be able to borrow one from your parents. The device will display your current location and can guide you to the geocache's coordinates.

> ***DID YOU KNOW?*** Websites like geocaching.com are treasure troves of information about geocaching. They provide details on how to participate, clues about hidden treasures, and tips for setting up your own geocache.

Creating Your Own Geocache Box

Part of the fun of geocaching is finding and creating treasure boxes. These are small containers filled with various items for finders to discover.

Here are some of the things you may find or could include in a geocache treasure box:

- **Tiny toys:** Like mini action figures, rubber ducks, or tiny puzzles.
- **Adventure tools:** Like a pocket-sized compass, a small magnifying glass, or a whistle.
- **Natural discoveries:** Interesting natural items you find, like unique rocks, seashells, or pinecones.

- **Handmade items:** Like friendship bracelets or painted rocks.
- **Message in a bottle:** Place a tiny message or a riddle in a small bottle.
- **Collectible coins:** You could add a unique or collectible coin to your geocache.
- **Artistic creations:** You could include small drawings, paintings, or other artistic creations.
- **Snack surprises:** A good idea might be to include some individually wrapped snacks or candies.
- **Stickers and decals:** This is a fun addition. You could include ones related to your geocache theme.

Geocaching can be a rewarding activity that's great fun with friends and family. But remember, it's not just about discovering the hidden treasure; it's also about the journey and experience of exploring.

CONCLUSION

. . . .

MAKE EVERY DAY AN ADVENTURE

It's fun to go camping and explore exciting new places, but you don't always have to travel far to find adventure. Being an adventurer is a mindset. It's about seeing the extraordinary in the ordinary, whether that's learning about trees in your neighborhood, spotting an animal in a far-away forest, or discovering rocks, minerals, and fossils in a nearby field.

Every corner of the world, no matter how close to home, holds the potential for adventure. All you need to do is get out there and search for it.

Here are some tips to help you get started on your journey to becoming an adventurer:

- **Plan your adventure:** Take time to plan your next adventure with your family and friends, whether it's in your neighborhood or further away.

- **Pack for your adventure:** Think about the things you'll need to take with you, whether it's just a small pack or a larger backpack.

- **Make notes:** Use your adventure journal to plan future explorations, or to relive fond memories of your past adventures.

- **Talk about it:** Sharing your dreams with your family might just help turn them into reality.

Remember, adventure is everywhere. You don't have to go to the South Pole or sail across the Pacific Ocean to find it.

JOIN AN ADVENTURE GROUP

Adventures are more fun when you share them. If you're keen to meet other adventurers, you might consider joining a group:

- **Join the Cub Scouts or become a Brownie:** For those between 8 and 10 years old, these groups offer a number of fun, outdoor-focused activities.
- **Join the Boy Scouts or Girl Scouts:** If you're over 10, you could join the Scouts. These organizations focus on wilderness skills and camping adventures.
- **Volunteer:** You could volunteer in community services, like cleaning up forest preserves, planting trees, or doing other outdoor activities where you can see and learn more about the world around you.

BE CAREFUL OUT THERE

Adventures can be fun and thrilling, but you should always play it safe.

Here are some safety tips for young adventurers:

- **Check with your parents:** If you're unsure about something, ask your parents.
- **Never go alone:** Adventures are safest with family and friends. Never go off on an adventure on your own.
- **Dress for adventure:** Wear appropriate clothing and sturdy shoes for your adventures. Dress for the weather, and don't forget a hat and sunscreen.
- **Stay hydrated:** Drinking enough water on your adventure is essential, especially on warm days. It keeps you energized and helps your body stay healthy.
- **Follow the rules:** If you're in a park or nature reserve, follow the posted rules. They're there to keep you safe and protect the environment.
- **Emergency plan:** Carry a basic first aid kit and know how to get help in emergencies.

Safety is the key to every great adventure. Whether you're exploring the hidden corners of your backyard or venturing into the wilderness, being well-prepared and knowledgeable will help you stay safe and make the most of your adventures!

Finally, remember that each day presents a new opportunity for adventure. If you live with the heart of an explorer, that adventurous spirit will always be a part of you. Who knows—perhaps one day this very spirit will lead you across the oceans or to distant lands few have ever visited.

Embrace curiosity, seek adventure, and let your spirit guide you to extraordinary places, both near and far.

Good luck!

APPENDIX

If you enjoyed this book and would like to read more about adventures or discover some inspirational tales, you might like some of the books below. Books are a great way to learn about adventures from the past and the present.

- *Kon Tiki: Across the Pacific by Raft*
  By Thor Heyerdahl

- *Journey to the Center of the Earth*
  By Jules Verne

- *Treasure Island*
  By Robert Louis Stevenson

- *The Lost World*
  By Sir Arthur Conan Doyle

- *The Call of the Wild*
  By Jack London

There are also movies about great adventures that can take you anywhere, including other planets. Here are some you may enjoy:

- *Balto*
  A true story about the lead dog of a sled-dog team named Balto, who traveled thousands of miles to bring medicine to a village in Alaska and save the lives of the townspeople.

- *The Black Stallion*
  The story of a boy stranded on a desert island and how he survives, along with a wild horse that is stranded with him.

- *The Man from Snowy River*
  The story of a man deep in the Australian outback trying to survive and live off the land.

Books About Nature and the Outdoors

- *National Geographic The Photo Ark: One Man's Quest to Document the World's Animals*
  By Joel Sartore

- *The World Encyclopedia of Trees: A Reference and Identification Guide to 1300 of the World's Most Significant Trees*
  By Toney Russell and Catherine Cutler

- *Insects of the World: An Illustrated Guide to the World's Most Abundant Creatures*
  By Paul Zborowski

- *Plants of the World*
  By Maarten J. M. Christenhusz and Michael F. Fay and Mark W. Chase

- *Complete Outdoors Encyclopedia: Camping, Fishing, Hunting, Boating, Wilderness Survival, First Aid*
  By Vin T. Sparano

- *Easy Campfire Cooking: 200+ Family Fun Recipes for Cooking Over Coals and in the Flames*
  By Peg Couch

THANKS
FOR READING MY
BOOK!

I truly hope you enjoyed the book and that the content is valuable now and in the future.

I would be grateful if you could leave an honest review or a star rating on Amazon.
(A star rating is just a couple of clicks away.)

By leaving a review, you'll help other parents discover this valuable resource for their children. Thank you!

To leave a review & help spread the word

www.ingramcontent.com/pod-product-compliance
Lightning Source LLC
Chambersburg PA
CBHW081707100526
44590CB00022B/3684